To Warwickshire College

With best wishes.

Chris Pitt

When Birmingham Went Racing

CHRIS PITT & CHAS HAMMOND

Best Wishes

Chas Hammond.

ABOUT THE AUTHORS

CHRIS PITT was born on an Easter Monday morning, the busiest racing day of the year. Birmingham races were on that very afternoon and the doctor charged with handing the delivery was going there. Talk about racing being instilled from birth!

He went to Bromford Bridge for the first time on Tuesday 12th June 1962. Luckily, his dad didn't need much persuading to take him. They'd catch one of the "special" race buses outside the Hall of Memory, or perhaps go by train to Bromford Bridge Station, which adjoined the course.

Chris recalls the first race he saw "live", won by a filly named Miss Murray, the mount of veteran Davy Jones, and has fond memories of all those boyhood visits to Bromford. Even now, whenever he hears the Migil Five's "Mockingbird Hill" on the radio, he is instantly transported back to the mound on the cheap side where they performed their biggest hit at an evening meeting all those years ago.

His previous book, *"A Long Time Gone"*, chronicling the stories of Britain's vanished racecourses, was published by Portway Press in 1996.

CHAS HAMMOND would take the day off school to go to Bromford races with his dad in the early 1960s.

He recalls going by bus to Erdington. His dad would call in at the Navigation for a drink, leaving Chas outside to enjoy his chocolate cigar, before walking down to the racecourse. Being under sixteen, he would get in free by jumping over the turnstiles.

During the National Hunt meetings he would run over to the far side of the course to see the runners jump the water, and then rush back to watch them jump the last.

Walking back up the hill after racing, Chas and his dad were often stopped by workers from nearby who would ask them what had won.

Happy days!

His previous book, *"Jump Jockeys 1830-1950"*, was published by The Complete Record in 2003.

DEDICATION

THIS book was intended for publication ten years ago to commemorate the thirtieth anniversary of the closure of Bromford Bridge. But it would not have been by us.

We first heard about it on 26th January 1995, when an article appeared in Peter Leather's "Hidden City" column in the Metronews. It reported that author Glyn Betteridge was charting its history by way of a book entitled 'Birmingham Racecourse 1895-1965'.

He wanted to hear from the ordinary punters and racegoers who had memories to share or information to impart. As we both had not just happy memories but also a number of items that we felt would have been useful, we wrote to Glyn, spoke with him on the telephone, and arranged a meeting.

The night of the meeting arrived. We waited and waited, but there was no sign of him. We rang his home to ask whether he'd forgotten about it. His wife answered the phone. Glyn had died the previous day.

We never met Glyn Betteridge but this book is dedicated to his memory. Hopefully, it's one he would have been proud of.

Front cover: Racegoers watch the finish of the Packington Novices' Chase at Bromford Bridge, 17th January 1956.
Back cover: A packed crowd at a Bromford Bridge evening meeting.

First published in 2005
by C.C.Publishing
(Chester)

Copyright © Chris Pitt and Chas Hammond

ISBN
0 949001 29 5

C.C.PUBLISHING, MARTINS LANE, HARGRAVE, CHESTER, CH3 7RX
TEL: 01829 741651. EMAIL: editor@cc-publishing.co.uk
WEBSITE: http://www.cc-publishing.co.uk

CONTENTS

Foreword   viii

Introduction   ix

Early Years   11

Birmingham and Solihull   13

Bromsgrove and Rubery (Lickey)   16

Great Barr – Home of Birmingham's First Steeplechases   18

Kings Norton   22

New Oscott (Birmingham Steeplechases)   23

Northfield   28

Dudley and Tipton   30

Birmingham Hunt   32

An Extraordinary Day at Aston Park   33

Knowle (Birmingham Steeplechases)   36

Henley-in-Arden (Birmingham Hunt)   40

Coleshill   43

Handsworth   45

Smethwick   47

Inkford Brook   49

Sparkbrook and Birmingham   51

The Wake Races -

Deritend Pool, Oldbury, West Bromwich   55

Cape Races   63

A 'Hoax' Race Meeting at Bordesley Green   64

Sutton Coldfield (Birmingham Steeplechases)   67

Sutton Park   72

Olton (Birmingham Steeplechases) 91

Four Oaks Park 95

Winners of the Birmingham Grand Annual Steeplechase 106

Four Oaks Park Coursing 107

Packington Park 110

The Small Heath Ladies' Race 114

Wordsley 115

Edgbaston and Quinton 117

Harborne 119

Hall Green 121

The Yardley Stud 128

Yardley Wood, Billesley and Ward End 131

The Mystery of Hay Mills Races 134

Shirley Park 135

Bromford Bridge 150

Bromford Bridge - Big Race Winners 204

A Groundsman's Memories 208

The Racecourse Tipsters 209

Those Nearby   (Brierley Hill, Penn Common,

        Redditch, Stourbridge, Tamworth) 212

Glossary 218

Bibliography 220

Index 221

FOREWORD
**by Jim Lewis, owner of triple
Cheltenham Gold Cup hero, Best Mate.**

IT is a great honour to be asked to write this foreword for a book that will rekindle the spirit of youth, and romanticise what were actually hard post war years. But so dear to us all now!

Immaculately researched and beautifully presented by Chris Pitt and Chas Hammond, it is also a history book that conjures up wonderful pictures in the mind of a bygone era that somehow survives in a modern form. Characters may change but the spirit and the emotions remain.

Born in 1934, I lived my childhood days less than a mile from the gates of Bromford Bridge Racecourse. It plays a pivotal role in my personal history because, as a young boy aged nine, I delivered newspapers to the racecourse and remember vividly "race days" when I would take a huge bundle of the *Sporting Life* and the *Sporting Buff* to Mr. Stonebridge, the course Manager, who would be waiting impatiently to relieve me of my heavy weight. He knew I had memorised every "Nap" selection for my Dad!

Dad would then send me to the illegal back street bookies in St. Margaret's Avenue to put the bets on, and when the horse didn't win he'd blame my poor memory!

Later, as a teenager from Ward End Road, I met a young girl called Valerie Dyzon. One evening we were standing in the dark on the hill over looking the racecourse. "The lights of Broadway", as we called them, were shining brightly, lighting up the course. With my arm around her waist, I whispered, rather shyly – "one day we will get married; one day I will buy you a house and a Jaguar car, and one day I'll buy you a racehorse". Yes, the memories of Bromford Bridge Racecourse mean so much to Jim and Valerie Lewis whose childhood dreams came true!

This book is a fond recollection of racing's earlier days; it is also a portrait of the characters that made the Sport of Kings accessible to a wider and more appreciative audience. It is a book produced by authors of nostalgia, who have a love for the sport, the determination to be accurate and the skill to make it absorbing, amusing and thought provoking.

For anyone whose passion is horse racing, this book is an essential purchase. A textbook to treasure and enjoy.

Jim Lewis

INTRODUCTION

SHORTLY after 9.30 p.m. on 21st June 1965, racing at good old Bromford Bridge came to an end. Now, forty years on, only the remnants of the paddock remain as a legacy of what was once one of the country's finest racecourses.

However, Bromford Bridge wasn't the only racecourse to have existed in and around Birmingham. Delve back in time to the nineteenth century and you'll find many, many more. Some, such as those at Sutton Park, Shirley and Hall Green, enjoyed long racing histories, whereas others had only brief flirtations.

This book has been a joint project. Chas Hammond has supplied much of the historical information, while I, Chris Pitt, have endeavoured to convert it into a readable story. We were both well aware that a work of this sort could have turned into a mass of repetitive data. Hence, while there should be plenty to interest the sporting and local historians, we hope that it will also be an entertaining read for those who, though not real horse racing fans, want to know something of what once happened in their area.

Various organisations, libraries, newspapers and individuals have helped us along the way. We apologise to any we have omitted, but in particular we would like to thank the following:

Librarians Marian Baxter and Sue Bates, plus the staff at Birmingham's Central Library for their patience and invaluable assistance.

Adam Fradgley of the Birmingham Post & Mail for providing some of the photographs.

Graphic designer John Griffiths for his painstaking attention to detail with several of the racecourse plans.

Racing historians David Boyd and Tim Cox for coming up with the answers to the most obscure of questions.

Pub historian Steve Penker for his help in identifying some of the early racecourse venues.

Racing journalist Mary Pitt for compiling the chapter on Yardley Stud Farm (and for coming up with the title for the book).

Trainer Sir Mark Prescott for supplying information on the history of coursing at Four Oaks Park.

Former amateur rider and trainer John Chugg for sharing his memories of Bromford Bridge.

Racecourse bookmakers Don Butler and Sammy Nixon for their stories of racing's characters.

Author David Ashworth for his contribution to the chapter on Racecourse Tipsters.

William Hiscox of Shirley Golf Club for assisting with the story of Shirley Park.

Although Birmingham's racecourses are no more, Chas and I will endeavour to take the reader on a tour of the long gone venues and convey something of their history. So please come with us and enjoy the journey.

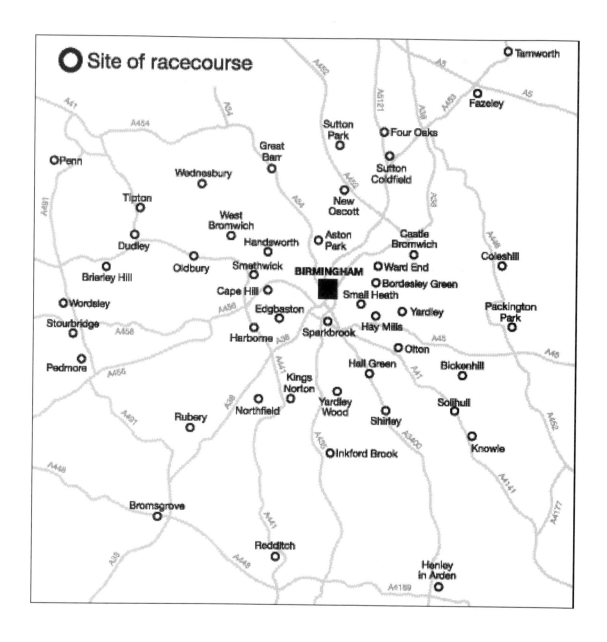

EARLY YEARS

When the House of Hanover ascended the British throne courtesy of George I in 1714, horse racing was already taking place all over Britain. However, during the reign of the four successive King Georges who presided over the country until 1830, the sport changed beyond recognition.

At the outset, the majority of races comprised matches between two horses, usually over distances between four and six miles. Then came races of three or more runners, which were mostly run in heats. A well contested race could involve as many as four four-mile heats, requiring horses to run up to sixteen miles in a day. Gradually, the format of the races changed. The distances became shorter and younger horses ran in them.

The horses changed too with the creation of the Thoroughbred, emanating from the three foundation stallions, the Byerley Turk, the Darley Arabian and the Godolphin Arabian, from which all modern day racehorses are descended. Thoroughbreds took over from the Galloway ponies, a smaller breed that had constituted the earlier form of British racehorse.

Royal Plates were competed for at the more important racecourses, while handicaps, weight-for-age races, sweepstakes and "give and take" races began to grow in popularity. A "give and take" race was one in which, for example, horses standing 14 hands high (1 hand = 4 inches) had to carry 10 stone, while horses under 14 hands carried less than 10 stone and those over 14 hands carried more. The weights were determined on a sliding scale of weight for size, the "give and take" element requiring that the bigger horse had to carry more weight than a smaller one.

One of the earliest "give and take" races took place in Warwickshire on Coleshill Heath on 9th October 1711. Offering a six guinea prize for the winner, it was restricted to "any horse, mare or gelding, that hath not won above the value of five pounds."

Birmingham's first recorded meeting was a three-day affair held on 27th, 28th and 29th May 1740. Although the actual venue is unknown, entries for the various races were declared at the Swan Inn at Snow Hill.

Moving ahead, *Aris's Birmingham Gazette* of Monday 25th May 1747 advertised a meeting to be held in Birmingham on Whit Monday, 8th June, featuring a race for £50 for any horse, mare or gelding that had never before won such a prize, to be run in three four-mile heats. The following day there was another £50 race, again in three four-mile heats, for horses "that never won a Royal Plate."

The advertisement stated that all entries for the races must be confirmed to Mr

Simon Whinnick at the Swan Inn on Monday 1st June, between midday and eight o'clock in the evening. A further, albeit curious, stipulation was that the horses could only be shod by blacksmiths that had subscribed half a guinea towards the prize money.

The first day's race was contested by Mr Warren's grey gelding Tamerlane, Mr Wass' bay mare Jenny Cameron, and Mr Bradley's brown horse Bolton, being won by the latter. As one of the conditions required a minimum of three runners in order for a race to take place, with only Mr Bradley's Arthur O'Bradley and Mr Griffiths' Nota Bene being entered, the second day's race was not run.

Nearby, Wednesbury enjoyed a brief racing history in the late eighteenth century, beginning with a meeting on 10th September 1776 held at Monway Field. An announcement in *Aris's Birmingham Gazette* dated 27th August 1781 stated that the meeting to be held on 12th and 13th September that year would be at a new course called Wednesbury Field.

The conditions stipulated that the first day's runners had to be shown "at the House of John Whitehouse, the sign of Sir John Falstaff," at ten in the morning on the day of the race, and for the second day at the Turk's Head, the property of William Smallwood. Wednesbury's meetings ended around 1790.

By then, racing had entered a new era of modernisation. The first St. Leger Stakes had taken place at Doncaster in 1776, and the inaugural Derby Stakes had been run at Epsom four years later. In 1791 James Weatherby published the first volume of the General Stud Book, which was to set the mould for similar publications throughout the world. As the nineteenth century dawned and progressed, horse racing continued to develop into a popular sport for participants and spectators alike.

In the last year of the Georgian era, 1830, a colt named Birmingham won the St. Leger. His owner, John Beardsworth, ran a horse repository in Birmingham's Cheapside district and can lay claim to being the first Brummie to own a Classic winner. Beardsworth died in 1835, aged 52, and was buried in St. Bartholomew's Churchyard. Birmingham, the horse, won 23 races during his career and earned £5,665 in prize money. Next to winning the St. Leger, his most notable accomplishment appears to have been his party trick of "following Mrs. Beardsworth around her dining-room table as if he had been a lap-dog or a tame cat."

In addition to those early Birmingham meetings during the mid-eighteenth century, horse racing had been staged locally at Solihull and Bromsgrove in the 1780s. But it was not until the middle of the nineteenth century that racing in Birmingham and its environs really came into its own.

BIRMINGHAM AND SOLIHULL

It all began at Lewd Heath, Solihull, with a two-day meeting on Monday 18th and Tuesday 19th September 1780.

The conditions of entry were pretty much standard in those days. One race each day, each worth 50 guineas, the best of three three-mile heats and open to any horse, mare or gelding that had "never won £50 at any one time (Matches excepted)." A typical sliding scale of weights dictated that three-year-olds carried 6st 7lb, four-year-olds 7st, five-year-olds 7st 12lb, six-year-olds 8st 6lb, and older horses 9st.

As was also customary, entries were made at local pubs on the day of the race. In this instance, those for the first day at Mrs Austin's George Inn, and for the second day at Mr Clarke's Holly Bush, between ten o'clock and midday.

However, what was unusual about that Solihull fixture was the imposition of a rule that the winners of both of the 50 guinea prizes had to "return to the Steward Forty-Five Guineas towards the next year's Purse." It was hardly an incentive for entering, having to hand back all bar five guineas of your winnings, but you have to hand it to the organisers for enterprise. Having said that, maybe that's why there were no more race meetings in Solihull for over half a century!

In 1835, a new two-day meeting was held on Tuesday 15th and Wednesday 16th September under the title "Birmingham and Solihull". Whilst it was not an ambitious affair, the *Birmingham Journal* reported: "These races attracted an immense concourse of persons, who came from all parts of the country; and it gives us much pleasure to say that the public are greatly indebted to the stewards for the attention they paid to their accommodation and comfort.

"The new racecourse is situated about half a mile beyond the (Olton) reservoir, the grand stand being placed with its back to the turnpike road, directly opposite the Seven Stars public house, and is, we are informed, about one mile in length. The course is flat, and at present heavy on the back part; but considering the short time allowed for making the necessary preparations, it was not only extremely well laid out and well defined and protected by substantial post and rails, but in every other respect the arrangements reflected great credit upon the stewards and other gentlemen by whom they were undertaken. We think, however, that the removal of the refreshment booths from the centre to behind the racecourse would be a very great improvement. As at present situated, they obstruct the view of the running for more than three parts of the course from all but those who are fortunate enough to have places on the grand stand."

On the Tuesday morning all routes out of Birmingham led in the direction of Solihull. The *Journal* reported: "Every description of vehicle was in requisition; and the road on both sides was for hours lined with pedestrians, male and female, hurrying forward to the place of the meeting. On arriving at the course, the numerous booths were speedily crowded; and in justice to the holders of booths (among whom was Mr. Bayliss, of the Old Crown, Deritend) it ought to be mentioned that, considering the immense number of visitors, the most liberal and excellent provisions were offered, upon payment, for their refreshment."

The races commenced at one o'clock. The main event was the Birmingham Stakes, which attracted a field of seven. It was run in four heats, the last two of which were won by Mr Fowler's brown mare Coquette, ridden by George Whitehouse, who was thus declared the overall winner. The *Journal's* reporter stated: "We have seldom seen a better contested race."

The second event was the Hampton Coppice Stakes, which included a silver cup valued at £25 for the winner. Mr Barber's Antelope took the lead from the start, was never headed and won both heats "in a common canter."

Just before the third and final race, rain began to fall heavily, not that this put off the racegoers, who stayed on to watch the Hurdle Stakes. There were only three runners, victory going to Cannon Ball after Harriet had fallen at the hurdle in front of the stand. The *Journal* reported that her rider, Mr Burton, was unhurt, adding: "This was the only accident which occurred during the day, if we except the ludicrous upset of a gambling booth by a horse and gig. No one was hurt, although the gamblers were all capsized and excessively frightened."

After racing, some seventy gentlemen sat down to dinner at the George Inn, Solihull. The *Journal* stated that the feast provided by the proprietor, Mr Taylor, "would have honoured the table of the finest hotel in the county." The various trophies were duly presented and Mr. Barber, "on receiving the cup, which was remarkable for taste and workmanship, requested the worthy host to fill it to the brim again and again, with prime old port."

The second day of the meeting again had three races, including the Solihull Stakes, "for horses of all descriptions." This had a good turn-out of nine runners, the first heat being won by Mount Eagle, the 6 to 4 favourite, and the second by Callban. Our correspondent records that the deciding third heat "was contested with as much truth as severity and was won by about half a length by Mount Eagle."

The next Birmingham and Solihull fixture was held on 20th April 1836, with entries being taken at the George Inn. A second meeting took place that year on 22nd and 23rd August, with four races on each day. Some 10,000 attended on the first day, but the second day provided "poor racing with very small fields."

There was again an April fixture in 1837, at which the Members of Parliament for

North Warwickshire added £40 prize money to a £5 sweepstakes of "twice round and a distance," and the promoters added another £95. This was followed by a meeting on the first two days of September, when it was observed that the stand was all but empty on the opening day.

The meeting on Monday 21st May 1838 had a programme of four races. The main event, the Birmingham Stakes, was run in four heats, two of which were won by Tom Speed's grey gelding Isaac, the mount of Sam Darling. Mr Speed had bought Isaac for "a trifling sum" in 1835 when the horse was a four-year-old and was well rewarded over the next three years as he won 38 times from 53 starts, mostly ridden by Darling. Isaac carried on racing until he was aged fifteen and won a great many races, including twenty at Worcester and Warwick. A contemporary writer declared that at such places as Oxford, Worcester and Warwick, "Darling was King, and his throne old Isaac's back."

Solihull's 1838 autumn fixture was held on Monday 1st and Tuesday 2nd October. Tuesday's programme featured a race for a Silver Cup valued at £40, for which there were ten runners, cups at that time providing plenty of incentive to compete. It was run in three heats, two of which were won by Theano. The North Warwickshire Stakes went to Prudence, ridden by a jockey named Bemetzreider.

At the meeting held on 28th May 1839, Betsey, who had won the Solihull Stakes the previous year, returned to claim victory in the Birmingham Stakes by winning two of the three heats. That year's October fixture was scheduled to take place on the 8th and 9th but actually took place the following week when a new course was used, though there is no confirmation of exactly where this was.

The last day's racing at "Birmingham and Solihull" took place on 23rd March 1840. There were three races, but only nine horses turned up to run in them. George Whitehouse, who had won the inaugural Birmingham Stakes in 1835, this time won both heats of the Solihull Stakes on Tivy.

The last race of that final meeting was over hurdles. This went the way of Mr E Hughes' Mary Wood, ridden by William Saunders, who walked over for the third and final heat after both of her rivals had fallen in the second heat.

Despite its promising start of five years earlier, when the *Birmingham Journal* had reported an "immense" number of visitors, 1840 saw the end of the meeting. It was in that same year that J. C. Whyte wrote *The History of the British Turf*, in which he remarked that "at Birmingham the stakes are small, few and trifling. They attract a poor attendance both of company and horses."

Perhaps the reason for its failure to survive may be gleaned from a newspaper article dated 6th May 1848, which commented: "Some eight or ten years back we recollect the inhabitants of the town bringing off their sports over a few miserable enclosures in the neighbourhood of Solihull; but this naturally fell into disrepute."

BROMSGROVE AND RUBERY (LICKEY)

Bromsgrove is one of the area's oldest racing venues, dating back to 1782, when a two-day meeting was held on 29th and 30th July at what is now Cliff Rock Road, Lickey, on the Lickey Hills side of Rubery. The first day saw a race for horses "that never won a King's Plate", while the second day had one for horses "that never won £50 at one time." Both races were run in four-mile heats. Only two horses turned up for the first day's contest, the winner being Mr Lowe's bay horse Sweet Robin. Five took part on the second day, with Mr Sanders' unnamed chestnut colt by Cicero taking the spoils.

The meeting was extended to three days the following year, when the last day featured a conditions race for four-year-olds and upwards, with the prize money being subscribed by "Gentlemen of Birmingham." Those same gentlemen extended their sponsorship to two of the three days in 1784. Both of their races were run in four-mile heats and, remarkably, were won by the same horse, Mr Thornton's Copperbottom, who beat two rivals in the first contest and three in the second.

The "Gentlemen of Birmingham" could not be enticed back in 1785 and the fixture reverted to two days the following year, when the races were won by Mr Lambourn's six-year-old brown horse Invalid and Mr Price's five-year-old grey horse Squib. Both were 2 to 1 on favourites.

The annual Bromsgrove race meeting was a very minor affair, never having more than three or four runners in each contest, but it continued until 1789, with all races being run in four-mile heats. Though not held in 1790, it was revived the following year at the "Lickey Course, near Bromsgrove" on Wednesday 10th and Thursday 11th August, the races comprising a "Maiden Plate for All-ages" and a conditions race for four-year-olds and upwards. The meeting was held there again the following year but thereafter appears to have ceased.

Racing at the Lickey Course was eventually revived with a two-day meeting on 14th and 15th October 1840. This time there were three races on the first day and two on the second. Mr V. Corbett's four-year-old filly Jenny Jones proved the star of the show, winning the Bromsgrove Stakes on the first day and the Handicap of "once round and a distance" on the second day. Her jockey in both races was the much-respected John Crickmere, who was later to write his name in the record books when winning the 1844 Grand National on Discount. Tragically, Crickmere died of consumption only two years after his 'National' victory, just two hours before his widow gave birth to a daughter.

A hurdle event was introduced to the programme in 1843 and Bromsgrove's annual August fixture attained greater respectability, with three, sometimes four, races a day. Easily the most successful horse to run there was Rory O'More, winner of the Woodrow Stakes, the Bromsgrove Stakes and the Bentley Stakes at the 1842 meeting. He won the Bentley Stakes again the following year, then captured the Bromsgrove Stakes and the Hewell Stakes in 1844. George Whitehouse rode him to five of those six victories.

The 1846 meeting, held on 18th and 19th August, was Bromsgrove's last under "proper" Jockey Club Rules. For endurance alone, the hero of the final day was the four-year-old colt Roebuck, who, having won the Hunters' Stakes in three heats, turned out again to win the Grafton Manor Stakes immediately after.

On Monday 17th September 1860 there was another revival, though not under the recognised rules of racing. Called "Chadwick Races" it was held in a meadow known as Roger's Tumps, on the racecourse near to the New Rose and Crown Inn at Lickey, where proceedings were enlivened by Mr Bate's brass band. The organisers confirmed they were satisfied with the arrangements made by Mr J. Perkins of the New Rose and Crown and added that they hoped to hold future race meetings there.

That was indeed the case, as the same venue was used the following year for a one-day fixture on 16th September. There was another meeting at Lickey in 1864 but we are not sure when this fixture ended or when it became known as Rubery races.

What we do know is that, in April 1895, horse and pony racing took place at Bromsgrove in the shape of a two-day meeting at Fox Walks Farm.

Rubery races were reported in 1899 as having been recently established on the old Bromsgrove Lickey Course, adjacent to the Rose and Crown, with meetings being held that year on 23rd May and 11th September.

The *Birmingham Daily Gazette* reported on Tuesday 4th June 1901: "The Rubery races were held in the fields opposite the Rose and Crown yesterday afternoon, and were fairly attended." It lists the results of the five races, all of which were for horses up to 16 hands and all bar one of them being over two miles.

Remarkably, a combination of just six horses competed in the five races. Three were won by Little Ada, who beat Dustman and Kitty in the Bromsgrove Lickey Open Flat Race; then beat Pot Boy and Kitty in the mile and a half Open Flat Race; and finished off by beating Barmaid and Kitty in the Rubery Open Flat Race. Kitty, having been soundly trounced in those three races, sprang a 33 to 1 surprise when beating Barmaid and Peter in the Open Hunters' Hurdle. Barmaid duly gained her reward for finishing runner-up twice by winning the Licensed Victuallers' Flat Race from Dustman and Little Ada.

Perhaps it was this lack of competitive sport that led to the demise of Rubery races after 1901, bringing to an end more than a century of racing at Lickey.

GREAT BARR

HOME OF BIRMINGHAM'S FIRST STEEPLECHASES

It was in Co. Cork way back in 1752 that two Irish sporting gentlemen, Edmund Blake and Cornelius O'Callaghan, inadvertently invented the sport of steeplechasing.

In order to resolve a wager as to who owned the faster horse, the pair agreed to a race. They started at the steeple of St John's Church, near the old castle at Buttevant, and galloped off on their chase, until reaching the steeple of St Mary's Church at Doneraile, owned by the St Leger family, a distance of some four and a half miles. They jumped whatever obstacles they happened to encounter along the way, and waded through the most natural of water jumps, the River Awbeg.

A brass plaque mounted on the wall of St Mary's Church commemorates that first steeplechase held in Co. Cork more than 250 years ago. It marked the birth of a sport that has thrilled both participants and spectators ever since.

The first steeplechase meeting ever held in Birmingham took place on the Sutton Coldfield side of Barr Beacon, Great Barr, on Monday 14th March 1836. Volume II of the Warwickshire Victoria County History records that: "A good course was flagged out from Sutton Coldfield in Warwickshire almost to the lofty, lonely eminence of Barr Beacon. Hunting people and farmers and miners and iron-workers assembled from all Warwickshire and from the sport-loving Black Country. The elite of Leamington Spa drove and hacked – a distance of over 20 miles."

The *Observer* reported: "On Monday last the Birmingham Steeple-chases came off in the neighbourhood of Great Barr, over ground belonging to Sir Edward Scott, and afforded a most excellent day's sport to a very numerous assemblage. The ground appeared to have been chosen with great judgement, as it enabled the spectators to see nearly every yard of the race.

"Probably many of our readers have been on the Manorial at Barr and will recollect that, in looking towards Birmingham, there is a valley which runs nearly parallel with the road and extends to Queslett. The line was distinctly marked out by red and yellow flags, placed in every fence, about 50 yards asunder.

"The starting place was in a fallow field on the Sutton Coldfield side of the valley, about a quarter of a mile from the Beacon, and clearly visible from it; the line then continued, bearing a trifle to the left, nearly to a farmhouse on the hill, and turning round a large red flag in a fallow field, came into a grass piece, near the Horns public-house, from whence the run in was two miles, in a straight line towards the Beacon, over rather light land, with a moderate rise all the way, making a distance of about three miles and a half. The fences were numerous and of a fair hunting like description."

Just three horses turned out for the first race, these being Mount Eagle (ridden by Mr F. Wallis), Turpin (Mr Parker), and Pharold (Mr Patrick). Mount Eagle won by about 100 yards, with Wallis triumphantly flourishing his whip. Second was Pharold and third came Turpin, both having been remounted. As Pharold had fallen in the latter stages when leading, it may be assumed that Mount Eagle was a somewhat fortuitous winner.

The were only two entries for the second race, the Warwickshire Stakes, this being a match between Captain Lamb's Manfred, the mount of Captain Martin Becher, and Mr K. Wallis' Creeper, ridden by Mr Ball. Though short on runners, it was by no means short on incident, as the *Observer's* correspondent duly noted: "Creeper led up to the fence at which Pharold fell in the first race, and, to the dismay of his backers, refused it. Captain Becher charged it, and his horse fell in exactly the same manner and spot that Pharold did. Mr Ball's riding at this crisis did him great credit; the quick and workmanlike manner in which he got his horse round to the fence, and handled him over, excited great and well-deserved praise. Becher, however, was not yet beaten; he was at work again in an instant, and gained ground upon his adversary at every stride; for Mr Ball, thinking he was safe, was sailing away very leisurely, and quite at his ease. Hearing, however, his friends cry out that 'the Captain was coming,' he shook his horse, and won in gallant style."

Captain Becher, of course, was immortalised after his mount, Conrad, refused at a post and rails fence in the 1839 Grand National. Seeking refuge from the following horses, he supposedly slid into the ditch on the landing side, thereby ensuring not only his own safety but also everlasting fame through Aintree's world famous jump which would thereafter bear his name, Becher's Brook.

A field of five contested the third and final race of the day, the Hack Stakes, run over two straight miles. Paganini, ridden by Mr Patrick, came in first, with Gadfly (Mr Main) second and The Doe (Mr Reynolds) third.

On Monday 27th February 1837 they raced over very nearly the same ground, though the course was rather longer and the fences generally easier with no timber or water. The races started and finished on the Barr Beacon. Only two races were held this time. The first of these went to Multum in Parvo, the mount of Mr Solloway, who left town the same night so that he could ride in the next day's prestigious St. Albans Steeplechase, which he won on Splendour. The other race at that year's Great Barr fixture was won by Woodley, ridden by Mr J. E. Beally.

An additional steeplechase was held on 28th March 1838, this being the Scott Cup, for officers of the Fifth Dragoon Guards. It was run in two heats and won by Spotless, owned and ridden by Mr Whitaker.

The following month, Barr Beacon was again the venue for the Birmingham Steeplechases meeting, the course having been devised by Sir Edward Scott and Lord Dartmouth. It was scheduled for Monday 16th April, but was postponed to the next day "owing to the tempestuous state of the weather." This time there were five races and Tom Olliver rode a double. He began by winning the Birmingham Stakes on The Grayling, beating Lady Teazle and Deceiver in a field of eleven, then added the Barr Beacon Stakes on Tom Leedham.

The Walsall Troop Stakes, which was run in three heats, was eventually won by Sir Edward Scott's The Shepherd, though only after a change of rider. The *Staffordshire Advertiser* covered the meeting and reported that The Shepherd "had no chance during the first heat, owing to the timidity of the rider. A fresh rider (Mr. Lowe) having been secured for the last two heats, Captain Scott's horse won in good style."

The Walsall Second Troop Stakes, run in heats of a mile and a half, went to Bessy Bedlam. The *Advertiser* noted: "The winner was admirably jockeyed by Mr. John Walker, whose riding did him infinite credit."

The day ended with a Sweepstake "run for by some Westbromwich (sic) gentlemen", which produced five runners and was won by Mr Bates' horse Gipsy. The *Advertiser* praised the gentlemanly conduct displayed by the riders as, after Mr Bagnall had been thrown from his mount at the second fence, the other four riders all slowed to a walk to check if he was okay!

The *Advertiser* also praised Sir Edward Scott for the layout of the course, stating that it was "admirably adapted for racing." However, it was not so complimentary about the title of the meeting itself. It was noticeable that the paper's report was headlined "Barr Beacon Steeple Races", with the writer complaining: "We were not a little surprised to find the Cards of the Races having the title 'Birmingham Steeple Races'! What pretensions Birmingham has to claim these races as its own we know not…we have no hesitation in saying that Walsall and Westbromwich might with better grace, have put in its claim to that honour; the gentlemen resident at the latter place having quite as effectually contributed to the gratification of the public and to the success of these races, by getting up a very spirited Steeple Race which took place at the close of the Races announced on the Cards."

Having got that off its chest, the *Advertiser* concluded its report by stating that, at the dinner that followed the day's sport, "the healths of Sir Edward Scott and Lord Dartmouth were enthusiastically drank."

On Friday 3rd May 1839, a Birmingham Steeplechases fixture was held "over about three miles of good hunting country in the neighbourhood of Erdington within five miles of the town." However, it appears likely that, despite this rather vague description, the course was still in its original location of Great Barr. There were just two races, both of which were won by the same horse and rider combination, namely Mr W. J. Godwin's Jack Robinson, the mount of Tom Olliver, beating four rivals in the first chase, then three in the second.

"Black Tom" Olliver was of Spanish-gypsy blood and was among the greatest cross-country riders of the mid-nineteenth century. He won three Grand Nationals, on Gay Lad (1842), Vanguard (1843) and Peter Simple (1853). He was also second in the race three times and third once.

His family's surname was Oliver but Tom is reputed to have added a second letter "l" because it was "as well to have an extra £ at hand!" Ironically, Olliver's handling of money was in direct contrast to his handling of horses. Ever gullible to beggars and to those with a tale of misfortune, he was nearly always bankrupt or on the verge of bankruptcy and was frequently imprisoned for debt. For a time he was landlord of The Star at Leamington and he later trained successfully at Wroughton, on the outskirts of Swindon, where he died in 1874.

During the years 1840-42 there was no racing of any kind in or around Birmingham. However, in March 1843 a steeplechase was held for the prize of a silver cup, given by Samuel Mayou. It was won by Mr Thornley's bay gelding Topthorn, beating Sir Watkin and five other runners.

Although the actual venue for that 1843 race was not stated, the likelihood is that it was held in the vicinity of New Oscott. Credence to this theory is given by the fact that the same Mr Mayou donated a silver cup when the Birmingham Steeplechases meeting was revived at New Oscott in 1845 and again the following year.

It wasn't quite the end of racing at Great Barr, however, for a meeting was held on Monday 1st October 1855, over a new course at Queslett, near the Horns Hotel. Chances are that this was probably pony racing rather than Thoroughbred, and the course could possibly have been at the Aldridge Road recreation ground. The *Birmingham Journal's* correspondent was in attendance and reported the Queslett Stakes had been won by Mr Newey's Harkaway and the Great Barr Stakes by Mr Lansdowne's Toper.

There was an element of controversy for the third race, the Sweepstakes, for which six horses started. Harkaway won it but a dispute occurred on account of it being thought that one of the stewards had a share in the horse's ownership, especially as many racegoers were decidedly of the opinion that Mr Whitehouse's Novelty was the winner. However, their protests were overruled.

"The company was very numerous," the *Journal's* reporter concluded, "and it bids fair to be a good meeting another year."

Alas, there was not to be another year and, following this one-off resumption, Great Barr races disappeared from the fixture list.

KINGS NORTON

Just one month after Birmingham's first ever steeplechase was run in Great Barr, another took place in Kings Norton on Friday 15th April 1836. The following report of the affair appeared in the *Observer* on 25th April:

"STEEPLE CHASE AT KINGS NORTON

"On Friday week a steeple chase came off at Kings Norton, between Mr. G. M. Barker, Mr. George Unett, Mr. W. Richards, Mr. J. O. Mason, Mr. R. Docker, Captain Timperley, Mr. Barber, Jun., Mr. J. A. Worthington, and Mr. W. Palmer, Jun.

"Mr. Richards rode Mr. Amphlett's horse, Captain Timperley a horse of Mr. Barber's, of Barston, Mr. Worthington his brother's horse, and the other gentlemen rode their own. The race took place at Urthwood Heath, and composed a circuit of ground of about three miles in length. The ground was heavy and the fences stiff.

"Mr. Richards took the lead, and kept it for about half the distance, when he was overtaken by Mr. Mason and Mr. Unett; the latter gentleman then took the lead and kept it, winning easily by at least 50 yards; Mr. Barber came in second, and Mr. Mason third. Mr. Amphlett's horse was badly staked, but is rapidly recovering, and there were many very heavy falls; nevertheless, the riding, upon the whole, was very creditable."

Despite being able to claim credit for staging only the second steeplechase ever held in Birmingham, there are no more records of horse racing in Kings Norton. However, it wasn't quite the end of its association with the sport because former jump jockey John Hurley trained for a few seasons at Meadow Hill Farm, Kings Norton, during the 1970s.

NEW OSCOTT

(BIRMINGHAM STEEPLECHASES)

Gibbett Hill, where Oscott College now stands, had a grim tale to tell. New Oscott gallows saw the end of many thieves who worked on the Chester Road, which had a reputation as being particularly dangerous. In 1729, John Johnson, a London silk-dyer, was murdered in the area and a local man, named Edward Allport, was eventually hanged for the crime. In 1742 another highwayman, named Sansbury, was caught drunkenly dozing in a field with an accomplice. He too was hanged.

On Friday 4th April 1845, a steeplechase meeting, comprising three races, was held on a course directly in front of Oscott College. It was about two miles round and contained seventeen jumps, including a brook, part of which is still there today.

The *Birmingham Journal's* report of Saturday 5th April stated: "This event, which since its announcement, has caused some excitement amongst our sporting friends, and that portion of the public who are glad to avail themselves of any excuse for leaving business and smoke behind them for an afternoon, came off yesterday, on the Rabbit Warren Farm, the property of Mr. Birch, situated about four miles from Birmingham, and one and a half from Perry Barr.

"The whole line of road from Birmingham, from eleven o'clock, presented one almost unbroken string of carriages, from the humble dog-cart, through all the graduations of gig, phaeton, britzka, and landau, to the dignity of a carriage and pair; the faces of the occupants thereof radiant with pleasure, and begrimed with dust, which stuck to the perspiration exuding freely by the agency of as lovely an April sun as ever shone. The ground was thronged with spectators, chiefly from Birmingham, who crowded the top and the sides of the hill which commanded a fine view of the whole course.

"The fences were principally thin hedges cut low for the occasion, but not stunted sufficiently to divest them of the appearance of being ugly leaps to go at. In the hollow, near home, two staked fences, about five feet high, with a dry ditch on the near side, tried the mettle of the nags – an untrimmed quickset hedge, and two hundred yards of a soft ploughed field that intervened between these fences and the winning chair, left very little puff in those that were not tailed off.

"The start was advertised for two precisely, but some of the horses not coming in time, allowed the amateur equestrians another hour to play some fantastic tricks, wherein empty saddles, bruised hats, dusty coats, and riderless horses were the most prominent features."

At three o'clock the riders mounted for the Birmingham Stakes, a handicap over four miles, for gentlemen riders. The winner's prize included a silver cup donated by Samuel Mayou, who was hoping to land it himself with the top-weighted Lottery. *(Note: This was not the famous Lottery, winner of the 1839 Grand National, but a horse of more modest ability.)*

Emperor set an easy pace, with the rest lying close behind, then Lottery took the lead at the eighth fence. Running up the hill past Oscott College, the field was tightly packed, but then the pace increased, with Emperor regaining the lead as Lottery weakened. Lottery refused soon after and Poverty also dropped out. Coming to the last fence, Emperor, Pretty Doe, Topthorn and The Plumber were all still in contention, but here The Plumber fell heavily. On the run in, Pretty Doe drew well clear to win easily, with Topthorn beating Emperor for second place.

After the race an objection was made to the winner, on the grounds that the rider was a professional. The committee considered the objection but decided to overrule it, which was somewhat surprising given that the winning rider, William Taylor from Uttoxeter, almost certainly was a professional. Agreed, Taylor was also a practising veterinary surgeon at the time, but he was certainly considered to be professional when winning the following year's Grand National on Pioneer.

The second race of the day was a Sweepstakes over two miles, with all runners carrying 11st 7lb. Each owner paid a £2 entry fee, and a whip was added to the winner's prize money. It drew a field of nine but only two horses completed the course, with the chestnut mare Kitty beating The Countess by two lengths after "an exciting struggle."

An objection was again lodged, this time on the grounds that Kitty had gone the wrong side of a post, but it was overruled. However, a second objection was then made on the grounds that Kitty's owner did not live within twelve miles of Birmingham, as required in the conditions of the race. Kitty's owner-rider, Mr John Shaw Walker, had in fact moved to take over the management of the New Hotel in Wolverhampton less than two weeks earlier. While the rules of the first race may have been laxly interpreted, this time they were strictly enforced. Kitty was disqualified and the race was awarded to the runner-up, The Countess, thereby providing a second winner for jockey William Taylor.

The third and final race was won by Mr Charles Richards' Duodecimo, ridden by his owner, beating Selina, with the only other runner, My Delight, falling at the last fence.

"In the evening", the *Birmingham Journal* reports, "upwards of thirty gentlemen, consisting of members of the committee, and others, sat down to an excellent dinner, at the house of Mrs. E. Mayou, Kings Head, Worcester Street. The silver cup, given by Mr. Mayou, is a beautiful piece of workmanship, made by Mr. Horton, silversmith, High Street."

The next year's races were held on Tuesday 10th March 1846, with Samuel Mayou acting as secretary. The *Birmingham Journal* reported that the course was "situated about two miles from Perry Barr," but took the view that, "it was one of the most unpleasant and severest which could possibly have been flagged out, the leaps being of an extremely trying character, and such, that if any accident transpired, it would be of a very serious nature."

The races started in the turnip enclosure on Rabbit Warren Farm. The first jump was a banked fence leading into a wheat field, "at the extremity of which was a very dangerous jump, consisting of a stiff bullfinch fence cut to the stakes, with a deep ditch of water prefacing it; this ditch was staked, so that the water from an adjoining pond might spread for two or three yards, and before this was placed a strong artificial hedge."

According to the report, the other obstacles, "about thirty-five in number", weren't much easier, for they included "a broken hedge and water, thickly interspersed with young trees", a "yawning bullfinch", a couple of "strong thorn fences on banks", and "a nasty over-grown hedge".

The sun shone brilliantly throughout the day, the reporter noting that "a vast concourse of spectators, of all ranks and sizes, in every description of vehicles, were attracted to the scene of the action, and, in general, took up their positions on top of the hilly wheat fields, where the winning flags waved; and from that point a delightful view of the whole of the sport could be obtained."

The first race was the Hunt Handicap Stakes, with a silver cup, once again donated by Mr Mayou, to the winner and a whip for the runner-up. It was run "over about four miles of a fair hunting country, for horses the bona-fide property of persons residing within ten miles of Birmingham." The winner was Ironmaster, ridden by Captain William Peel, of whom more later.

In the second race, the North Warwickshire Stakes, Jerry, ridden by William Archer, was first past the winning post but was disqualified for going the wrong side of a flag. The race was awarded to the runner-up, Safety Valve, the mount of William Saunders. The last race, the Pack Stakes, went to Worcester, ridden by John Parker.

Samuel Mayou again officiated as secretary at the 1847 meeting, which took place on Tuesday 9th March. The stewards included a couple of local MPs, Messrs C. R. Colville and Charles Newdegate, the latter gentleman having been born in Oscott and educated at the College. Although only two races were held that year, the *Journal's* correspondent reported: "The company assembled to witness the novel sport was very great, notwithstanding the coldness of the air, and the lowering aspect of the weather."

There were thirty-four fences that year, seventeen on each circuit, including a wide variety of hedges, ditches, thorn fences and bullfinches, plus "a pleached fence (whatever that may have been), broken in several places, with a rivulet before it."

The start was in a piece of fallow land at the foot of the hill overlooking the finish. The runners headed off in a straight line for Fulford's farmhouse. Keeping to its left, they turned left at the first flag behind the farmhouse, climbed an ascent at the rear of Oscott College, then turned left again into a fallow field, heading towards Witton Church. After clearing a thorn fence, another left turn was made, bringing them in a straight line for the College by the side of the Sutton Coldfield road. They ran through a hilly meadow and, after crossing an area of ploughed land, entered a wheat enclosure, at the bottom of which lay a bank-leap out of a rugged cartway, leading into some ascending wheat pasture, about three hundred yards to the left of Oscott College. Here they turned towards Barr Beacon, jumped three fences and ran into a grass field, turning sharp left and passing the starting point to do it all over again.

The three-mile steeplechase was won by the 4 to 1 shot Maid of Llangollen, ridden by Neptune Stagg, catching the trailblazing Twilight, the mount of William Taylor, to score by three-quarters of a length.

The Birmingham Stakes, run over four miles, produced fourteen runners, with Lord Strathmore's chestnut gelding Belahazzar being installed the 4 to 1 favourite. Mr J. Brown's Red Hawthorn was second favourite at 5 to 1, with British Yeoman, Ballybar and Richard I all trading at 7 to 1.

It seems that Rabbit Warren Farm had been aptly named, for Red Hawthorn, after clearing a bullfinch, put his foot in a rabbit hole, fell and rolled on his hapless owner-rider, "smothering him with dry soil, and for a while depriving him of his sight." Pluckily, Mr Brown remounted and went on to finish fourth. The race was won by Richard I, ridden by the aforementioned John Shaw Walker.

Of far more interest, however, was the third placed horse, an eleven-year-old named The Chandler, who was having his very first race. The Chandler had been bred by Sir Edward Scott of Great Barr. He took an instant dislike to the horse, referring to him as a "fiddle-headed brute", so passed him on to a Mr Wilkinson from Sutton Coldfield, who was himself a chandler – a man who deals in candles, oils, soaps and groceries – hence the name. Wilkinson used the horse to pull his chandler's cart.

Wilkinson then sold him to Robert Garnett of Moor Hall, who used him to pull his gig to the meeting of his local hunt, the Bonehill Harriers. It was there that The Chandler first caught the eye of Captain William Peel. When Peel's intended mount arrived lame at the hunt, Garnett unhitched The Chandler from the gig and offered him to Peel to ride. Peel was so impressed by the horse that he promptly bought him for 20 guineas.

Peel hunted The Chandler for five years and in 1847 sold a half-share to another officer, Captain Josey Little, and put him into training. It quickly turned out to be a good idea. Following his third place at New Oscott, he won his next start at Warwick by twenty lengths and followed up by winning that year's Worcester Grand Annual Steeplechase and also the Leamington Hunt Chase, which was then one of the most important races in the calendar.

The Chandler went on to win the 1848 Grand National, ridden by Captain Little, who was having his first ride at Aintree. Captains Peel and Little are reputed to have won £7,000 off the bookmakers – a tidy sum for the mid-nineteenth century. The runner up that day was a horse called The Curate, ridden by Tom Olliver. Ironically, it was Olliver that had coached Captain Little on the finer points of how to ride the gruelling Aintree course.

(Note: There is a degree of uncertainty among Aintree experts as to whether the horse was called simply Chandler or The Chandler. Most record books list him as 'Chandler', although John Maunsell Richardson and Finch Mason's 1909 work 'Gentlemen Riders Past and Present' refers to him as The Chandler. He is also listed as The Chandler in Osborne's 'Steeple Chase Calendar and Hurdle Race Epitome' for 1849-50. For the purposes of this book we have elected to call him The Chandler, although we remain open to persuasive arguments to the contrary.)

The races were held at New Oscott for the fourth and last time on Friday 17th March 1848. "The weather", lamented the *Birmingham Journal's* reporter, was "exceedingly unfavourable, it having rained chiefly throughout the day."

It had been intended at one stage to use Sutton Park's racecourse, which had opened four years earlier, as the farmer on whose land the New Oscott meeting was previously held refused to allow the fixture to take place. However, he relented at the last moment and the meeting once more took place at Rabbit Warren Farm.

There were three races. William Taylor rode a double, initiated by the victory of Tamworth, the 5 to 2 second favourite, in the four-mile Birmingham Stakes and completed by Emperor in the Scurry Stakes.

Captain Josey Little (of The Chandler fame) won the other race, the three-mile steeplechase, on Carlow, the 5 to 4 favourite, following an exciting tussle with top jockey Arthur Yates on Mind Your Own Business. Carlow was declared the winner by a head but there was a good deal of grumbling at the decision, for many believed that the runner-up had his head in front on the line.

Little, a prominent amateur rider of that time, had been commissioned into the King's Dragoon Guards but then lost much of his money in a bank failure and was forced to transfer to the less expensive 81st Foot Regiment. No doubt the rewards gained from The Chandler's Grand National victory helped boost his beleaguered finances!

NORTHFIELD

The Black Horse at Northfield is a well-known and popular pub, but the Birmingham suburb's links with horse racing are minimal. In fact, the "Birmingham Hunt Steeplechase", held on Tuesday 20th March 1849, with a gold cup for the winner, is the only race ever to be staged in Northfield itself.

The *Birmingham Gazette* reported on the event in its edition of 24th March: "The weather proving delightfully fine, a great number of persons were congregated on the ground. The ground, liberally granted for the occasion by the proprietor, Charles Richards, Esq., principally consisted of a picturesque breadth of grass land, situated in a fine open country, exceedingly well adapted for sporting pursuits.

"The turf was in fine galloping condition; the leaps were of ordinary hunting character, and by no means 'teazers;' (sic) yet the country, though not 'big,' was a delightful one in its characteristics for drawing out the qualities of both steeds and riders. Two miles of Mr. Richards's tract of land constituted the course, which being twice traversed, gave the required distance – four miles."

Nine horses were originally entered for the race but only five actually started, these being:

Mr C. Millward's Black Satin, 12st 7lb (Mr Harrison)
Mr H. Gem's The Barber 12st (ridden by the Owner)
Mr T. Hancox's Varmint, 11st 12lb (Mr T. Eccles)
Mr Boddington's Valentine, 11st 12lb (Mr Carey)
Mr Cooper's Clarendon, 11st 4lb (Owner)

Whatever the race lacked numerically, it made up for in terms of excitement. There were no problems in the early stages, as Clarendon set a slow pace followed by Black Satin, with The Barber third, Valentine fourth, and Varmint in the rear. But on reaching a bye-lane leading to the turnpike road, all bar Varmint refused to jump the hedge. Varmint, skilfully avoiding the melee in front of her, leapt the hedge into the lane and, in the words of the *Gazette's* reporter, "left her companions, some of whom were dismounted, and others completely stunned and bewildered by coming so closely into collision with each other, to extricate themselves out of their awkward position as well as they could, while her rider made the most of the disaster by getting a quarter of a mile ahead."

The others had managed to make up most of the lost ground by the time the turnpike road was reached, where Varmint still held a slight lead, with Black Satin close at her heels. But the latter refused again, encouraging the other three to follow suit. This left Varmint well clear again and it looked as though the race was over.

But it wasn't only the fences that proved troublesome, for on re-crossing the turnpike road, "Varmint and her rider nearly met with a serious accident, in consequence of a person on horseback riding so close to them as to oblige the mare to swerve from her course, and compel her to leap a high gate-post instead of the regular fence which was intended. The mare, however, soon recovered herself, and cantering to the winning post, won the race cleverly by at least 300 yards. The Barber came in second; Black Satin, much farther in the rear, third; Valentine fourth; and Mr. Cooper's Clarendon no-where, his rider having previously pulled him up."

The day ended with a dinner for some thirty people at the Black Boy and Woolpack, in St Martin's Lane. The *Birmingham Gazette's* reporter concluded: "The pleasures of the festive board were kept up with great spirit and good humour till a very advanced hour of the night."

DUDLEY AND TIPTON

Flat racing was held at various locations in the area from the early part of the nineteenth century. There are records of a meeting held on 24th and 25th July 1826 at Dudley Port, with declarations to be made at the Anchor public house to its proprietor, Mr Blewitt.

A meeting advertised as "Dudley, Tipton and West Bromwich Races" was held on Monday 24th and Tuesday 25th July 1837. It was reported that the races "have been well attended every year," implying that they had been taking place for some time.

For this meeting a new, circular racecourse on the Earl of Dudley's property at Tipton was used, measuring "one mile and a distance" round, with an almost straight run-in of 400 yards. The track was described as being a fine newly laid out course lying between Castle Hill and the Tipton Road. It ran from the railway station and railway line towards the Earl of Dudley's limestone kilns to the north, and down the New Tipton Road. The grandstand was backed up against the Castle Ground Walls, "and the race ground extended in an oblong course, running from the New (Tipton) Road to the Lime Kilns."

Clerk of the course was Edward Challingsworth of the Saracens Head, Dudley, and the subscribers (sponsors) included The Right Honourable Lord Ward, Edward Dixon, jun. Esq., and Sir F. L. H. Goodrick, Bart MP. On the Monday, the first race was the Dudley Castle Stakes, then came the Horseley Stakes for four-year-olds, and lastly, the Tipton Stakes. The second day comprised the Worcestershire Stakes, the West Bromwich Stakes, and the Himley Hunt Stakes.

The two-day July fixture was held again the following year, when Tom Speed's Isaac, ridden by Sam Darling, won both the Dudley Castle Stakes and the Tradesmen's Purse. Isaac was back in 1839 and again won twice, repeating his win in the Dudley Castle Stakes and then adding the Worcestershire Stakes for good measure.

An interesting innovation at Dudley was the Yeomanry Stakes, which was restricted to grey horses only. It was first run in 1839, when it was won by a gelding named Forester. Mr Thomas' mare Deceiver won it in 1840, when the course was said to have been much improved.

Deceiver won the Yeomanry Stakes again in 1841, by which time the "West Bromwich" element had been dropped from the meeting's title. The second day of that year's fixture, held on 20th and 21st July, included the Forced Handicap of "once round and a distance", this being won by Mr Key's filly Marialva. A "forced handicap" was a race run on the last day of a meeting in which all those horses who had run previously at the meeting and were still sound were supposed to compete. The "force" was not quite literal, because an owner could make payment to avoid running his horse – presumably if he didn't much care for the weight allocated.

The annual Dudley and Tipton race meetings were traditionally held during the second half of July. The Ashwood Hurdle Stakes, run in heats of one mile and a half and containing six 4ft high leaps, was introduced in 1844. From 1845 the formbook refers to the fixture simply as "Dudley".

The meeting held on 20th and 21st July 1846 was not only a bleak one for the jockey Neptune Stagg, who broke a collarbone on the second day, but was also the last held at this racecourse. The land on which it stood was later taken over by the Oxford & Wolverhampton Railway.

Following the loss of their course, the organisers lost no time in finding a new one, this being about one mile round, located on the opposite side of Tipton Road. The 1847 meeting took place at the new course on 19th and 20th July, entries having been declared at Priory Street (precise location not stated). The five-year-old Reliance provided jockey William Archer with two of his three winners at the meeting by winning the Dudley Castle Stakes and the Selling Stakes. Archer's third success came courtesy of Fat Jenny in the Ladies' Purse.

Alas, this was a short-lived affair. The last recorded racing here was a two-day meeting in July 1848. The second day's three races comprised the Dudley Castle Stakes, won by Flora, the mount of John Livesey; the Selling Stakes, which went to Novel, who won two of three heats; and the Ashwood Hurdle, in which Tugford Lass won both heats. Like its predecessor, this course was also taken over by the Railway Company.

From then on the local race meetings took on a nomadic existence. Tipton Wake Races took place in 1859. Then came Wyrley Races on 29th October 1860. These were also held on 27th October 1862; and finally on 29th and 30th October 1866.

A meeting called "Bilston & Sedgley" was held on 4th and 5th November 1861 at Hallfield. Finally, a "Rowley & Blackheath" fixture took place on 13th and 14th September 1869, on the "old course, opposite the Hawthorn Tavern."

BIRMINGHAM HUNT

Meetings were staged under the auspices of the Birmingham Hunt at various locations, beginning in 1850 and 1851 at Bickenhill, near to where the National Exhibition Centre now stands.

At the 1851 meeting, held on 15th April, the Handicap Hunt Sweepstakes, over about three miles, produced eleven runners and was won by Mr James Harrison's gelding The Profligate, ridden by the owner. The winner carried 13st 2lb and started at 5 to 1. The only other race on the card was another sweepstakes, run over the same distance, this going to Brown Rappee, the mount of Mr John Parker.

In 1852 the Birmingham Hunt moved its meeting to nearby Knowle, where the races took place on Monday 12th April. They were held at Knowle again the following year, and from then on the Birmingham Hunt fixture took place there spasmodically until 1863.

We can trace no record of a Birmingham Hunt meeting in 1864, but it returned to Bickenhill on 11th April 1865, on a new course "about 8 miles from Birmingham, in the neighbourhood of Elmdon and Bickenhill, near the clock at Bickenhill, adjoining the Coventry Road." The course was mostly grass, over about fifteen natural hunting fences, and there were three races. All three winners were ridden by their respective owners. The meeting opened with the Mutual Handicap Steeplechase, won by Jerry, owned and ridden by Mr J. Sankey. The second race, the Presentation Plate, went to Mr H. Holmes' Yorkshireman. The final event was a Scurry Steeplechase, which was won by Wasp, the mount of his owner Captain Hodge.

There were no further meetings at Bickenhill, as the Birmingham Hunt switched its meeting to Henley-in-Arden on 20th April 1866. There appear to have been no Birmingham Hunt meetings in either 1867 or 1868.

The Birmingham Hunt returned to Knowle on Tuesday 16th April 1869 and stayed until its last fixture there on Tuesday 19th April 1872. Its title was changed from "Birmingham Hunt" to "North Warwickshire Hunt" (which had previously staged meetings at Henley-in-Arden) when it moved to Packington Park in 1873, after which the name disappeared from the fixture list.

AN EXTRAORDINARY DAY AT ASTON PARK

The annual Birmingham Steeplechases had hitherto been taking place in the peaceful rural confines of Knowle. However, getting there wasn't easy for the majority of Brummies and so in 1855 it was decided to bring the fixture closer to the city centre. The chosen venue was Aston Park, home of the historic Aston Hall.

The meeting took place on Monday 26th March. It turned out to be one of the most extraordinary day's racing in the sport's history.

A mile and a quarter, circular, all grass racecourse with seven jumps – comprising three natural fences, two sets of post and rails, and two flights of "pleached hurdles" - was laid out next to Victoria Road, lying between the hall and the pool. A temporary grandstand was acquired from Coventry and erected by the side of the pool.

A crowd estimated at being in excess of 16,000 came to the park that day. Amongst them was the racing correspondent of the *Birmingham Mercury*, who reported: "At the entrance to the park were seated many sham sailors, each deploring the loss of an arm or leg, such members, it was observed, being closely strapped or bandaged in such a manner as to excite the commiseration of passers by."

The notion of charging one penny for admission to the course was soon abandoned when gangs broke down the barrier rails and simply marched through into the course. This show of force was merely a precursor to the havoc that was to follow between the races, with fights breaking out throughout the afternoon.

The first race was a handicap steeplechase over three miles. Bullfincher, ridden by his owner, Mr R. James, started the heavily backed favourite at 2 to 1 on and, despite pulling hard, made all the running to win "by three or four lengths."

The Birmingham Grand Annual Chase was run over four miles, meaning that the runners had just over three circuits of the track to negotiate. Spring, the mount of William Archer, was made the 6 to 4 favourite in the six-runner race, with Diana, ridden by Daniel Meaney, at 3 to 1, then came Boundaway at 4 to 1, Escape at 5 to 1, and 10 to 1 the two outsiders, Peltz and Star of England.

Escape made the running until nearly halfway when he fell, leaving Spring in front. Spring continued to lead until half a mile from home, where Star of England and Diana closed on him. The three of them fought out a fine finish with Star of England, strongly ridden by George Stevens, winning by a length from Diana, with Spring a length and a half further back in third. Stevens was then the recipient of a walk over on Soho, the only one of the original five entries to turn up for the Selling Steeplechase.

George Stevens, despite weighing less than nine stone, was one of the nineteenth century's greatest steeplechase jockeys. The following year (1856) he was to ride the first of his five Grand National winners (a record that still stands today) on Freetrader, the others being the sisters Emblem (1863) and Emblematic (1864) and twice on The Colonel (1869-70). Star of England was the first of his three Birmingham Grand Annual victories, being followed by The Comet (1858) and Emblem (1863).

Ironically, having survived a career as a National Hunt jockey virtually unscathed, Stevens died on 2nd June 1871 following a fall from his cob, The Clown, the previous day while out riding on Cleeve Hill. A gust of wind blew his hat off and, as a passer-by retrieved it and handed it to him, The Clown shied, whipped round and bolted down Cleeve Hill, flinging Stevens head-first against a stone. A plaque still marks the spot where he fell.

Incidentally, in addition to Stevens, three other Grand National-winning jockeys also rode at the Aston Park meeting, namely, John Tasker (1854 on Bourton), John Hanlon (1855 on Wanderer), and William Archer (1858 on Little Charley).

The next race on the Aston Park card was the Birmingham & Warwickshire Hunt Steeplechase, worth £100, for which Helen the Fair, ridden by Walter White, started the 2 to 1 favourite in a field of nine. Second favourite at 3 to 1 was Harry, with The Captain and Golden Hue both at 6 to 1. The weights ranged from 13st to an enormous 14st 3lb carried by top weight Golden Hue, the mount of John Tasker. Harry made most of the running but faded badly from the bottom turn, where The Captain, Helen the Fair and Golden Hue all passed him. Those three scrapped it out over the last half mile, with The Captain, ably assisted by Mr Charles Walker, winning by a length from the favourite, with the top weight a further two lengths back in third.

By the time of the last race, the Hunters' Steeplechase, the fights had become so numerous and ferocious that the three amateur riders due to ride in it refused to leave the relative safety of the weighing room. Professional jockeys had to be substituted. There was no betting on the race, in which Reveller, the mount of H. Bell, won by three lengths, despite bolting several times during running.

After the meeting had finished, the *Mercury* reporter noted that: "several thousands of the spectators, including the riff-raff of the town, were seized with a sort of military ardour, so they determined to indulge themselves with a mock fight in imitation of the heroic efforts which have lately transpired in the Crimea, or perhaps rather out of rivalry to the 'Battle of the Alma', now exhibiting at the Theatre Royal."

The mob ripped up racecourse rails and fence posts and made off to the open ground behind Aston Hall, where they divided into two groups of allies and Russians, the former, about 7,000 strong, occupying the valley, while the other, about 4,000, took possession of the hill. Racecourse flags were converted into ensigns and the

Battle of the Alma commenced, the larger body impersonating the British and making a vigorous attack on the Russians posted on the hill.

The *Mercury* continued: "Bludgeons and sticks of considerable length were brought into requisition as weapons, and those who formed the Russian ranks were driven into the gardens attached to the hall. Several encounters took place, in which much personal injury was done on both sides. Two lads had their eyes cut out, and others were much bruised and wounded about the head."

This open warfare continued all the way into the city, with 200 or more of the combatants arriving in Dale End at around half-past seven, brandishing sticks and creating uproar. There, the *Mercury's* reporter observed, they broke the window of a baker's shop and assaulted anybody that got in their way, two of the rioters striking a person named Savage about the face and ears. The culprits were apprehended and the fracas was eventually ended by the plucky Constables Heverin and Nadin, who "drew their staffs, and with difficulty dispersed the mob, thus putting an end to the affray.

"We should add," concluded the *Mercury*, "that several of the rebel party entered the town through Newtown-row and Summer-lane, where some of them were very violent. Whilst passing the old asylum they threw stones and other missiles at the remaining windows of the building, many of which were demolished. We hear that the authorities intend interfering to prevent a recurrence of so disgraceful an affair."

A total of sixteen people were taken to hospital and the saga ended with three men being sent to prison.

Not surprisingly, the experiment of bringing the Birmingham Steeplechases closer to the city was not repeated. That was the one and only day's racing ever staged at Aston Park. The steeplechases returned to Knowle the following year.

KNOWLE

(BIRMINGHAM STEEPLECHASES)

An announcement in *Aris's Birmingham Gazette* refers to a race meeting taking place on 31st July 1787 on the "old course" at Knowle, which logically implies that racing had taken place there even earlier.

Its next association with racing was a Birmingham Steeplechases meeting in 1852. Plans had been put in place to stage this in Sutton Coldfield during the first week of April, but when the corporation refused to sanction the fixture, it was transferred to Knowle, finally taking place the following week on Monday 12th April.

Knowle's racecourse was located to the left of the turnpike road at the entrance to the village, about two and a half miles from Hampton Railway Station. It was a triangular circuit of about two miles and the fences included a natural brook. The grandstand was situated on the crown of the hill nearest to the village. Four races were run at that 1852 meeting, with the main event, the Grand Midland Steeplechase (the forerunner of the Birmingham Grand Annual), being won by Tipperary Boy, ridden by William Archer.

The fixture was repeated the following year on Monday 28th March, but this time over a new course, half a mile from Knowle (now Dorridge) Station. The course ran adjacent to the road towards the railway station and was principally of grass but with some ploughed land, containing "30 hunting leaps and a water jump."

A crowd of some 20,000 saw Shinrone, ridden by Charles Boyce, win the main event, the Birmingham Grand Annual. Boyce, the son of classic-winning Flat jockey Francis Boyce, was destined to win the 1857 Grand National on Emigrant, riding with one arm strapped to his body as the result of a hunting accident. The other races that day were the Free Handicap Steeplechase, the Birmingham Hunt Steeplechase, and the Selling Steeplechase, the latter event going to a horse named Tom Bowling, partnered by Mr E. S. Davenport.

The following month a single steeplechase was held at Knowle under the auspices of "Birmingham Hunt", this being won by Stanhope, ridden by Mr Cary.

A second day was added to the 1854 fixture, held this time "near Knowle, within one mile of Knowle Station," on Monday 27th and Tuesday 28th March. The precise course layout was not stated, though it reputedly ran "through the meadows, up and down the hill into the course," and contained "a sharp turn to the right."

On the first day, Sam Darling Jun. rode two of the winners, landing the Knowle Steeplechase on Ace of Trumps, along with the Birmingham and Warwickshire Hunt Steeplechase on California. The Grand Military Handicap Steeplechase was won by

Torrent, the mount of Captain Hutchinson.

The second day saw Chris Green ride Needwood to victory in the Birmingham Grand Annual. Surprisingly, Burnt Sienna, who had completed the course in that year's Grand National on his previous start, was a faller, injuring Burrows, his rider. Green also won the Solihull Steeplechase on Blue Stockings. A top-class jump jockey, Green had by this time already ridden one Grand National winner on Abd-el-Kader in 1850 and was to win another on Half-Caste in 1859. He later became private trainer for Lord Poulett and saddled The Lamb to win the 1871 Grand National.

The final race on that second day, the Scurry Handicap Steeplechase, went to Beckbury Lass, partnered by William Archer, who had won the Grand Midland Steeplechase on Tipperary Boy two years earlier. Like Charles Boyce and Chris Green, Archer was also to taste Grand National glory, courtesy of Little Charley in 1858. Archer had three sons, one of whom, Fred, was to become the greatest Flat jockey of the nineteenth century, riding 2,748 winners and being crowned champion jockey thirteen times.

Rural Knowle had quickly become the established home of the Birmingham Steeplechases. However, it had its opponents and there were those who wanted to bring the fixture closer to Birmingham in order to make it more accessible to the masses. Thus, the 1855 fixture took place in the grounds of Aston Park. In the light of what transpired (see Aston Park chapter), it was hardly surprising that the meeting returned to Knowle the following year.

An advert for that 1856 meeting appeared in the *Birmingham Journal*, stating that five races would be run on Monday 7th April. It went off peaceably enough compared with the fiasco of the previous year, as the following report confirms:

"The disorderly and disgraceful conduct of a large number of Birmingham worthies, expressively denominated 'roughs,' at our steeple chases, held at Aston last year, induced the managers of this annual sport to fix upon the vicinity of Knowle for the celebration of the good old English pastime for the year 1856, Knowle being less easy to access. Accordingly, thousands of the inhabitants of Birmingham yesterday took their way to that place, in monster excursion trains along the Great Western line, in omnibuses, and almost every description of vehicle.

"The spot selected for the running can scarcely be called other than 'fair hunting ground;' but it certainly was very trying to the horses, being peculiarly hillocky, and abounding with awkward hedges and ditches in addition to the artificial fences. An improvised grand stand was tolerably well filled, but the betting ring was by no means crowded, and the business done did not appear excessive.

"Hosts of thimble riggers, card-sharpers, and other 'professionals' of that delectable genus, infested the course and, despite the proverbial 'cuteness' of Brummagemonians, contrived, by their cleverly arranged dodging, to draw large amounts of cash from gullible spectators. Not a policeman was to be seen, order being preserved as well as it could be by a few solitary amateur preservers of the peace. The pickpockets, who mustered in goodly numbers, profited immensely by the occasion, as they were enabled to practice their vocation without fear of a 'peeler's' surveillance, and with the full enjoyment of a conscious immunity of law.

"One unlucky member of the picking and stealing tribe was detected by a gentleman entering the betting ring taking his hands from his pocket. Discovery of a missing purse followed the detection, and the thief was dragged into the betting compartment. He was searched, the purse was not found upon him, a nimble accomplice having doubtless secured that, but his pockets disclosed a number of cigar cases, some mounted in a costly manner, silk handkerchiefs, and other articles, the proceeds of prior successful pocket dippings.

"As there was no policeman to hand the rascal over to it was suggested that lynch law should be adopted to meet the exigencies of the case. The delinquent was at once surrounded by a number of indignant individuals, and one person took upon himself the task of administering to the thief a sound whipping. Having received his salutary chastisement, he was ignominiously ejected into the open course, but only to meet with a worse castigation, for a vast crowd of onlookers closed round the ejected one, beat and kicked him for upwards of five minutes, at the end of which time the youthful rogue sneaked away, the sorer, if not the wiser, for the summary thrashing which he had received."

The day's big race was, as always, the Birmingham Grand Annual Steeplechase, a four-mile handicap with £100 added. It attracted a field of seven including the star French steeplechaser Franc Picard, owned by Baron de la Motte and ridden by Harry Lamplugh, who started at the generous odds of 6 to 1. Cupbearer, ridden by William Archer, was the 5 to 2 favourite, with Janus (Walter White), who had finished fourth in the previous year's Grand National, at 4 to 1. The third choice, at 5 to 1, was British Sailor, with Boxall on board. The field was completed by The Minor (Chris Green), Rosa (Weaver) and Goodlad (Ben Land, jun.).

Cupbearer made the running, followed by British Sailor and The Minor, while Franc Picard trailed in last place. Rosa shied at the first fence, took the next two badly and finally refused at a hedge. Cupbearer and British Sailor alternated the lead on the first circuit, followed closely by The Minor. Cupbearer stumbled at the hedge nearest the stand and it was British Sailor who led the field out onto the final circuit, followed by The Minor, Goodlad, Cupbearer, Janus and Franc Picard.

Goodlad fell at a ditch and immediately afterwards British Sailor came down, his rider, Boxall, breaking four ribs in the fall. Up the hill opposite the stand, The Minor took the lead, while Franc Picard made swift progress from the rear to move into second, with Janus third. Franc Picard and The Minor duelled over the last two jumps before the French horse drew ahead on the run-in to win by a length. Janus came in third, six lengths behind The Minor, with the exhausted Cupbearer a distant last of the four finishers. Franc Picard was to win a second Birmingham Grand Annual in 1859.

The Birmingham Grand Annual was moved to a new course at Sutton Coldfield in 1857 and never again returned to Knowle. Indeed, there is no record of any further meetings at Knowle until an announcement in the *Birmingham Post* of one to be held "over the old course" on 12th April 1861.

The Birmingham Hunt Steeplechases were held at Knowle on 4th April 1862, "on the usual course," when the three races comprised the Hunters' Stakes, the Knowle Hunt Stakes and the Post Entrance Stakes. This fixture was held there again on 2nd March 1863, with entries being declared at the Greswolde Arms Hotel. After brief flirtations with Bickenhill and Henley-in-Arden, the Birmingham Hunt meeting returned to Knowle on Friday 16th April 1869.

That year there was once again a grandstand for the benefit of spectators. Three races were run, with the same horse and rider winning two of them. Shooting Star and Mr Arthur Dabbs began the afternoon by carrying 12st 3lb to victory in the Hunters' Stakes, over about three miles, defeating four others. They then turned out again in the Hunters' Plate over the same distance, finishing alone after all five rivals failed to jump round. The remaining race, the Hunt Cup, over about three and a half miles, attracted no less than seventeen runners and was won by the 10 to 1 chance Hops, the mount of Mr C. Halford.

The Birmingham Hunt races were held at Knowle for the next three years, always on a Tuesday in April. In 1870 Mr Halford won the Ladies' Welter Cup on the half-bred mare Hampton Lass. Messrs Halford and Dabbs were both back in the winner's enclosure at the 1871 meeting, Dabbs winning the Knowle and Solihull Ladies' Purse on Topthorn, while Halford rode his own horse Albion to victory in the Hunters' Steeplechase.

The final Birmingham Hunt meeting at Knowle took place on 19th April 1872. The five races included the United Hunters' Steeplechase, won by Stumcarty, who humped 12st 13lb to victory, partnered by Captain Holyoake. Joe Cannon won the Packington Park Stakes on the four-year-old filly Industry.

Packington Park then became the new venue for the Birmingham Hunt meeting, although its title was changed from to "North Warwickshire Hunt" when it moved there in 1873.

While 1872 was the last time that horse racing took place at Knowle itself, it wasn't the end of its racing connection. Syd Mercer trained there between 1948 and 1954, while fellow trainer Ken Bridgwater lived at Elvers Green Cottage in Elvers Green Lane for many years prior to basing the family's racing operation at Lapworth.

HENLEY-IN-ARDEN

(BIRMINGHAM HUNT)

Henley-in-Arden's steeplechase meetings were held at Castle Hill, Beaudesert Mount, and lasted from 1845 to 1875.

An announcement of the 1854 fixture stated that it would take place on Tuesday 28th February, "over the finest Steeple Chase Ground in England." The two races comprised the Town Stakes, to be run in heats of one mile and a half, and the Birmingham Stakes, of £3 each, with £15 added. The Clerk of the Course was Mr G. Blower and Mr G Harris officiated as Secretary.

The *Birmingham Daily Post* wrote of the 1858 meeting, held that year on Easter Monday, 5th April: "The Henley-in-Arden sports came off yesterday; and that rural retreat being only a dozen miles distant of Birmingham, the officers quartered there mustered in strong force; and the 'lower ten thousand' of that great town, despite the badness of the times (for it is reported that there are upwards of fifteen thousand hands out of employment at Birmingham just now,) also assembled numerously, the monster 'busses and pleasure vans filled with joyous hearts, exciting the wonder of Henley yokels, and their local friends.

"The weather was bitterly cold – a nipping, piercing easterly wind prevailing, which doubtless kept some hundreds away, particularly of the feminine gender. Still, there was a goodly sprinkling of the latter, buxom and smiling, fair specimens of Warwickshire beauty, symmetry and affability."

Also present were several members of the North Warwickshire Hunt, three of whom, including the Master, were officiating as stewards. The *Post* was highly critical of their performance, commenting: "our duty, as impartial chroniclers, compels us to remark it is a pity that either one accepted office, inasmuch as one of them never showed when most wanted, and the other two had pecuniary interest in the Hunt Chase, and an unpardonable attempt was made to exclude as many strangers as possible. It is true that Lieutenant-Colonel Yates was called in to 'aid and assist,' but the gallant officer had to fire the bullets that had been specially manufactured for the occasion."

One of the problems stemmed from a clause in the conditions of the Hunt Chase, whereby all horses must have been regularly and fairly hunted during 1858 with any established pack of hounds and *ridden by their owners*, a certificate to that effect being required from the Master of Hounds. "We wonder," mused the *Post*, "how many members of the N.W.H. dictated the wording of that clause.

"But it was a badly arranged meeting altogether," the paper chastised, "and where there is neither impartiality or a thorough business system, such meetings ought to be 'knocked on the head.'

"The ceremony of weighing for the first two races was performed in the town, in a little place where no one could have swung a cat round without beating its head against each of the side railings, and yet the enclosure was allowed to be indiscriminately filled with men, women, and dogs. Neither the officiating stewards nor clerk of the course exercised the authority nor courage to demand the expulsion of intruders, although two police officers were staring on open mouthed the whole of the time.

"Indeed, there was nothing but confusion, and the disgraceful scene was considerably enhanced by a bevy of objections being raised as to the qualifications of certain animals and certain riders. A dozen horses had been entered for the Hunt Chase, and all had arrived, but five or six of them were objected to, and three were disqualified; because the very unusual words "ridden by their owners," had been omitted in the certificates from the Masters of Hounds.

"The disgraceful proceedings in the town were followed up on the course; for when the Leicestershire horse, Little Yeoman, won in a canter - Jenny Jones tiring under the heavy weight, Telegram not being up to the game, and the remaining half dozen meeting with disasters - a cry was raised that he had not carried his proper weight; that the second was to be disqualified also, and Telegram entitled to the stakes! The weigher, however, was an honest man, as good as he was tall, and he passed Mr. Audinwood (the winning rider) as 'all right.'

"An interval of two hours or more was then allowed for carrying out the old custom here of dining between the races, after which the 'scaling act' was repeated under the Town Hall. An adjournment was then made to the course, where the spectators were amused by a lady from Leamington, well known in the midland hunts, taking her horse over the whole of the steeple chase line, and without making the slightest mistake."

Mr. Edwards, the *nom de course* of top amateur rider George Ede, won both the last two races on Goldsmith and Innkeeper by dint of superior jockeyship. However, he had a nasty shock prior to the first of his victories, being unseated on the way to the start.

The *Daily Post* reported: "He was mounted on Goldsmith, a fine horse, but a hard puller, who had completely overpowered Fred Page in the hunt race, and had treated that worthy with an extraordinary leap over a hay-stack, a bolt through a cabbage garden, and a visit to the kitchen of an antiquated dame in the

George Ede, alias "Mr Edwards".

town, and the venerable lady voluntarily declared that in the whole course of her pro-longed career she had never seen or heard of the like before. Goldsmith capsized Mr. Edwards before starting, and stunned him for a short time, but afterwards went as straight as an arrow, and won in a canter. Innkeeper's victory was just as easy.

"Thus ended Easter Monday's recreation at Henley-in-Arden," the reporter con-cluded. "What was done in the Terpsichorean line, or at other reunions, social or oth-erwise, we do not know. We had had quite sufficient of the racing transactions and their day-time concomitants, and were glad indeed to get our willing and honest 'Jarvey' to bring us back to Leamington in time for the first available evening train over the well-regulated iron road of the London and North Western Company.

"One word of advice to the Messrs. Blower and Co. as to their future anniver-saries, if it shall ever so happen that there will be racing at Henley again. Discard aristocratic dictation for exclusive purposes; and let the weighing be got through on the ground. You have one of the prettiest little steeple chase courses in the country, and a right jovial creditable meeting might be raised. Receive the hints in the good spirit they are offered, and act up to them. Then *floreat Henley*."

The organisers evidently took note, for Henley-in-Arden Steeplechases contin-ued, eventually forging a link with the Birmingham Hunt, which staged a meeting there on 20th April 1866.

There was also a fixture on Monday 19th April 1869, when the main event was the Open Hunt Stakes, of about three miles. Four runners went to post, the winner being Baron Slow, a 4 to 1 chance ridden by Mr Eldridge, who defied top weight of 12st 13lb to beat the 6 to 4 favourite Flying Scud, with Gypsy Lass a distant last of the three finishers. The other race that day was the Farmers' Hunt Plate, also over about three miles. This was won by Hampton Lass, ridden by W. Page, beating Barley and Red Knob.

The last day's racing at Henley-in-Arden took place on 28th April 1875. The results of some of the races are not recorded because they were worth less than £20, while the North Warwickshire Stakes was declared void (reason not stated). The remaining events were the Farmers' Plate and the Birmingham Open Hunters' Plate, the latter being won by Mr J. Walker's Zealand, a 5 to 2 chance, beating two rivals.

COLESHILL

As mentioned in an earlier chapter, a "give and take" race took place on Coleshill Heath on 9th October 1711. The "give and take" theory was based on a sliding scale of weight for size, meaning that the bigger horse was obliged to carry more weight than a smaller one.

The race was run in three heats and offered a six-guinea prize for the winner. The conditions stipulated that it was for "any horse, mare or gelding, that hath not won above the value of five pounds, the winning horse to be sold for 10 pounds." Entries were to be declared by six in the evening on Friday 5th at the Swan, in Coleshill. There was also "a plate of less value, to be run for by asses."

A steeplechase meeting was scheduled for Coleshill on 3rd March 1847, although the results do not appear in that year's *Racing Calendar*, hence it is possible that it may have fallen foul of the weather.

The next mention of racing in the vicinity comes in the form of an announcement that appeared in the *Birmingham Journal* of a meeting to be held at Coleshill on Monday 13th October 1856. It was stated that the course was "within five minutes walk of Forge Mills Station, (near Hams Hall), Derby Line," and that the races were for ponies not exceeding 131/2 hands high.

The two races comprised a four-guinea stakes, to be run in heats, entrance fee 7s 6d; and a two-guinea stakes, again in heats, entrance fee 3s 6d. The supporting events included a £1 foot race, while the announcement concluded: "Refreshments of the first quality may be obtained on the Ground."

The following Saturday, the *Journal* published a report of this meeting, stating that it had been revived "after an interval of some three or four years," thereby confirming that racing had taken place there previously.

Said the *Journal*: "A committee has been formed, and although many obstacles had been thrown in their way, they combined to bring about a day's enjoyment for the townspeople, and a fair sprinkling of visitors from the surrounding neighbourhood, as well as many lovers of the Turf from Birmingham. The day was gloriously fine. The ground was some beautiful meadow land, the property of Mr. Heywood, to whose kindness the committee are indebted for the opportunity. Although somewhat hastily got up, there was no lack of amusements upon the ground.

"The races commenced around three o'clock, and although some little wrangling occurred about the weighing stand, relative to the weights of the respective jockeys, they were conducted throughout in a very satisfactory manner; the Steward, Mr.

Messenger, acting with the most praiseworthy attention and impartiality.

"In the course of the day, a well-contested half-mile foot race was run for a purse of money. There were four competitors, and the prize fell to the lot of J. Meadows, alias the Coleshill Clipper."

The first pony race was won in two heats by Little Harry, the mount of Jonas Cooke. The second race, however, was more keenly contested. Joseph Page's Pretty Boy, ridden by his twelve-year-old son Johnny, won the first heat but was beaten in the second by Black Bess, partnered by J. Haddock. The deciding third heat saw Black Bess defeat Pretty Boy again to land the spoils.

The *Journal's* report concluded: "A considerable balance remains in the hands of the committee, and it is intended next year to have races upon a more extended scale."

The committee kept its word. Two more pony meetings were held in 1857, the first on Monday 13th April, the second on Monday 6th July. The *Birmingham Journal* carried the following advertisement relating to the latter:

"COLESHILL WAKE RACES

THESE RACES will take place on MONDAY NEXT, July the 6th, over the Old course, near the Forge Mills Station, (Derby Line).

FOR PONIES

Applications for Booths, Stalls & c., to be made to the Proprietor, Mr. William Heywood, Lamb Inn, Coleshill."

Despite its popularity, we can trace no further records of racing at Coleshill after 1857, although Over Whitacre races were held in the vicinity, near to Shustoke Station, on 14th November 1870 and again on 13th November 1871.

But that wasn't the last time Coleshill was to be mentioned in the same breath as horse racing. Fast forward a hundred years to the mid-1970s and along comes Bob Burns, a retired minibus operator from Sutton Coldfield.

Having failed to persuade the Birmingham District Council of the merits of building a racecourse in the grounds of Sutton Park, Mr Burns put forward a scheme for a new super racecourse to be built near Coleshill. His dream was certainly on a grand scale for he dubbed the proposed new course "The Royal Ascot of the Midlands." He acknowledged that it would need financial backing from the Horserace Betting Levy Board and that obtaining planning permission would be difficult.

In terms of location, there was reason to believe that such an enterprise could have been successful, with the motorway network, the rail terminal and the rapidly-expanding Birmingham Airport all close at hand. Alas, once again, Mr Burns' race-course scheme was doomed to failure.

HANDSWORTH

Pony racing was held at Handsworth during the mid-nineteenth century, although it may have started much earlier than that. Possible locations include land adjacent to Heathfield Road, or at Sandwell on the Leveretts. The Leveretts certainly looks a likely spot, lying just off Oxhill Road, part of the A4040 Birmingham ring road, and within half a mile of West Bromwich Albion's ground, The Hawthorns.

The first definitive records are of a meeting at Handsworth held on Monday 7th and Tuesday 8th October 1844. Mr Hammond's grey mare Nora won both heats of the one-mile Sweepstakes on the first day, beating Mr Clayton's bay gelding Cigar. Nora also finished runner-up to Mr Worley's Ivanhoe in the Hack Stakes and would do so again the next day in the Innkeepers' Stakes.

The highlight of the second day was undoubtedly the one-mile hurdle race, over five flights of hurdles. Mr Lowe's bay gelding Ugly Buck beat Mr Timmings' chestnut mare Fanny in the first heat but the positions were reversed in the second heat. The deciding third heat was, claimed the *Birmingham Journal's* reporter, "one of the best contested races ever run, the Ugly Buck clearing the hurdles in fine style, and winning by half a head."

An advert appeared on the front page of the *Birmingham Journal*, dated Saturday 27th May 1848, which read:

HANDSWORTH SPRING RACES AND GIPSY PARTY
GROVE FARM, SUMMER HOUSE INN, GROVE LANE
A GIPSY PARTY will take place on Monday next;
Admission to the Grounds 6d each.
The RACES are fixed for Whit Tuesday, the 13th of June.

The meeting held on Monday 1st and Tuesday 2nd October 1849 is regarded as being Handsworth's first under the 'proper' Rules of Racing. The racecourse was said to be located one mile from Handsworth & Smethwick station. The *Birmingham Journal* reported that it was held "in a field which has been occasionally used as exercise ground for the cavalry stationed in Birmingham, and was also the intended site, we believe, for the central barracks for the Midland District, the erection of which was spoken about two or three years ago."

Credit for arranging the race meeting was given to Henry Bolton, proprietor of the New Inn, upon whom lavish praise was heaped. The *Journal* commented: "Taking into account the many difficulties which were in the way, everything went off as well as could be desired, and in such a manner as to go far to secure a capital meeting next year. Although the weather was unfavourable on the first day, still there was a large attendance throughout. Some excellent horses were entered and the running was such as to give general satisfaction, being really very good in a few of the races."

There were four races on the first day and five on the second day. Three horses won on both days: Forget-me-Not, ridden by T. Clay, took the opening race, the Hack Stakes, carrying 9st 10lb, and the Ladies Purse, carrying 10st 8lb; Red Robin won the Handsworth Stakes, "of two sovs. each, with fifteen sovs. added from the Racing Fund", then followed up in the Innkeepers' Stakes; while Faith won the first day's Pony Race and the final race of the meeting, the Consolation Stakes.

The annual Handsworth race meetings continued to be held on the first Monday and Tuesday of October from 1850 to 1854, with entries for the races being taken at Mr Bolton's New Inn.

There was an unprecedented attendance of upwards of 20,000 being present on the first day in 1854. The *Journal* reported that this "must suffice to show that if the indefatigable promoter of these meetings, Mr. Bolton, be supported, there is no reason to doubt but that Handsworth's meeting may soon be an attractive assembly."

Mr Smith's Miss Talbot was the star performer that year, winning both the Handsworth Stakes and the Abbey Stakes on the first day. It was noted that: "In two races, one of the favourites, Mr. C. Dyde's Clio, overpowered her young jock and ran out of the course, thus destroying all chance of her winning."

The 1854 meeting was the last to be staged in Handsworth. Although still officially called Handsworth, the 1855 fixture, which took place on 8th and 9th October, was actually held in Smethwick, at a new course "in juxta-position with the Blue Gates, Smethwick." It appears that the race meeting was transferred to Smethwick because of the Council's reluctance to hold it at Handsworth itself. The precise reason is unclear, but it was probably because no suitable land was available. This seems the most likely explanation judging by the *Birmingham Journal's* statement that "the whole affair will be brought before the public in a few days at a public meeting in Handsworth, and so our word now stands only thus – had land for a course been to be had in Handsworth, these last races would not have come off at Smethwick."

Today it is hard to envisage horse racing having taken place in Handsworth, but at one time the "Township of Handsworth" covered about half the ancient Parish of Handsworth, which stretched all the way to Sutton Park. Even looking at an 1872 map of the village, two years before the "Township" became the urban district of Handsworth and long before the local council had purchased the land for Handsworth Park, racing still seems to have been an unlikely pastime. However, "The Grove" estate, the eventual site of Handsworth Park, was most certainly once a venue for the Sport of Kings.

SMETHWICK

The first reference to racing at Smethwick is of a two-day meeting that took place on Monday 16th and Tuesday 17th October 1854, on a flat, mile and a half course situated at the back of Mr Rudge's Swan Inn, within five minutes walk of the Stour Valley Railway. The *Birmingham Journal* reported: "The attendance was good on Monday; but on Tuesday the course was not so fully attended, owing to the meeting at Warwick, and the unsettled state of the weather. An excellent stand was erected, from which a distinct view of the running could be obtained."

The first race on Monday was the Brewery Galloway Stakes, which was won by Shamrock Lass, beating Creeping Sam and Butcher's Darling; next came a Handicap Hurdle Race, this being won by Alma, beating Larry o'Gaffe, Louisa and Little Gipsy. The third and final race was the Smethwick Stakes which went to Gaffer Green, beating Little Emma and Peggy cleverly in both heats.

Only two races took place on Tuesday, the Innkeepers' Stakes (for which there were five runners) being won by Little Gipsy, and the Consolation Plate going to Gaffer Green. James Davies, a young Birmingham man already well known to the police, was committed for trial after being caught trying to draw a watch from the waistcoat pocket of Mr Job Bates, a colliery agent. The *Journal* reported: "Inspector Dew and Police-constable Hillcox were close at hand, and the latter took the adroit, but for this time disappointed, thief into custody. We say thief, because the bare removal of the watch constituted a felony."

In 1855 the *Racing Calendar* lists the results from a meeting at "Handsworth" on Monday 8th and Tuesday 9th October. This took place at a new racecourse, upwards of a mile in length, which had been laid out by Henry Bolton, proprietor of the New Inn. In fact, the meeting was not held in Handsworth at all, being located at Smethwick, adjacent to the Blue Gates. The meeting had been transferred from Handsworth to Smethwick because of the Council's reluctance to hold it at Handsworth itself (see Handsworth chapter).

The *Birmingham Journal* reported: "No less than nineteen or twenty thousand persons were tempted by the extraordinary fine weather, the novelty, and the general arrangements, to attend. There were numerous improvements, a nice paddock abutting upon the grand stand, a square space in front, etc. The successful efforts of the police, too, under Inspector Dew, were beyond all praise, and with the exception of two detected cases of pocket-picking on the first day, and a few similar ones on the second, all went off exceedingly well.

"The grand stand was quite full, and here after each race, according to regulations, the winning horse was offered for sale by auction, by Mr. Samuel Rodway, of Birmingham, and in some cases his well known efforts were very successful."

There were three races on the first day and three more on the second. Monday's programme began with the Handsworth Stakes, which, after three heats, was won by Vestige, beating Tomyris, Resignation and five others in a well-contested race. A hurdle race, over four flights of hurdles, ended in Mr Findon's Rosa beating three others. "The Ladies' Purse," notes the *Journal's* reporter, "was taken after rather a severe struggle by Mr. Baker's Resignation, beating three others."

Tuesday opened with the Innkeepers' Stakes, over two miles, which Cock Sparrow won by a length, beating three opponents. The hurdle race drew only two runners, Rosa and Tomyris, but, according to our reporter, "was one of the best contests ever witnessed over a minor course, and after three severe and well contested heats Rosa won the stakes." The concluding Consolation Plate, run in three heats of once round and a distance, resulted in another victory for Cock Sparrow, beating The Despised and Resignation. The *Journal's* reporter ended: "This brought on six o'clock, and terminated a most exciting and successful meeting."

However, the next day brought another race. The owners of Tomyris and Cock Sparrow, Mr Green and Mr Phillips, made a match for these two horses to run for a £40 prize over the Smethwick course. Jockeys were duly mounted and, on the given signal, off they went, twice round and a distance, in excess of two miles. After a close battle between the pair, Tomyris (having his seventh race in three days) beat Cock Sparrow (having his eighth race in three days) by a neck.

With regard to the two instances of pick-pocketing, Mary Wilson, of Livery Street, was charged with having stolen a silver watch from Peter Oldcroft, a miner, and was committed for trial; and Michael McCarty was also sent for trial, despite protesting his innocence, accused of stealing a silk pocket-handkerchief and a race card from John Walford, a stock-keeper at the Smethwick Iron Works.

The following Monday, 15th October, pony racing was held at Smethwick over the "old mile course", said to have been close to Dudley Road and Grove Lane, within five minutes of the railway. There is then a gap of eight years before a two-day meeting took place "on the old course" at the back of the Swan Inn, Spon Lane, on 19th and 20th October 1863.

In 1866 an advert appeared for a race meeting at West Smethwick Park to be held on 15th and 16th October. This was again to be held on the "old course" at the back of the Swan Inn, courtesy of Mr B. Darby of the Holly Lane Tavern.

The last references to racing in Smethwick came with the announcement of a race meeting to be held on Oldbury Road in 1867, for which we have been unable to trace any results.

INKFORD BROOK

A race meeting took place under the auspices of the Warwickshire Hunt at Inkford Brook, near Wythall, on 1st April 1856, when a twelve-year-old local lad named Johnny Page rode a horse called Pat Manley to win the four-mile chase. Later that year, on 8th September, he gained his first pony race victory on Pretty Boy at Birmingham's Sparkbrook races.

Red-haired Page had come to Birmingham in 1854 with his family who operated a livery stable. His father, Joseph, later ran the Bulls Head on the Stratford Road. The Hall Green Steeplechases, which began in 1871, were held on his land.

Young Johnny, who had started out on his father's hunters and ponies, left school unable to read or write but that didn't bother him, for all he wanted to do was become a jockey. He became apprenticed to Joseph Dawson at East Ilsley, Berkshire, and rode his first "proper" Flat winner at Liverpool in 1858. During his brief spell as a Flat jockey he won the 1860 Northumberland Plate on First Lord.

He switched to riding over fences and scored his initial success in that sphere on Telegram at Sutton Coldfield on 15th February 1864. He went on to become champion National Hunt jockey in 1867 and 1868 before going to ride in France, where he won many races, both on the Flat and over jumps, including the Grand Steeplechase de Paris twice. When Harry Lamplugh was killed in a race fall, Page took over his stable in France and combined riding with training for the Duke of Hamilton.

Page rode in the Grand National eleven times, winning it twice, on Cortolvin in 1867 and Casse Tete in 1872. He also won the 1871 Birmingham Grand Annual on Moose, plus the 1867 Scottish Grand National on The Elk, and the Great Metropolitan Chase in 1869 on Chevy Chase.

It was also in 1869 that the North Warwickshire Hunt elected to stage a race meeting at Mr Frappells' farm at Inkford Brook. Members of the Hunt's committee, which included Johnny Page, met at the Bell Inn, Bristol Road on 23rd March and decided that the meeting should take place on Monday 5th April. The programme would consist of four races.

An announcement in *Aris's Birmingham Gazette* on Saturday 27th March listed the races, which comprised:

The Hunters' Handicap Stakes, for horses the *bona fide* property of gentlemen, farmers or tradesmen since 1st January 1869, that had been regularly hunted with the North Warwickshire Hounds.

The Open Hunters' Plate Steeplechase, for *bona fide* hunters that had never won a steeplechase, hurdle or Flat race value £20, or horses that had never run in a handicap steeplechase or hurdle race, or been in any public training stable since 1867.

The Galloway Steeplechase, for horses not exceeding 15 hands; with a cup for the winner and a cup for the second horse.

The Consolation Stakes, for beaten or maiden horses that had been regularly hunted with the North Warwickshire Hounds. The prizes included "a present of a race glass for the second horse."

The announcement concluded: "The course will be over Mr. Frappells' farm, at Inkford Brook, that gentleman having kindly given permission to the committee for its use, and fine weather is the only thing required to make it a successful meeting."

A further announcement was published in *Aris's Birmingham Gazette* on Saturday 3rd April:

"INKFORD BROOK HUNT STEEPLECHASES will take place on Monday next, April 5, to commence at 1.30. A small fee will be charged for admission to the grounds. Omnibuses from 11 to 12.30 from the Swan Hotel, New Street."

This appears to have been the last race meeting held at Inkford Brook.

As for Johnny Page, he retired from riding in 1880 and took over Grove Farm at Hall Green, which he held for some years. He later ran the Wylde Green Hotel. He retired to live in Shirley in 1907, dying there ten years later, aged 74. He was buried in the family grave at Boldmere, Sutton Coldfield.

The Inkford Brook area does have other associations with horse racing. During the 1950s Jack Lea trained nearby at Station Road, Wythall, while Jim Edmunds of Houndsfield Farm, Wythall, trained for some twenty years between the early 1960s and 1980s.

Nowadays the area is represented by Ian Williams, whose successful training operation is based at Dominion Racing Stables, Portway, a stone's throw from junction 3 of the M42.

SPARKBROOK AND BIRMINGHAM

The first race meeting at Sparkbrook took place in 1850. Pony racing was held there on Monday 9th September, on a course at the back of the Angel Inn, bounded by Highgate Road, Main Street and Kyrwicks Lane.

The Angel Inn, which had opened in 1849, was also the venue in 1851 when a two day meeting was held on Monday 18th and Tuesday 19th August. The course, which was described as being "very pretty", measured 1,000 yards round and was formed out of three large fields adjoining Turnpike Road, a few yards from the inn, situated one mile from Birmingham on the Warwick Road. Charles Whitworth, landlord of the Angel Inn, ran the meeting and many thousands attended.

The Angel Inn was again the venue the following year and also in 1853, when the "Birmingham and Sparkbrook Races" became a three-day affair, held on August 15th, 16th, and 17th. The programme was as follows:

FIRST DAY

HIGHGATE STAKES. – For Ponies under thirteen hands. 15s each, with £3. added; catch weights. Heats, twice round and a distance.

INNKEEPERS' STAKES. – For Galloways under fourteen hands. £1. each, with £5. added. Three years old, 6st.; four years, 7st.; five years, 8st.; six and aged, 8st. 10lb. Heats, three times round. The winner to pay 10s. 6d. towards expenses.

SPARKBROOK STAKES. – For Horses of all denominations. £3. each, with £15. added. Three years old, 7st ; four years, 8st.; five years, 8st. 10lb.; six and aged, 9st. The second Horse to save his stake. Heats, three times round and a distance.

SECOND DAY

LADIES' PURSE. – For ponies under twelve hands. 10s. each, with £2 added. Heats, once round and a distance.

BIRMINGHAM STAKES. - For Horses of all denominations. £3. each, with £15. added. Three years old, 7st.; four years, 8st.; five years, 8st. 10lb.; six and aged, 9st. The winner of the Sparkbrook Stakes to carry 7lb. extra. The second Horse to save his stake. Heats, twice round and a distance.

HURDLE RACE. - For Horses of all denominations. £2. each, with £7. added. Over two flights of Hurdles. Three years old, 8st.; four years, 9st.; five years, 9st. 10lb.; six and aged, 10st. The winner of any Hurdle Race in the years 1852 and 1853, once 7lb. extra; twice 10lb extra; thrice 14lb extra. Heats, three times round and a distance. The winner to pay 10s. 6d. towards expenses.

THIRD DAY

LADYPOOL LANE STAKES. - For Galloways under fourteen hands. £1. each, with £5. added. The same conditions as the first day, with 5lb. added for winning. Winner to pay 10s. 6d. towards expenses.

BOOTH STAKES. – For Beaten Ponies under thirteen hands. 15s each, with £3. added. Catch weights. Twice round and a distance.

STAND STAKES. – Hurdle Race for Beaten Horses. £2. each, with £5. added. To be Handicapped by the Committee. Heats, three times round and a distance. The winner to pay 10s. 6d. towards expenses.

A MATCH, for £20.

The announcement concluded: "The Grand Stand will be the only one allowed on the ground. Any person obstructing the roads will be dealt with according to law. Police will be in attendance to enforce these regulations. No Gambling allowed."

It seems a strange proviso, that no gambling was to be permitted at the race meeting!

Nonetheless, there was a crowd of 15,000 on the opening day. The lack of proper fences to keep the public off the course was a serious cause for concern. It was reported that, on the first day, a cab driver named William Mason ran onto the course and "finding the horses close on him he turned to return, but was knocked over by a man following into the path of the oncoming horses. He was hit by two of them, breaking both his thigh and spine, paralysing him."

A Flat meeting was held on Monday 7th and Tuesday 8th August 1854, with crowds of 20,000 being present on both days. In 1855 a two-day pony racing fixture took place in September. Ponies were measured at the Angel Inn on the day of the races, with admission to the grandstand costing one shilling. It attracted a crowd of between 10,000 and 12,000 each day. Following the accident to the cab driver two years earlier, this time several people were injured when a section of scaffolding that supported the temporary grandstand collapsed.

In 1856 pony racing took place on a new course located two miles out of town on the Warwick Road, to the left of Ladypool Lane. The meeting was run by Henry Keeten and took place on Monday 8th and Tuesday 9th September.

The 1857 *Racing Calendar* announced that that year's Sparkbrook and Birmingham meeting would take place on Monday 3rd and Tuesday 4th August, over the same ground as the previous year but with an additional field, making the course three-quarters of a mile round. There was a large grandstand and two races on both days to keep the customers satisfied. However, it appears that going racing at Sparkbrook still had its dangers. This time a greengrocer named John Floyd, of Ward Street, was knocked down and had his left leg fractured in two places.

The first day began with the Innkeepers Stakes. It was run in two heats of three times round, both of which were won by Miss Hatch, beating Peter Snipe and Our Jim. Then came a hurdle race, also run in heats of three times round. This time it was Our Jim that won both heats, beating Miss Hatch and Peter Snipe.

Those same three horses, despite having each run four races on the first day, all turned out again for the hurdle race on day two. Again it was run in heats of three times round, and on this occasion it was the turn of Peter Snipe to win both heats, beating Our Jim, Billy and Miss Hatch. The final event was the Sparkhill Stakes, run in heats of – yes, you've guessed it – three times round. Not satisfied with having raced six times already, Our Jim won the first two heats, thereby defeating Peter Snipe "and one other", presumably either Miss Hatch or Billy.

Hence, the extraordinary Sparkbrook meeting of 1857 featured four races comprising a total of eight heats, with just four horses competing in all of them. They certainly earned their corn in those days!

Our Jim, in fact, ran in seventeen races that year comprising twenty-six heats, having had his name changed twice. When appearing at the Coventry April meeting he was known as Challow Boy, but his lack of success there must have induced his new owner, Mr Massey, to change his name to Dick Taylor for the June Redditch meeting. Having 'only' won the last race there, the Beaten Handicap, there was another change of owner, a Mr Hurst, who raced him as Our Jim at Sparkbrook with greater success.

It was assumed that the annual Birmingham and Sparkbrook races would again be held at the course near the Angel Inn in 1858. That year, however, there was an alternative fixture, due to be held on Monday 19th and Tuesday 20th July "on the New Course" on land belonging to Samuel Melsom, proprietor of the George Inn, Sparkbrook. It was located opposite the George Inn, between Ladypool Lane and St. Paul's Church, by Moseley Road, comprising two fields extending from the railway line at Brighton Road Station to Ladypool Lane. However, the course was narrow and the turns were considered somewhat dangerous.

This meeting was called simply "Sparkbrook". Admission to the grandstand cost a shilling; traps one shilling and sixpence; and four-wheeled carriages two shillings. The first race each day was scheduled for two o'clock precisely and the numerous side-shows included an "exhibition of educated monkeys."

The various conditions and stipulations of the meeting included: "Any jockey riding in false colours to be fined 5 shillings", along with "fictitious entries will be disqualified" and "Every horse to walk and canter past the stand before starting." All applications for booths were to be made to Mr Melsom at the George Inn, and nobody would be allowed to sell wines, spirits and ales, except the booth-keepers.

The first day of the meeting would feature the Moseley Selling Stakes, in heats of three times round; a hurdle race, run in three heats, over six flights of hurdles; the Birmingham Stakes for horses not exceeding 14 hands high, run in heats of "about one mile"; and the Kings Norton Stakes, for ponies not exceeding 11 1/2 hands.

Day two was to open with a hurdle race, again run in three heats, over six flights of hurdles; followed by the Sparkbrook Stakes in heats of three times round; the Highgate Stakes, also in heats, twice round; and conclude with a handicap race.

However, a subsequent announcement stated that the annual Sparkbrook meeting would take place a fortnight later "on the Old Course, near The Angel, Sparkbrook, one mile from Birmingham on the Warwick Road," on Monday 2nd and Tuesday 3rd August 1858. The Angel Inn was now run by Tom Parker who also presided as a Steward at the race meeting.

The August meeting duly went ahead. It opened with the Handicap Plate, both heats being won easily by the six-year-old Perseverance, ridden by Ennis, beating Michael and Clover. Blink Bonny, despite having to carry 15lb more than the allotted weight of 7st, was an equally impressive winner of both heats of the Birmingham Stakes, defeating Clover and Snipe. Perseverance then lived up to his name when reappearing to win both heats of the Innkeepers' Selling Stakes from Michael and Sir Richard.

In what was the most exciting event of the meeting, the Sparkbrook Stakes, Michael beat Clover by a neck in the first heat, with Clover turning the tables by a length and a half in the second heat. Clover then won the deciding third heat easily. Michael and Clover clashed again in the very next race, a Sweepstakes over three laps of the course, with Michael coming out on top this time, winning both heats.

The paucity of runners meant that both Michael and Clover ran in nine heats during the two days. Other races at the meeting included two hurdle races, plus the Aston Stakes for ponies, which was won by Birmingham Lass.

The "New Course" on Mr Melsom's land opposite the George Inn, Brunswick Road, was used for the second (and last) time on Monday 1st and Tuesday 2nd August 1859. There is no record of any Sparkbrook meeting having taken place in 1860.

In 1861 a "Sparkbrook & Shirley" meeting was held on Monday 5th and Tuesday 6th August on another new course, at the back of the Saracen's Head, Shirley, about four miles from Birmingham. The Stewards were Messrs Weaver (who ran the Saracen's Head), Parker and Wamsley.

We can trace no reports of any Sparkbrook meetings between 1862 and 1867. However, racing returned on 3rd and 4th August 1868 on "the old grounds at Ladypool Lane." Henry Keeten, who had officiated at the 1856 meeting, was again in charge.

The 1869 Birmingham and Sparkbrook meeting, held on 2nd and 3rd August, again on the old grounds at Ladypool Lane, was to be the last. The curse that had bedevilled the early meetings returned with a vengeance when two accidents occurred on the first day. A young lad named Frederick Ford was badly injured when running across the course and being struck by a horse. Half an hour later, sixteen-year-old John Watts was also knocked down.

Maybe it was these accidents that led to the ultimate demise of racing at Sparkbrook, for there are no records of any further meetings being held there. Walking round today's built up district of Sparkbrook, it is hard to envisage that it was once home to so many racecourses.

THE WAKE RACES

DERITEND POOL

The Deritend Pool races were held at Mill Pool, Heath Mill Lane, on a piece of land lying between Fazeley Street and Little Ann Street. They were purely for ponies and donkeys and formed one of the attractions of the annual Wake fair. Announcements advertising these meetings first appeared in local newspapers in 1848.

The 1851 fixture was held on 28th and 29th July, with entries for the races being taken at the Forge Tavern, Fazeley Street. A grandstand was erected for the comfort of the spectators.

In the *Birmingham Journal's* report of the 1853 meeting, held on 1st and 2nd August, its correspondent eulogised: "This ancient local institution, which nearly 500 years ago first had an ecclesiastical formation, and which exists to this day, if somewhat metamorphosed in character, yet scarcely less spiritual than of old, was celebrated on Monday and Tuesday, the festivity, however, having commenced on Sunday evening. The extensive piece of ground, the old mill pool, which has been levelled, afforded an excellent field for the annual sports, but more especially for the races, which were of a character very much superior to those of former years. Wombwell's menagerie, and abundant shows of all kinds, crowded the ground; and thousands of persons participated in the amusements, and in the good things of this life, supplied at innumerable booths."

The 1854 meeting took place on Monday 31st July and Tuesday 1st August, with the following year's being held on the last two days of July at a "well tanned course" of only three-quarters of a mile.

On 31st July 1855 the *Birmingham Daily Press* wrote of Deritend Pool Races: "None but a locally 'raised' man can thoroughly comprehend this phrase. The wake is easily enough imagined. Its booths, round-abouts, shooting galleries, gingerbread, American ice, buns, Banburies, pop, pork pies, and brandy snap, and their inspectors, visitors, and purchasers, male and female, young, old, and middle-aged, respectable, dubious, and bad, are common to every wake in the kingdom. The addition of the races was in itself nothing remarkable; but that these races should have for a course a pool – the pool – Deritend Pool, known to our boyhoods as the only urban sheet of water where we could play 'ducks and drakes', sail paper boats, catch sticklebacks, bathe, slide, and skate – this is a step above the common, and gives to this annual gathering a classic interest – Brummagem classics, of course.

"Of the thousands assembled yesterday on the course, the greater portion, it is probable, indulged in some reminiscences of the pool when it was a pool, recalled, it maybe, the swallow sporting on its banks, the mishaps of bygone winters or the grief of still earlier years. Reminiscences, however, did not prevent the crowds who yesterday thronged the Pool from thoroughly enjoying the present.

"The amusements were of the usual character, but the booths were rather more numerous than is customary. Many persons are of opinion that meetings such as these are objectionable. So, no doubt, in some points of view they are, but their advocates have also several strong arguments. They say that anything that brings people together for mutual recreation is beneficial, as strengthening that bond of union among all classes was never more needed than now. They also say that 'wakes', fairs, and public meetings are calculated to keep what have been termed 'the dangerous classes' from indulging in amusements and pursuits of a less innocent tendency.

"A large number of more respectable visitors say, 'I want amusement and I am not very particular what it is. I enjoy those opportunities for pleasure and relaxation that are afforded me, and I don't care to analyse them very deeply. I eat my dinner, and I don't go into the kitchen to see how it is cooked; if I did, I might find the cook not remarkable for cleanliness, and I should leave my plate of meat disgusted, but still hungry.'

"While, therefore, these meetings seem destined for a time to exist, it is quite as well to see that they are carried out with some regard to propriety, and the good temper and orderly conduct exhibited by the vast crowd must have been a subject of congratulation to all. The police, too, fulfilled their office with much discretion, and the whole affair passed off with less drunkenness and disturbance than would have been expected.

"Mr. Keeten, and the gentlemen who acted with him as a committee, had made the best arrangements possible, and had their efforts to provide tolerable sport crowned with success." (Henry Keeten, who died on 28th January 1874, was a prominent promoter of horse racing in and around Birmingham.)

The first day's races opened with the Trial Stakes, for ponies not exceeding 12 hands, in which Mr Burdett's Little Dwarf beat Kitty and Mr Bucknell's unnamed brown pony. This was, noted the reporter: "A good race, but marred by the crowded state of the course."

The second event was the Deritend Pool Stakes, for ponies not exceeding 13½ hands, this being won by Hobbie Noble. In the third and final contest, the Aston Stakes, for ponies not exceeding 13 hands, Mr Jones' Deceitful defeated Little Dwarf in a tight race comprising three heats. The only other runner, Hobbie Noble, fell, the report remarking that "Her rider, we are sorry to say, received some rather serious injuries." It added that: "Mr. Jones's claim to the stake is disputed, his pony's qualification being questioned. The matter will be settled this day."

Sadly for the *Birmingham Daily Press* correspondent, that 1855 fixture seems to have been the last race meeting held there. Confirmation of its demise came with the following advert which appeared in that same newspaper on Friday 27th March 1857.

DERITEND POOL ESTATE

LOWER FAZELEY STREET, HEATH MILL LANE AND FLOODGATE STREET. The Proprietors having completed the NEW BRIDGE in FLOODGATE STREET, are now prepared to SELL or LET, on BUILDING LEASES this important ESTATE in lots, suitable for MANU-FACTORIES or other WORKS with Frontages to the above Streets and the River Rea.

Apply to Messrs. James G. and Lister Lea, 47, Union Passage, Birmingham.

The "ancient local institution" of the wake had succumbed to the relentless growth of an industrialised Birmingham.

OLDBURY

Most towns had their Annual Wake but there were some locals who believed the "Oldbury Wake and Races" to be the greatest festival of the year.

Few racecourses were as good as Oldbury's. It was considered the best for miles around Birmingham, and thousands of people from neighbouring towns flocked there for the races.

The Wake was held on the ground lying between the Flash Brook and the canal and in a northerly direction from the Birmingham Road. There was racing on the first three days of the Wake, predominantly races for ponies, and winding up with a donkey race.

The racing was well organised. A grandstand was erected each year and the course was marked out with a combination of posts and rails, or ropes. Immediately before each race a bell was rung and a horseman in hunting dress rode round to clear the course of people.

Every publican of importance had a special licence to sell alcohol on the race ground. They occupied large booths and also supplied hot and cold meats and other types of food. The booths were placed as near as possible to the grandstand with one end opening out onto the course itself.

In addition, there were roundabouts, swing-boats, shooting galleries, coconut shies, a boxing booth and other amusements, plus stalls selling toys and sweets, accompanied by brass bands and other forms of musical entertainment. It was, quite literally, "all the fun of the fair". Many of the adjoining streets had similar stalls lined along the edge of the footpath. At night, lamps illuminated the whole gigantic affair, as festivities continued into the early hours.

Oldbury Wake traditionally took place during either the last week of August or the first week of September. Precisely when the Wake itself started is unclear but we do know that there were races held on 3rd September 1838 and on 31st August 1840. There then appears to have been a break, as an announcement of the 1849 fixture states that the races were being revived "after 8 or 9 years".

There was a meeting in September 1850, and another on the first three days of September 1851, held at the "old course" near to the Parrot Arms.

The 1852 renewal took place on Monday 30th and Tuesday 31st August. Despite the showery conditions, the *Birmingham Journal* reported that nearly 6,000 persons were present, "the ground being covered with shows and all descriptions of amusements."

The stewards were certainly kept busy. The first two events on Monday, the Galloway Stakes and the Sweepstakes, passed off peaceably enough, but the six-runner Silver Cup, for ponies not exceeding 12 1/2 hands, made up for that. In the first heat, Little Wonder and Whistling Jemmy collided with each other and unseated their riders. Then, after Mr Gregg's Jenny Lind had won both heats, Mr Turner, owner of third-placed Cambrian Lass, lodged an objection on the grounds of the winner being 12 hands 3 inches high, rather than the maximum allowed 12 hands 2 inches. The *Journal* stated that "the matter is to be referred to *Bell's Life*", who were evidently the recognised arbiters of such matters.

Tuesday opened with further controversy after Mr Howe's Young Dutchman had finished alone in the first heat of the Gentlemen's Stakes, his sole rival, the aforementioned Cambrian Lass, having struck a post and lost her rider, who suffered a fractured left arm in the fall. In a display of gamesmanship hardly appropriate of a gentleman, Mr Howe immediately objected and claimed the stake, unless the same jockey rode Cambrian Lass in the second heat, which was, of course, impossible. After some delay, Howe's objection was waived. In the end it was all academic, for Young Dutchman won the second heat in a canter to land the spoils.

After a considerable delay at the starting post, Mr Nightingale's Sugar won the first heat of the Ladies' Purse by a length, then followed up with an easy victory in the second heat from Mackerel and Banker. Neddy Darby was disqualified, having bolted with his rider. Mr Roose's Shamrock Lass followed up her victory in the previous day's Galloway Stakes by winning the final race, a Silver Cup, "for horses not thorough-bred."

The *Journal* ended its report by noting: "An ordinary was provided each day at the Parrott (sic) Arms by Mr. Turner, to whose exertions the inhabitants are mainly indebted for the races this year."

In 1853 an announcement proclaimed:

"OLDBURY WAKE and RACES,

Monday, Tuesday, and Wednesday, August 29, 30, and 31.

FIRST DAY – MONDAY.

THE AMUSEMENTS OF THE WAKE.

SECOND DAY – TUESDAY.

The OLDBURY STAKES, for Ponies, under 13 hands high, for £3. Entrance 5s. Catch weight.

A PONY RACE for a Silver Cup, for Ponies under 12 1/2 hands high, added to the entrance of 7s 6d each. The second horse to save his Stakes. Catch weight. Heats.

A HANDICAP FOOT RACE, for Two Sovereigns. Entrance 2s 6d. Heats.

THIRD DAY –WEDNESDAY

The INNKEEPERS' STAKES, for £5. Entrance 10s 6d., for Horses of all denomi-nations, the property of residents of Oldbury. Weight to commence at 8st. 10lb., and 7lb. added for every inch. Heats.

The GALLOWAY STAKES, for Four Guineas. Entrance 10s. Second horse to save his Stake. To be handicapped on the Morning of the Race. Heats.

BOOTH STAKES, for £3, for Beaten Ponies, under 13 hands. Entrance 5s. Heats. Entries for this race to close on Tuesday, before Ten o'clock p.m."

The conditions stipulated that a minimum of three horses must start for each race, with all entries, along with the colours and names of the jockeys, to be made in writ-ing and submitted to the Clerk of the Course at the Parrot Arms, Oldbury, by ten o'clock on the Saturday evening, 27th August.

It was also stipulated: "No Person allowed to sell Excisable Articles except the Booths on the Ground. Any Person selling, or obstructing the Roads, will be dealt with according to law. Police will be in attendance to enforce these regulations. All applications for Booths to be made to Mr. Turner, at the Parrot Arms, on or before Tuesday, the 23rd."

A similar announcement appears for the following year, declaring that: "Oldbury Wake and Races will be held, as usual, on the Old Course adjoining the Parrot Arms, on Monday and Tuesday, September 4th and 5th, 1854."

The first day's races comprised the Oldbury Stakes, for ponies under 13 hands high; a Silver Cup, for ponies under 12 1/2 hands; and a hurdle race, over five flights of hurdles, for ponies under 12 hands. The second day opened with the Booth Stakes, for ponies under 13 hands; then came another Silver Cup, this one for ponies under 12 hands; and finally, the Trial Stakes, for beaten ponies under 11 1/2 hands.

As before, entries, with colours, were to be made at the Parrot Arms. Conditions included that any jockey starting without wearing colours would be fined five shillings. Applications for Booths, costing £2 each, would be decided by ballot, these being the only outlets allowed on the course for selling ales or liquors. Admission for brewers' wagons cost 10s each; with carriages 2s 6d; gigs and carts 1s 6d, and a saddle horse 6d.

Curiously, directly below this announcement is an advert for "Oldbury Races", to be held on the very same days, 4th and 5th September 1854, "at the back of the Old Crown, and opposite Mr. Charles Hickin's, the Engineer's Arms."

Here the races comprised the Innkeepers' Stakes and the Oldbury Stakes, both restricted to ponies not exceeding 13 hands; plus the Trial Stakes and the West Bromwich Stakes, both for ponies not exceeding 12 hands. All four races were to be run in heats of twice round and a distance, with the winners being called upon to pay ten shillings to the Race Fund.

Was this a rival meeting? Did it even take place? The concept of two pony racing fixtures being held in Oldbury on the same days seems ludicrous. However, with both of them taking place adjacent to pubs, at least there would have been somewhere for racegoers to celebrate their winnings or drown their sorrows!

Reports and results of the 1855 Oldbury races, held on Monday 3rd and Tuesday 4th September, appeared in the *Birmingham Journal*. On Monday, there were three races, beginning with the Trial Stakes, "of 5s each, with £3 added from the Oldbury Race Fund", which was won in two heats by Mr Ashford's Tiny, formerly named Little Dwarf. The Oldbury Stakes, "of 10s each, with £5 added", went to Mr Owen's Deceitful, who beat Hobby Noble and Kitty Cut-a-Dash. The last event was a Handicap, "of 5s each, with £1 added", which was contested by three horses, Tiny again being the winner. Tiny added further to his tally when winning Tuesday's first race, the Innkeepers' Stakes. Hobby Noble won the Handicap for beaten ponies, and the Railway Stakes went to Deceitful in two heats, beating two others.

Immediately above the report of that year's races was the following item, entitled:

"ROBBERIES ON THE RACE GROUNDS"

It stated: "On Tuesday, a youth from Birmingham, named Samuel Rands, was charged with stealing a cotton handkerchief from the pocket of James Walters, a farm labourer, of Worley Wigorn, on the race grounds, on Monday evening. He was shown to be a regular associate of thieves, and the Magistrates, in exercising their extended jurisdiction, sentenced him to three months hard labour.

"John Thomas, from Nottingham, was also charged with stealing under similar circumstances, a pocket handkerchief, the property of William Knipton, of Yorkshire, who was on a visit to his Oldbury friends. Although the prisoner's hand was felt in the prosecutor's pocket, the property could not be found, and the accused not being able to give a good account of himself, he was sentenced to three months hard labour as a rogue and vagabond."

Sentences of three months hard labour for stealing a handkerchief give some indication of the draconian punishments that existed during those times.

Oldbury Wake's annual races continued at the back of the Old Crown throughout the 1860s and early 1870s, being held during the last week of August or first week of September. The last specific report of racing at Oldbury covers the two-day meeting held on 31st August and 1st September 1874. However, the revelry of the Wake and its horse races was enjoyed by the masses right up until 1885.

During its later years, the Wake and the races were held on the opposite side of Birmingham Street, in a field between that street and Stone Street. But the racecourse was much smaller than its predecessor and nothing like as good. Furthermore, with licences to sell alcohol invariably being refused by the local magistrates, neither was it as well attended. Eventually, the ground was required by the Tharsis & Copper Extracting Company, and the Wake was again moved, this time to a site in Bromford Road, but, alas, without the races.

WEST BROMWICH

It is thought that pony racing may have been going for some years in West Bromwich. Its name was also associated with the "Dudley, Tipton and West Bromwich Races" during the 1830s, although the "West Bromwich" element was dropped after 1840.

An 1853 announcement in the *Birmingham Journal* proclaims:

SWAN VILLAGE. WEST BROMWICH.

WAKE SPORTS,

ON MONDAY and TUESDAY NEXT, 7th and 8th November, 1853.

FIRST DAY – MONDAY

A PONY RACE, of 5s each, with 3 sovs. added, for Ponies not exceeding 13 hands high; heats, twice round the course; three to start, or no race; the second horse to save his stake. Open to all England.

A MATCH, for 10 sovs. Three times round the course.

The INNKEEPERS' STAKES, of 10s each, with 5 sovs. added, for Horses of all denominations, the property of Gentlemen the residents of West Bromwich; heats, twice round and a distance; three to start, or no race; the second horse to save his stake.

FOOT RACING, BAG RACING, and other amusements.

SECOND DAY – TUESDAY

A PONY RACE, of 5s each, with 3 sovs. added, for Ponies not exceeding 13 hands high, the property of Gentlemen the residents of West Bromwich; heats, twice round; three to start, or no race; the second horse to save his stake.

The HANDSWORTH STAKES, of 10s each, with 5 sovs. added, for Galloways not exceeding 14 hands high; heats, twice round the course; three to start, or no race; the second horse to save his stake.

A MATCH, for 10 sovs. Two miles round the course.

FOOT RACING and other amusements.

We are not quite sure what the "bag racing" constituted, other than presumably a sack race of some sort. However, the horses could be entered to run in the "proper" races by applying to William Minshaw, who ran the Swan Inn in Swan Village.

There was a similar announcement in the *Birmingham Journal* the following year:

WEST BROMWICH WAKE

SWAN VILLAGE RACES

WILL take place on MONDAY and TUESDAY, November the 6th and 7th, over the Old Course, adjoining Mr. Minshaw's, the Swan Inn.

The races were of a similar nature to those of the previous year, although there were some minor amendments to the conditions of entry. Stipulations included: "Colours to be named at the time of entry; Jockeys deviating from colours named to forfeit 10s to the racing fund."

On 8th and 9th August 1855, pony racing took place at a new Wake meeting, near to New Church, Union Cross Inn, in Greets Green. The next reference to racing in the area is for a meeting on 29th and 30th June 1863, held at Newtown, near Great Bridge.

A three-day "Newtown Wake & Races" fixture was staged at the Phoenix Inn, Ryder's Green, West Bromwich, on 2nd, 3rd and 4th July 1866.

The two-day "West Bromwich" meeting, held on 28th and 29th June 1869, back at the Newtown venue, near Great Bridge, appears to have been the last recorded meeting in that area.

CAPE RACES

As with West Bromwich, the Cape Races may have taken place for many years, although the first positive reference is an advert dated 15th October 1855, which spoke of pony racing on the old mile course. The course is said to have been close to Dudley Road and Grove Lane.

The *Birmingham Daily Post* of 11th September 1861 carried the following announcement:

"CAPE RACES AND OX ROASTING
WILL TAKE PLACE on MONDAY and TUESDAY NEXT, September 16th and
17th, at Mr. Gordon's Cape of Good Hope, Smethwick.
Applications for Stalls, Booths, Shows, & c., apply to Mr. J. Gordon."

They raced there again the following year on 15th and 16th September, though there is no further mention of the ox roasting!

Although racing appears to have been spasmodic, August meetings took place in four consecutive years between 1866 and 1869. The 1866 fixture was held on 20th August, while the 1867 meeting of 26th and 27th August was supplemented by a two-day October meeting.

The latter was announced in the *Birmingham Daily Post*, stating that: "Birmingham and Smethwick Autumn Hurdle and Flat Racing will be held on the Cape Grounds on Monday and Tuesday, October 14th and 15th, 1867."

That October fixture appears to have been a one-off, for the only racing there in 1868 was the traditional two-day August affair. However, ox roasting or no, time was fast running out for Cape Races, and the meeting held on 23rd and 24th August 1869 appears to have been the last.

A 'HOAX' RACE MEETING
AT BORDESLEY GREEN

Back in the second half of the nineteenth century there were lots of minor once-a-year race meetings nestled in obscure locations. They included barely heard-of venues such as Netton Hunt, Little Bridge, Shilbottle and Wrangle Common. The clerk of the course usually sent the list of runners to one or both of the two daily racing papers – the *Sporting Life* and *The Sportsman* – for publication, and then, after the last race had been run, would telegraph them with the results.

In 1898, *The Sportsman* received a letter signed by Mr G. Martin, clerk of the course of Trodmore Race Club, Cornwall, containing the entries for the Trodmore Hunt's forthcoming fixture on August Bank Holiday Monday.

The results were duly wired to *The Sportsman* and appeared in Tuesday's edition. The *Sporting Life* hadn't been notified of the meeting but spotted the results in its rival paper and published them the next day. However, the *Life* gave the starting price of one of the winners, Reaper, at 5 to 2 instead of 5 to 1, which had appeared in *The Sportsman*. The bookmakers queried the discrepancy and so it was decided to contact Mr Martin to ascertain the correct SP. But where was Trodmore? Somewhere in Cornwall, but where exactly? The police didn't know, neither did the Post Office. In fact, there was no such place.

Trodmore Hunt turned out to be a fictitious race meeting, allegedly devised by a group of Fleet Street journalists who knew exactly how the process worked. They then simply wrote their own results and went round the next day collecting their winnings. Once the perpetrators realised they'd been rumbled, they quickly went to ground. Although the journalists came under very strong suspicion, nobody was apprehended and the instigators of the plot were never found.

Some twenty years earlier, the front page of the *Birmingham Daily Mail* of 2nd August 1877 had carried the following announcement:

BORDESLEY GREEN RACES
(BANK HOLIDAY)
ON MONDAY, AUGUST 6, 1877
Ten minutes walk from Saltley Station and three minutes walk from Saltley College, and five minutes walk from the Custard House.

STEWARDS:
Mr. FRANK HORSFALL; Mr. THOS FLETCHER

Committee Room :- FOUNTAIN INN, CHEAPSIDE

YARDLEY STAKES OF 10 GUINEAS

For Ponies 13 hands 2 inches, 9st.; 7lbs allowed for every inch under. Winners 7lb extra. Entrance, one guinea. About three-quarters of a mile.

STECHFORD STAKES OF 15 GUINEAS

For Galloways 14 hands 2 inches, 10st.; 7lbs allowed for every inch under. Winners of any race in 1877 to carry 7lb extra. Entrance, one guinea. About one and a half miles, over six flights of hurdles.

INNKEEPERS STAKES OF 20 GUINEAS

Over hurdles, for horses 15 hands, to carry 10st.; 7lbs allowed for every inch under. Winners of any race in 1877 to carry 7lb extra. Entrance, two guineas. About one and a half miles.

THE BIRMINGHAM STAKES OF 20 GUINEAS
THE FIRST ANNUAL

This race will consist of horses the bona-fide property of Cab Proprietors, and will be ridden by bona-fide proprietors, their sons or drivers. No other horses will be allowed to compete in this race. The winner, in addition to the stakes, will be presented with a massive Silver Medal, with the name of the horse and rider engraved thereon.

For bona-fide cab horses 15 hands to carry 10st.; 7lbs allowed for every inch under. Entrance, one guinea. About one mile and a half on the flat.

MATCH FOR £50
SCURRY WELTER

This race to name and close on the day of the races. The second horse to receive one third of the stakes. To carry 10st.; 7lbs allowed for every inch under 15 hands.

Each nomination must be accompanied by the entrance fee, and the colours named at the Committee Room. Owners at a distance will please send height and colours, with entrance fee. Post Office Orders to be made payable to Mr. H. Luckman.

The Stakes will be paid over to the winners the same evening at the Committee Room.

NOTICE TO TRADESMEN

Owners of Ponies, Galloways, and Horses, wishing to make matches between themselves to be run on the above course, can do so. The amount of Stakes, name of Stakeholder, and names and colours must be sent not later than Friday, August 3rd, to the Clerk of the Course, at the Committee Rooms, so that they can appear in print.

Starter – Mr. THOS COLLINS.   JUDGE – Mr. JAMES CORBETT.

Mr. HENRY LUCKMAN, Clerk of Course and Scales.

NOTICE

The owners of Ponies, Galloways, and Horses, are respectfully informed that the Course can be used for Exercising and Training, with use of Hurdles and attendance, up till the 4th of August. Admission Tickets, 5s each, to be had at the Committee Room. All enquiry for Booths, Stalls, Shows, &c., apply at Committee Rooms.

The meeting was to be staged adjacent to the Old Guy in Digbeth. The programme of events looked genuine enough, if somewhat innovative, what with a race for cab horses and the winner receiving a "massive Silver Medal". The tight deadlines meant that anyone wishing to "make matches between themselves", or nominate an entry in time for the Scurry Welter race, would have needed to – well, scurry.

When racegoers turned up at Bordesley Green on August Bank Holiday Monday to watch the races, there were no races.

The *Birmingham Daily Mail's* 'Table Talk' column the following Saturday, 11th August, opined: "As predicted by many, the projected 'Bordesley Park Races' turned out a shameful hoax. Most decent people rejoice at the *fiasco* – a 'consummation devotely (sic) to be wished' by all. Some of the greatest roughs in Birmingham assembled at the rendezvous and as a whole the gathering was of the most 'rowdy' description. The prime mover in the affair is non-est, and if wise will keep out of the way.

"One person must have felt grateful for this 'meeting' – a local publican, whose entire stock was drunk up by the crowd. All things considered, the victimised pleasure seekers were wonderfully good humoured and forbearing."

This 'hoax' accusation brought forth an immediate response, which appeared in the *Birmingham Daily Mail* on Monday 13th August:

"THE BORDESLEY GREEN 'RACES'

With reference to the remarks in 'Table Talk' on Saturday regarding the 'races' at Bordesley Green, Mr. H. Luckman, 'clerk of the course', writes that he was on the ground from 12 till 6 p.m.; that an excellent racecourse had been laid out at great expense, and the sole reason the races were postponed was a misunderstanding with the county police for the supply of men to protect his interests."

In fact, the 1877 Bordesley Green races appear to have been abandoned rather than merely postponed, for there are no announcements of a revised date, nor can we trace any results of such a meeting.

So, was it merely an elaborate hoax or not?

Interestingly, some credence to the course's existence is given in Showell's 1885 Dictionary of Birmingham, which refers, firstly, to a racecourse at Walmer Lane (Newtown Row) and then, crucially, also mentions that there was one at Bordesley. There was a Horse & Jockey pub in Newtown Row and also one of that name in Mills Street, Bordesley Park.

Having said that, our researches could not uncover any further references to horse racing in the Bordesley Green area.

Rather like the syndicate of journalists who devised the fictitious Trodmore Hunt meeting, could it perhaps have been the local publican trying an unusual way of drumming up trade? We'll never know for sure.

SUTTON COLDFIELD

(BIRMINGHAM STEEPLECHASES)

The name 'Sutton' denoted the 'South Tun' or 'South Town' lying to the south of Tamworth. The 'Coldfield' derives from the days when charcoal burners were present in the surrounding forest. 'Col' or 'cole' was the old name for charcoal, whereas the coal in use today was then termed 'sea-cole'. An alternative derivation for 'col-field' is a field on a hillside, the French word for hill being 'colline'.

Sutton Coldfield staged its first steeplechase in 1852 at a course to the side of the Lichfield Road. A more permanent venue was then found adjacent to Moor Hall Park. Moor Hall itself had been built for Bishop Vestey in 1527 and had been extended in the eighteenth century. The course was situated on the opposite side of the Lichfield Road to the original one, being "just through the town of Sutton, and past the Toll Gate," with Tamworth Lane to the south, the Lichfield Turnpike Road on the west, Little Sutton Lane to the north, and Moor Hall Park to the east.

Sutton Coldfield's Moor Hall racecourse was to be the home of 'Birmingham Steeplechases' from 1857 to 1873. It was a circular course with eight fences to a circuit. The main event, the Birmingham Grand Annual Steeplechase, was three times round, making 24 fences in all. A local reporter claimed: "The course, from the undulating character of the ground and the splendid scenery round, forms one of the finest Steeplechase Courses in the country."

The inaugural meeting at Moor Hall took place on Tuesday 24th March 1857. The Birmingham Grand Annual was won by Sting, ridden by Edwin Weever.

The *Birmingham Post* covered the 1858 meeting, which took place on Monday 22nd March, and reported: "These annual affairs came off yesterday at Sutton Coldfield, under the able management of Mr. John Sheldon, jun., and passed off with *eclat*. Indeed the steeple chases, under the present auspices, appear to be 'looking up,' and we have no hesitation in saying will become second to none, as every sporting man seems duly to appreciate the fresh 'infusion of blood'. Thirty-nine horses ran for the five events, and we are glad to say that falls were 'few and far between,' despite the racing pace at which some of the stakes were run."

The course was the same as the previous year's, described as being all grass apart from one field of wheat and another of turnip. The *Post* reported: "The start was effected from a wheat enclosure rather on the ascent side of the Tamworth Road, to leave which a stump hedge and bank had to be topped; after which the competitors bore to the right, and had a long run of some 300 yards through a turnip field, and a laid fence brought them to another turning flag, when a direction straight for the

Grand Stand was taken, two nasty drop leaps intervening there, and some hurdles at the entrance into the winning field. The course then continued past the Stand, and a sweep to the right was made over a stiff hedge at the rear of Mrs. Hayward's dwelling house, parallel with the Lichfield Road; leaving which the horses diverged again to the right, over a made fence by the side of the Tamworth Road, leading down to a bank fence, prefaced by an insignificant rivulet, the approach to which was rather awkward, owing to the ground being rather uneven and unsound. The starting point was then gained, and the circle ridden over a second (and third) time."

It was a lovely spring day and the racing attracted a crowd of between 30,000 and 40,000. The seven miles of road between Birmingham and the racecourse was, said the *Post*, "lined, to and fro, with an uninterrupted succession of bipeds, quadrupeds, and vehicles. Indeed, it was a great holiday for all, and the scene *en route* was animated in the extreme."

The Birmingham Grand Annual was run over three and three-quarter miles and attracted nine runners. The race was won by George Stevens riding The Comet, beating The Huntsman and Moire Antique. The *Birmingham Post's* reporter gave a most comprehensive description of the race, one that today would receive fulsome praise. However, of the Hunters' Stakes, he admitted: "We shall not attempt to give a detailed account of this affair, five out of the eight horses being ridden in similar colours, which caused considerable confusion."

In 1859 permission was obtained allowing the races to be run through Moor Hall Park itself. The course was considerably enlarged and improved, being now more than one and a half miles round. The fences were nearly all natural. It also became a two-day meeting for the first time, that year's fixture taking place on Wednesday 23rd and Thursday 24th March.

On the first day there were two Sweepstake races 'for Officers of the Army', one of which was won by Goldsmith, ridden by Captain George Warwick Hunt. They turned out again the following day to win the Grand Military Gold Cup. Born near Plymouth, Captain Hunt was responsible for leading the charge of the Light Brigade in the Crimean War. He lived in France for many years and died in Torquay in October 1906, aged 73.

The crack French steeplechaser Franc Picard, ridden by Harry Lamplugh, won the Birmingham Grand Annual for the second time (he had won it when the race was held at Knowle three years earlier). Franc Picard won the Grand Steeplechase at Dieppe a record seven times.

George Stevens rode two winners at the 1860 Sutton Coldfield meeting, and did so again the following year. Bad weather dogged both days of the 1862 fixture. Penarth won the Birmingham Grand Annual, thus giving his rider, George Holman, back-to-back wins in the race, having won it on Doubtful the year before.

The 1863 meeting, held on Monday 23rd and Tuesday 24th February, was the first after the opening of the railway line between Birmingham and Sutton the previous year. The front-running Xanthus, who had run prominently in the last five Grand Nationals, finishing third twice and fourth once, won the Erdington Steeplechase, ridden by George Holman.

The Birmingham Grand Annual was by now worth a healthy £350 and was second in importance only to the Grand National. The seven-year-old mare Emblem, ridden by George Stevens, won the 1863 running and was measured at having covered 36ft 3ins when taking one of the jumps. The following month Emblem and Stevens won the Grand National itself by twenty lengths.

The course's proximity to the railway station – barely ten minutes walk – certainly helped swell the turnout, and given decent weather, attendances of 25,000 to 30,000 quickly became the norm. The Birmingham Steeplechases fixture was at its height, and a local periodical sang the praises of the racing committee, "whose attractive programme always justifies the expectations of the most ardent admirer of this division of our national sports."

A crowd of 30,000 was present on the Monday in 1864, when George Holman won the Birmingham Grand Annual on Chamade, his third and final victory in the race. Local lad Johnny Page rode his first winner over jumps on Telegram in the Erdington Steeplechase. Page then won the following day's Licensed Victuallers Plate on the same horse. There were new stands in place for the following year's meeting, at which George Stevens won the Erdington Steeplechase on Jesuista.

In 1866 Sutton Coldfield staged not just its traditional two-day Birmingham Steeplechases fixture but also an additional meeting, held on Friday 23rd March under the auspices of the North Warwickshire Hunt Steeplechases. This was something of a moveable feast, being held at various venues such as Kineton, Leamington and Packington Park. It comprised four steeplechases, none being of any great importance. The North Warwickshire Hunt's meeting returned the following year when it had to contend with ferocious gales which caused damage to the grandstand. Fortunately, nobody was seriously hurt.

Top amateur rider E. P. 'Ted' Wilson rode two winners on the second day of the 1867 Birmingham Steeplechases, including the Birmingham Grand Annual on 10 to 1 chance Tiger. The son of a Warwickshire farmer, Ted Wilson rode on and off for more than 35 years. He twice won the Grand National, aboard Voluptuary in 1884 and Roquefort the following year.

The crowd on the second day of the 1868 meeting was so huge that it forced down the railings at the rear of the Stewards' stand. The vast throng of spectators saw John Wheeler ride The Nun to a 9 to 2 victory in the Birmingham Grand Annual. More significantly, although racegoers may not have appreciated it at the time, the

Farmers' Steeplechase was won by The Colonel, ridden by Mr John Goodwin. The Colonel went on to win the Grand National not once but twice, in 1869 and 1870, one of just a handful of horses to do so.

Speaking of the Grand National, three amateur riders who rode winners on the first day of that 1868 meeting all went on to win the great race.

Fred Hobson, who won the Maiden Hunters' Plate on Black Swan, had been the previous year's champion amateur rider with 36 winners, despite his somewhat unorthodox style of catching hold of the back of the saddle when landing over a fence. In 1877 he won the Grand National on his own horse Austerlitz.

Mr Edwards, who won the Sutton Handicap Plate on Ace of Hearts, was just a month away from winning that year's (1868) Grand National on Lord Poulett's grey The Lamb. 'Mr Edwards' was in fact the *nom de course* for Eton-educated George Ede, who was not only a top class amateur rider but also a noted cricketer. He scored 1,200 runs in 1863 and together with Lord Poulett founded Hampshire Cricket Club. Ede rode a total of 306 winners before being badly injured when falling in a steeplechase at Aintree in March 1870. He died of his injuries three days later, aged 36.

Thomas Pickernell, who rode as 'Mr Thomas', won the last race on both days of that 1868 Sutton Coldfield meeting. Pickernell, who was born in Shrawley, Worcestershire, rode three Grand National winners – Anatis (1860), The Lamb (1871) and Pathfinder (1875) – and rode in the race seventeen times. He lost the sight of an eye and broke his jaw in three places in a horrific fall at Sandown in 1877 and was forced to retire. He then became the first National Hunt inspector of courses and occasionally started races at Sutton Park. He lived in Valentine Road, Kings Heath and acquired a reputation for being a hard drinker. He died at his home in 1912 and was buried in Moseley Parish Church, Birmingham.

A reporter observed in 1869: "The severe hill to the left of the stand has been done away and a turn formed nearly opposite the enclosure by which the runners got to the far side." Ted Wilson achieved his second Birmingham Grand Annual victory that year, this time on the 10 to 1 shot Meanwood.

The second day of the 1870 fixture had to be postponed due to severe weather. It was eventually held on Monday 21st February, when Hippolyte won the Birmingham Grand Annual, giving jockey John Wheeler his second win in the race. Johnny Page won the following year's Grand Annual on Moose, who carried 11st 5lb and started at 100 to 30.

Tommy Pickernell, alias "Mr Thomas".

Another large crowd turned up in 1872, when the meeting was held on a Thursday and Friday. It was reported that the course now comprised "only one field of ploughed land and a couple of seeds, the first thoroughly rolled." Lord Anglesey's Corfu, a five-year-old carrying 10st 3lb, won the Birmingham Grand Annual, ridden by Jimmy Adams.

Easily the best horse on view that year was Lord Aylesford's four-year-old Reugny. Ridden by Joe Cannon, he won Thursday's Erdington Plate and the Craven Cup on Friday, both races being over three miles. He was sold subsequently to Captain James Machell, for whom he won the 1874 Grand National, partnered on that occasion by Mr John Maunsell Richardson.

The 1873 meeting took place on Wednesday 12th and Thursday 13th March, later than planned after having been postponed from the previous week. The 3 to 1 favourite Dodona carried 11st 5lb to victory in the Birmingham Grand Annual, but the meeting was marred by the accident to a spectator named William Wiseman, of Nechells, who was knocked down by a horse during one of the races. It was an inauspicious end for what was to be the last meeting in the grounds of Moor Hall.

The encroachment of the builder spelt the end of the Moor Hall course. Owing to it being required "for purposes other than racing," the lease was not renewed and a new track had to be provided from the 1874 meeting. The new racecourse, at Anchorage Road, located immediately adjoining the Station and to the left of the Royal Hotel, was far more confined than that at Moor Hall Park. Part of it had been used in 1852-53 for the very first Sutton Coldfield Steeplechases.

The new course was considered unsuitable and lasted for just that one meeting. The Birmingham Grand Annual was run for the final time at Sutton Coldfield and won by Morning Star, the mount of Fred Lynham. Before turning his attentions to National Hunt racing, Lynham had been a successful jockey on the Flat, winning the Cambridgeshire Handicap on Adonis in 1870.

There were no steeplechase meetings in Sutton Coldfield for the next two years, although pony racing took place at nearby Mere Pool. Jumping returned on Tuesday 3rd April 1877, when a Sutton Coldfield Steeplechases fixture was held at the back of the Halfway House pub. The clerk of the course, Mr J. Tyler, organised a seven-race card and, despite the heavy rain that fell from mid-afternoon until the last race at 7.00 p.m., there was a large crowd. However, the racing was moderate at best, with no more than three runners in any of the races, and the Sutton Coldfield News published a scathing report of cheating, the reporter adding that one of the jockeys (unnamed) at the meeting had done the same earlier in the year at Olton.

Olton had by then become the new home of the Birmingham Grand Annual Steeplechase, and that low-key Sutton Coldfield fixture of 1877 was the last to be held there. A sad end, perhaps, for a racing venue that had seen horses such as Emblem, The Colonel and Reugny ply their trade before tasting glory in the world's most famous steeplechase, the Grand National.

SUTTON PARK

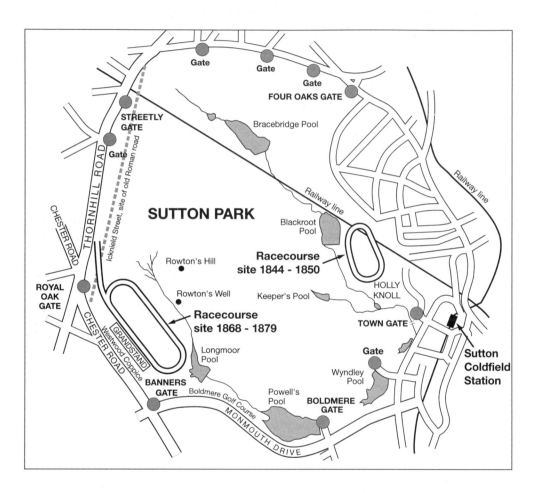

It was May 1892. The old labourer shuffled around Sutton Park, lending his hand to any odd job that needed to be done, from cutting gorse to pruning trees, repairing a fence, or cleansing a water-course. He'd been there for more years than he cared to remember, but not just in a labouring capacity.

His name was Escott. John Escott. He'd once trained racehorses on the fine old turf of Sutton Park. His gallops had been in the neighbourhood of Holly Knoll, and he'd tell you that here was as good a mile and a half of galloping ground as was to be found in the whole country. He'd also say that he once trained a Derby winner.

There were many people who had been prepared to swear that William I'Anson's filly Blink Bonny never did win the 1857 Derby, as the record books show, and that the real winner was Adamas, the little colt trained by Escott that had learned to race in the grounds of Sutton Park. Escott was convinced of it, and he gave a graphic description of the race, for which there were thirty starters.

"Yes," he said, "I can see 'em finish now, five of 'em, all of a cluster. A sheet would have covered the lot. Mine had lost a lot of ground at the start, but had made it up after."

It was a desperate finish between Blink Bonny, Adamas, and 200 to 1 outsider Black Tommy, but Escott was sure his horse had won, and this was confirmed when the number of Adamas – number thirteen – was put into the frame in first place. "When I saw my number thirteen go up I never had such a feeling in my life. I turned round to wave my hand to someone who was standing at the back of me, and when I moved my eyes again to the number board I was dumbfounded to see my 'oss's number shifted and Blink Bonny's in its place. Instead of first they put him third."

It was true. Adamas's number had been taken down in favour of Blink Bonny's. When Adamas returned to the paddock, his jockey, Sutton Coldfield-born and raised John "Tiny" Wells, said, "I don't care where they've placed me. I know I've won".

"Then," recalled Escott, "he burst out crying with vexation, and so did I. Ah, sir, you don't know what a difference losing a Derby makes to you, especially when you've made sure you've won it."

Escott never fully overcame his disappointment of seeing the Derby cup of victory dashed from his lips. Whereas Wells was to win the next two runnings on Beadsman and Musjid and add a third on Blue Gown in 1868, Escott never got another chance.

Now, thirty-five years on, Escott went quietly and conscientiously about his work, deriving only whatever consolation could be gained by still insisting that 1857 was Adamas's year.

Escott had trained at Sutton Park during the 1850s, but to trace the full history of horse racing there, we need to go back a further two decades.

The First Racecourse

The first Sutton Park racecourse lasted from the 1830s until 1843, though by all accounts, it was in the wrong location. It was described as being "of the most confined and dangerous description, over which it was impossible to let a horse of any value run, even had there been the inducement of good stakes to contend for."

Held under the title of "Sutton" rather than "Birmingham", the restrictions placed by the Corporation of Sutton, who had sole jurisdiction of the parish and manor, plus the opposition from some of the inhabitants, meant that it was always going to struggle to survive.

Around 1838 a group of local sporting gentlemen applied to the corporation for permission to build a proper racecourse in the park, there being many parts of it well adapted for the purpose. Their request was denied, even though it was backed by an offer to spend £1,500 on a grandstand, which would eventually be given over to the corporation at the end of twenty years.

Racing came to an end there on Tuesday 20th June 1843 with a programme of four races. A mare named Victoria won both heats of the Sutton Park Stakes; Heigh Over won both heats of the Hack Stakes; an unnamed colt won the Galloway Stakes, and the Hurdle Race went to a mare called Kitty.

Luckily, by then, various changes in the municipal body resulted in a more liberal spirit being shown towards racing in the neighbourhood. The new racecourse was only a year away.

Holly Knoll Racecourse, 1844 to 1850 (Birmingham Races)

The first properly organised racing came to Sutton Park the following year, courtesy of John Wiggan, who ran the Royal Exchange in Whittall Street. Wiggan was a wealthy, retired gunsmith who lived in a white house near to the course. On Monday 20th November 1843, the front page of the *Observer* previewed the venture, commenting that the racecourse was almost completed and "will be inferior to few in England."

It reported: "In shape it is oblong, has a straight run-in, up rising ground, of nearly six hundred yards, and is a mile round. It lies on a piece of table-land, in the neighbourhood of the most romantic part of the park; and we believe that, for beauty of situation, combined with every qualification for a racecourse, it will be found almost unrivalled."

This new racecourse cost £1,000 to build and was located on the same side of the park as the original one, but occupied the area to the north side of Holly Knoll, immediately in front of Blackroot Pool. The pool had been created in 1757, originally to operate a leather mill, though it later became a water-powered sawmill.

The first half mile of the course was flat, followed by an awkward descent, then a gentle rise for about a quarter of a mile, with the rest being level. On the opposite side there was a slight ascent at the Four Oaks turn.

The inaugural meeting took place on Wednesday 19th and Thursday 20th June 1844. The clerk of the course was Mr T. S. Wilkins, who announced in his advertisements that "no money will be added in any case unless three horses start."

John Sheldon Sen., of The Swan, Snow Hill, Birmingham printed the race cards for the meeting. Indeed, it was at Sutton Park that Sheldon, a printer by trade, first became acquainted with the duties of a racecourse official, a direction to which he then devoted himself, rising to become one of the most respected officials under

Jockey Club and National Hunt Rules. Sheldon, who lived at Ewe Tree House, Chester Road, Erdington, and later ran the Coach and Horses pub, promoted racing in and around Birmingham along with Ben Palmer, who kept the Anchor in Bradford Street. By the time Sheldon died, aged 89 in June 1896, his son, also named John, had followed in his father's footsteps, being responsible for perpetuating racing at Sutton Park besides running the courses at Olton, Four Oaks and Packington.

The main event at that first meeting was the Windley Pool Handicap Stakes, for which six horses ran. The easy winner was Counsellor, a five-year-old chestnut son of the 1835 Derby winner Mundig, on his return home from Ireland where the previous week he had defeated a field of top hurdlers at the Curragh. Counsellor carried 7st 4lb and was ridden by a jockey named Pilsbury, wearing Mr T. Wesley's colours of red, with white sleeves.

Neptune Stagg rode three of the winners at Holly Knoll's inaugural meeting, including the first race ever run there, a Match, in which Mr Barton's chestnut filly Glideaway beat Mr Fowler's black filly Filby. Born in Bingham, Nottinghamshire in 1824, Stagg was a well-known jockey and rode the first winner of Newmarket's Cesarewitch Handicap, landing a major gamble on the Irish-trained Cruiskeen in 1839. He also won the 1841 Chester Cup on Cruiskeen and rode in both the Derby and the Grand National.

After he retired from riding he kept the Coach and Horses Inn in Birmingham's City Centre between 1851 and 1864, described as "one of the oldest sporting houses in Birmingham." In 1877 Stagg, aged 53, was found drowned in a water butt in the yard of his home in Tindal Street, in Balsall Heath, Birmingham. His mother-in-law discovered him head downwards, with his feet protruding from the top. He had, said the coroner, "evidently remained in the water for some considerable time."

A one-day meeting was held on Tuesday 22nd October 1844. However, the four races were of poor quality and plans to make the October fixture permanent were abandoned after that one meeting. From thereon Sutton Park races would be just the two-days in June. The organisers quickly caught onto the notion of how best to present the racing to the public by imposing a £5 fine on owners whose horses, after being saddled, did not pass in front of the grandstand before the race. (Modern day trainers, please note!)

The amount of stake money on offer for the 1845 meeting exceeded £500. Of this, £217 was the prize for the inaugural running of the Birmingham Stakes, won by Roderick, who beat Marian Ramsay and a trio of others. The last event on the card was a hurdle race, over four flights of hurdles, each 4ft high. This went to Mantrap, who won two of the three heats, his task being made easier when the winner of the first heat fell in the second heat, his rider receiving a nasty cut on the head.

Blazing hot weather accompanied the opening day in June 1846, when, for the first time, the racecourse was turfed throughout. There had been a hitch two months earlier when the temporary grandstand had burned down, but it did not stop the meeting going ahead with a replacement stand. Hednesford-born jockey Robert Denman, who later was to ride in France, won two races on the first day.

The total value of the stakes for the meeting was now £920. An unnamed brother to Sir Henry (afterwards christened Sir George) won the Birmingham Stakes, worth £625, gaining a clever victory from Mystery.

The 1847 Birmingham Stakes, to which £200 was added by Birmingham sportsmen, was won by Lord Chesterfield's Lady Wildair, ridden by reigning champion jockey Nat Flatman, the Lester Piggott of his day, beating The Wizard, Fitzwilliam, Roderick and Alliance. Flatman, who had won Goodwood's Stewards' Cup on Lady Wildair the year before, was champion jockey for seven consecutive years from 1846-52, his best season being 1848 when he rode 104 winners.

Sutton Park's 1848 fixture took place on the Monday and Tuesday of Whitsun week. A local newspaper enthused: "The sporting circles of this great 'emporium of commerce' have displayed great liberality within the past few seasons in attempting to establish a good annual turf gathering, and will ultimately, there is no doubt, effect a successful standard meeting."

It continued: "The course which is about one mile in extent, is in first-rate order, the committee having paid great attention to the turning, manuring and fencing, a very large sum having been expended by them. In the course of another year or so, should the consent of the corporation be obtained, it is intended to erect a beautiful stand, which will not only be the means of ensuring comfort to a fashionable company, but considerably enrich the funds of the race-authorities, and enable them to increase the quantum of sport. We hope no petty obstruction will be thrown in the way by the Corporation; they ought to bear in mind that the national pastimes of the country, and more particularly in such a populous district as this, should have every encouragement."

The sum of £100 was donated by the residents of Sutton Coldfield to that year's Birmingham Stakes, the tradesmen clearly wishing to encourage the perpetuation of the races, which brought a good deal of extra business to the town and put plenty of money into their coffers. The race attracted 22 entries, though only ten of these were declared to run. They included Lady Wildair, but this time she was no match for the winner, Brandy Face, ridden by George Abdale. The successful horse and jockey were reunited the following day and won the Windley Pool Handicap. Interestingly, neither of these races was run in heats, which was very much the norm at the time.

There was an additional race this year, the Cavalry Stakes, restricted to military riders. The local paper noted that "a new stake has been added, in which, we understand, those officers quartered at our barracks are to appear in the pig-skin; J. Joel,

Esq., generously adding a handsome gold cup."

Jockey John Dodgson was praised for his riding at the 1849 meeting. On the first day he won the Innkeepers Stakes on Jack Cade, then on the second day he landed the Edgbaston Plate on Exhort. The runners were said to have raced behind a red barn, located on the far side of the course. The Windley Pool Stakes apparently started by the barn itself.

Sutton Park's annual two-day race meeting had become a very popular event. The *Birmingham Tradesman's Advertiser* dated 8th June 1850 carried a whole page of adverts from a dozen or so of the various traders who had taken booths at the racecourse. The *Birmingham Journal* reporter described the course as being: "well covered with human beings of every class – a greater number never before seen at Sutton."

William Sharpe took the riding honours that year, winning four races. After winning the Birmingham Stakes on Wild Rose on the first day, he then scored a second day hat-trick, landing the Sutton Park Stakes on Shilamalia West, the Windley Pool Stakes on Keleshea, and the Edgbaston Plate on Imperial. He collected a gold mounted whip, value six guineas, for winning the Birmingham Stakes, and a silver one for winning the Windley Pool Stakes.

Alas, all did not go well that year. There were crowd problems, with the police being called upon to stop people bathing in the pool contiguous to the grandstand, and there was confusion and acrimony following the running of the West Bromwich Stakes. This was run in three heats and had just three runners. Clara, ridden by George Whitehouse, won the first, then Yates' mount La Malhereuse won the second.

Sarah, ridden by Turner, was then awarded the third heat after both the other horses were disqualified for going the wrong side of a post. Protests were lodged by connections of the disqualified pair, and the stand-in Steward, Mr Sadler, was called upon to adjudicate on the dispute, which he duly resolved but not, apparently, to the universal satisfaction of all concerned.

The *Birmingham Journal* reporter, who appeared to disapprove of races being run in heats, was far from impressed by the outcome and opined: "No respectable racing authorities continue heats on their ground; they always engendered ill feeling, and a congregation of leather flappers in this way is but a certain forerunner of that fraud and robbery, of which the public are the victims."

The cup for the Sutton Park Stakes.

Perhaps it was the *Journal's* swingeing criticism that led to the racecourse's demise. If so, it was an ignominious end, for that Sutton Park meeting, held on Tuesday 18th and Wednesday 19th June 1850, was the last to take place at the Holly Knoll course.

Whatever the reason, the racecourse's fate was quickly sealed, for, among the items on the front page of the *Birmingham Journal* on 3rd August 1850 was the following announcement:

THE GRAND STAND IN SUTTON PARK.

TO BE SOLD BY AUCTION,

BY SAMUEL KEMPSON, on the spot, on TUESDAY NEXT, August 6th, at Eleven o'clock in the morning – the above STRUCTURE, being eighty-five feet long by fifteen feet wide, and comprising excellent, well-seasoned Leal Planking, Elm Boards, and strong Uprights; together with sixty-five yards of OAK PALING, five feet high, and Three OAK GATES and POSTS, being the Paddock in front of the Stand. Auctioneer's Offices, Union Street, Birmingham, and Sutton.

Although all traces of the track have disappeared from the open ground between Blackroot quarry and the Hartopp Road Railway Bridge, part of the course can still be seen clearly where it curves through a cutting in the north side of Holly Knoll. And the two banks which comprised the spectator enclosures are still there today.

The following item appeared in the *Birmingham Mercury* on Saturday, 22nd June 1850. The author had made a point of travelling to Sutton the day before the race meeting in order to see the preparations for himself. We reproduce his account here because we feel it captures the atmosphere of a day at the races in the mid-nineteenth century…

SUTTON RACES
BY "OUR COMMISSIONER"

This going down to the scene of action on the day previous is a rule to be followed, on all convenient occasions, by every reasonable man; by so doing you do not injure your pocket, and you consult comfort, and endure a hundred pleasures, which are incompatible with the contrary method.

Even the short journey from Birmingham to Sutton is accompanied by many disagreeable circumstances. You don't know how to dress for the road, and appear respectable at the same time; if you put indifferent clothing on, you feel the consequences, regret the act during the day; and if you dress, the road undresses you. Then the heat, the dust, and the shaking puts a man out of condition for thorough enjoyment; he is not perfectly at ease with himself; the primal diurnal elasticity has vanished, and to be pleased requires an effort, even if it be at all attainable.

The way to get out of this is to put the labour on one side of a night's sleep, and the pleasure on the other. Should any doubt, let them try our method, and we know what result will follow the experiment. Our mode has another advantage, not an insignificant one either – it permits you to see everything there is to be seen; and the visitors to Sutton races who came from home on Tuesday did not see the whole affair.

They did not see, as we did, the clean old town sleeping in peace at early dawn, seemingly unconscious or indifferent, to the dawning of the eventful day, which flung robes of golden light around its old church tower, and brought substantial metal, of a like colour, to the pockets of the citizens before its close.

Perhaps we are wrong, though; this quietness may be merely superficial, and consciousness and interest may be shaping their dreams; traders may be calculating expected gains; sportsmen testing their books, and maidens marking down conquests behind the natty white-curtained windows which attracted our gaze.

But these are 'things not seen,' and what we do not, just now, wish to see, for we prefer sleeping Sutton to sleepless Epsom or Newmarket; not that we mean it to be understood that the town is innocent of everything beckoning the coming day and its business – behind yon gate there is a yard, and stabling, and horses, and grooms; round the corner there are more stables and their furniture, and here is a carefully-tended animal returning from its breathing coming up the street, and an anxious owner, with his jockey, walking slowly down.

We follow the latter into the park, brushing the dew in showers from our path, and wind up the hill to the course; and what a course it is, to be sure, for position we hold it unparalleled in England; for its nature it might be better, and would be so, we dare say, if the means to make it such were not lacking. Here stretches along before us a fine extent of open country, rendered valuable by the cultivation which improves rather than detracts from its natural charms; here Sutton becomes picturesque, and its woods, arrayed in June's magnificent robes strike us with their sober grandeur, and fill us with a something akin to awe.

These are the haunts of meditation, these
The scenes where ancient bards th' inspiring breath,
Ecstatic, felt; and, from this world retired,
Conversed with angels and immortal forms,
On gracious errands bent.

To these woods Thompson's words may be truly applied, as no mean authority on such questions gives a central Druidical station to Sutton; and as the Druids, we know, had an eye for a wood, the theory seems highly creditable. Lord! if one of those masterful and white-robed and bearded old gentlemen could just step up to the crest of the hill for a minute or two, and watch the movements of the people engaged in erecting tents and booths, he would go back a wiser man.

There is so much doing, and what is done is of such a nature, that an aboriginal would take it for a town in progress of building, and not a convenience for a day. It's a building of Babel that is before us now; the gathering in of the people and the confusion of tongues will follow beyond a doubt. What knocking, and fixing, and shouting, and swearing there is; we will retire and contemplate. Do not be alarmed, dear reader, and skip this passage, we shall cut it short, be assured; but we must say that looking on this labour makes a man able to appreciate the comfort it furnishes him with, makes him satisfied with rough boards, and thankful for the accommodation provided.

You who came late this morning will see nothing of all this, and, probably, never even think of it; not you, you came to be amused, and that is all, and will disclaim all interest in the means which assist in the obtainment of the end. Yet you would not injure the end, by knowing something of the means; and, perhaps, might even find pleasure in the knowledge.

Here is a whole family hard at work on the hill; three dogs, barking and slipping, the old woman pulling in front, the patriarch shouting, swearing, and shoving, and the young hopefuls helping the wheels round. There are half a score of these carriages on the hill together, and licensed victuallers', brewers', and soda water manufacturers' vehicles in a somewhat similar fix. You would think, at a little distance, that they never got any further, for as one succeeds in reaching the top, another takes his place at the bottom, and these are the first arrivals on the course.

A queer assemblage they make up, too, contrasting vividly and oddly with the native influences of the spot; the erections are being made of such opposite materials, transformations so dextrous take place, that the whole thing works like a trick in some great pantomime, or large puzzle intended for the children of the primeval giants. We should not like to be compelled to show the relation of the parts of a dog-cart, as a cart, with the same thing transformed into a gingerbread stall.

Odd contrasts! There are glazed calico flags, stuck up among verdurous leaf panoply – a hand piano grinding away beneath a lark 'at Heaven's gate singing' – camp fires sickening under the burning glances of the morning sun – a ballad singer chaunting, with the cuckoo for a chorus; and, if these are not strong enough for your taste, place the whole of the labour going on here beside the ploughing and hoeing which you can perceive in the distance.

But contrasts are odious; and we leave the course and walk townward to breakfast, a gentle lounge, across the park, winding the dusty road and horse exhausting hill, brings us to the gate, where we find certain of the free commoners of Sutton debating the policy of entrusting their cattle to the chances of the day, of which debate the cattle seem to be aware, and await their owners' decision, evidently conscious that there is something unusual in the wind, and that they are, under the circumstances, incapable of taking care of themselves. One old lady was 'afeard they ud be kicked by the horses, which were so skittish, being kept, poor things, in stables under the ground.'

We take breakfast, fresh – mark, fresh – eggs, a slice of grilled ham, country fed and chimney dried, salads crisp as hoar frost on brambles, the grassiest of butters, and the coolest of cream; then we look to our toilette, lounge through the garden, and retake the field, to observe the arrivals.

First among the straggling pedestrians come the inferior members of the predatory tribe of sharpers, the beastly looking men, principally Irish and Scotch in their extraction, who earn a living by the 'tanner' on a stick, the pegs, and the garter. The latter require a stage for their performance, and they make one, and a very suitable one, too, of the empty barrel which they carry on a shoulder. The barrel is placed in some catching spot, and the list is twisted, and the stick offered to any who have a penny to throw away; and if a policeman, or other suspicious person approaches, the barrel is easily tossed aside, and its owners walk away for a time.

With this species of the genus sharper comes another, the professional beggars. Let it be noticed that, on the race course, as in life, the joys and the sorrows, the grievous realities and the foul pretences of life are to be seen side by side; and the maimed and the blind appear there, to obtain a copper from our holiday-furnished pockets, and to force a serious thought into our pleasure-seeking minds. We must exercise our charity with discrimination, but not forget it entirely, although the art of the undeserving, and the need of the deserving, make both classes appear as one.

Now come also the petty traders, the dealers in knacks and trifles, the penny brooches, gingerbread, and piemen, and with these should come, according to rule, the nondescript vendors of the only correct card, but they do not till later in the morning; and thanks to the management, when they do come, there is a most unorthodox similarity in their wares, Sheldon's list being the satisfactory staple. You are not surprised to see so many men 'padding up,' whose dress betokens an acquaintance of some sort with the stable; probably you may think that a love of the amusement brings them here; you will perceive the error by and by when you see them earning their bread.

The Course

Well covered it is, too, with human beings of every class – a greater number never before seen at Sutton; booths, shanties, and vehicles, three or four deep. Hark! why it is barely half past one, the time announced for starting, and there goes the bell, followed by a rush of people off to the course; up they come from all sides, from dingle and bushy dell – from the shady alleys and shingle walks by the pool – from booths and tables, to creep or push into the circle, to climb the tops of vehicles, or ascend the stands. Very fine, certainly, very fine, is the scene from the grand stand – the clear course hedges in a crescent of faces and accompanying bodies, fair forms are perched on doubtful parts of carriages, decked in wreathed smiles; over head a warm sun, screened by clouds; around us life and action, flags, gay dresses; away yonder the glorious uplands, church towers, and shade providing woods.

Another bell, another settling of the company, and out comes the graceful racer, with his silk-jacketed managing sprite, to charm the eyes and whet the desires of gazers; another follows, and yet another, until there are eight horses in the field for the Stand Stakes. Again the bell, announcing the approaching start – now gallop the course clearers, shouting and smacking their whips – now lads creep underneath the rails and lie level with the horses' hoofs – now the poor dog, who has found his way onto the course, runs wildly up and down, amid shouts from all sides, vainly seeking to find his way out. Now the flag is lifted, the horses placed, and a breathless calm falls on the multitude, while 'expectation stands on raised toe.'

Here they come, well together at the start, stretching along bravely, led by the Marshal, followed closely by Gaffer Green, and the others well up. 'Well done for the Marshal – the pace increases, yet he maintains his position.' 'Bravo Gaffer, the Gaffer is the man, he gains on the Marshal.' 'Bob, the horses are not to be seen from the stand.' 'A sovereign the Gaffer heads the hill first.' 'Done.'

Hurrah, in sight again, Fazeley in the front, shoulder to shoulder with the General, and the rest close behind, led by the Marshal. Now for the hill, fatal to so much horse power; it has broken up the ruck; settled the Gaffer completely, and left the running home between the General and Fazeley. A right brave run it is, hand over hand, pell mell, broadside to broadside; the General – Fazeley – the General – no – I say, yes! Hurrah! Hats off. In goes the number; it is the General; won by a nose!

We could have wished a man in our place who affects to look upon horse racing with contempt, he would have felt the thrilling interest, the rushing of the blood, the enthusiasm as we did; aye, and would spasmodically have clapped his hands and shouted, albeit he had no sordid interest in the issue.

Now for a ramble. Do you want refreshment, what will you take? Anything from sheeps' trotters and curds and whey to lobster salad and champagne, may be had on the course. Who do you patronise – Stewart, Clements, or which other of these favourite purveyors? Plenty to eat and drink, and, wonderful to say, at the regular market prices. Peel's principle, extended consumption, compensating for reduced prices, has penetrated the national trading mind to the benefit of consumers, and, we believe, to all concerned.

We can't, it is of no use attempting it, describe all we saw, of what was to be seen in the park; a dry catalogue would fill a column. Here is a queer triumvirate, a machine to determine your weight and height, another to test your muscular strength, and a third to resolve the condition of your lungs. 'Know thyself,' said the old Greek, and he thought that the task would be difficult; you may comply now at the cost of a few coppers.

Shooting galleries by the pool, swings, picnics, and impromptu stabling among the trees. Shows for the yokels, merry go-rounds for children, and something for everybody, even to tea on the grass, provided and supplied at a penny a cup.

Ah! our old acquaintances the gambling sharpers are here – here in shoals. 'Luck's the lord and fortune is the spoil,' still sounds in the ears of many; the table is down; the thimbles are down, as we live, here is a sharp gentleman going to outsharp the sharper. He has not done it yet, but he is convinced that money may be won, and that he is the man to win it; bless you, he knows where the pea is now, and he whispers the information in the ear of the fair-haired, open faced girl who leans on his arm, boards his two sovereigns, and loses the bet.

But he has more, oh yes, he has more; gold shone through his purse, and there are men there, beside himself, with gold in their pockets, who bet, aye, and win too, or seem to do so. Perhaps the latter, who knows? Not he, for he listens, produces his purse – how anxious are the hawks covering their prey, till they have fleshed their beaks – empties it on the table, and in a moment stands plucked. The table vanishes, and kind friends tell him that he is verdant, and has been robbed; how consoling. We saw this fish rise at the bait, we saw many others hooked during the day, and we said to ourselves, the warning will do, experience alone is their teacher.

****

Longmoor Valley Racecourse, 1868 to 1879 (Birmingham Races)

Things had moved on since the closure of the Holly Knoll racecourse in 1850. The population of Sutton Coldfield had grown to 4,662 by 1861. The following year the Birmingham to Sutton Coldfield railway line was completed, being followed in 1879 by the line running through the park, linking Sutton with Walsall. The latter, which cut through the northern part of the old Holly Knoll racecourse, also led to Blackroot Pool being reduced in size in order to accommodate the railway cutting.

Sutton Park's Royal Promenade Gardens opened in 1868. It was that same year that saw the arrival of the second racecourse. It was located in Longmoor Valley, alongside Westwood Coppice, Banners Gate, near to Rowton's Well and also near the Parson and Clerk pub, a portion of the course crossing that ancient landmark, the Roman Road.

Before describing the new racecourse, it is perhaps worth noting some of its geographical and historical landmarks. The Roman Road, part of the 112-mile long

Icknield Street, was built in the first century AD and runs from Bourton-on-the-Water to Templeborough in South Yorkshire, spanning Sutton Park's western side for 11/2 miles. It enters the Park near the Royal Oak Gate and pedestrians can follow its course all the way to Streetly.

Rowton's Well was for some time regarded as a holy well, with tales of the miraculous healing powers of the waters, particularly in relation to eye diseases. The name itself denotes 'the camp on the hill' and may have been used by the Romans for their water supply.

Longmoor Pool in Longmoor Valley dates from 1733. A mill was built there and was used for producing buttons and, later, for milling flour. In 1923, following a severe thunderstorm, the Pool burst its banks, resulting in a rush of water downstream, which eventually reached the town and flooded many of the shops.

The Longmoor Valley course was much larger than the previous one, being constructed "at considerable expense" by John Sheldon Jun., son of the much-respected racing official at Holly Knoll. It was an elongated oval of about a mile and a quarter, with a nearly straight seven-furlong course, making the "distance" (i.e. from the start of the seven furlongs course to the winning post and then one full circuit) one mile and three quarters. The course was 35 yards wide, and there was a (temporary) grandstand capable of holding about 800 people.

In return for being permitted to stage a race meeting in Sutton Park, the racecourse executive undertook to pay the Park authorities an amount equal to the latter's takings on the best day in the year, thus ensuring that it would be a source of profit to all.

The *Birmingham Journal* previewed it on 4th July 1868, as follows: "The course is more than a mile and three-quarters long, and the straight is seven furlongs. Gentle elevations at various points surrounding it will afford excellent vantage ground for thousands of spectators. The grand stand has been let to Mr. Ward, of the Fox and Hounds, Tottenham Court Road, London. It commands striking and varied views of the surrounding country, but will probably be valued more by those who take possession of it at the races for its admirable position with respect to the course. It will be gratifying to orderly persons who intend going to the races to hear that a strong body of police will be present to enforce the regulations.

"The soil is much better adapted for the purpose than that of the old racecourse, being comparatively soft and having some degree of elasticity, even after the very parching weather we have had recently. We are informed that experienced trainers have examined it, and have expressed a very high opinion of its suitability."

In fact, the ground was sometimes a problem at the Longmoor Valley course. Being near to Longmoor Pool, the going was apt to get very heavy and the course soon became known by racegoers as "The Morass."

The inaugural meeting took place on Thursday 9th and Friday 10th July 1868, under the stewardship of the Earl of Coventry and Captain Douglas Lane. It was reported that extra trains had to be put on for the crowds to get to Sutton Park. The *Birmingham Daily Post* announced that: "Special Trains will run from New Street Station, Birmingham, as often as required, from Eleven a.m. till two p.m., calling at Lawley Street, Bloomsbury, and Aston only. The Return Trains will commence running to Birmingham at 5.30 p.m. and will continue till 10 p.m. The Tickets will be available to and from Sutton Stations only." The first class return fare was 1s 9d, or 1s 3d in the covered carriages.

Entry to the course was through the Royal Oak Gate, opposite the Parson and Clerk. Sutton Coldfield railway station was about a mile and a half away, but as the road to the course ran right through the park, it presented a pleasant and delightful walk. By road, the distance from Birmingham was six miles.

It was no longer the custom to run races in heats. Thus, the first race on the new course, the Two Year Old Stakes, worth £75, was a single event over five furlongs. The winner was a horse named Ben Block, ridden by Walter White. The big race of that first day was the £215 Birmingham Handicap Stakes, run over a mile and a half. This went to East Lancashire, who won by four lengths from Toy, with Barnabo another six lengths back in third.

There were two three-figure prizes on offer during the second day's sport and both were won by odds-on favourites. Barnabo, at 5 to 4 on, turned out again to win the £160 New Hall Welter Cup, over one mile, while the £100 Great Barr Cup, a six-furlong handicap, went to the 11 to 8 on favourite Haymaker.

Unfortunately, that first meeting was plagued by unruly gangs wielding sticks and stones, while a welching bookmaker was beaten up and forced to spend the remainder of the afternoon being guarded by police in a toilet.

Nor were things much better at that year's autumn meeting, held on the last two days of September, with a man being robbed during the afternoon of the first day. The feature race was the Birmingham Autumn Handicap, worth £110 and run over a mile and a half. It was won by Barnabo, supplementing his victory at the inaugural meeting.

The Sutton Park Cup, a five-furlong handicap worth £125, was the highlight of the second day, this being won by Moonbeam, ridden by Jimmy Adams. However, the day was marred by a serious accident in the second race, a four-furlong handicap for two- and three-year-olds. In the closing stages of the race, Turn of Luck, ridden by a jockey named E. Beechey, swerved right across the course towards the chains near the finish. In doing so the horse jumped the chains into the crowd, striking a spectator and smashing his skull. The man died an hour or so afterwards, while Beechey was severely injured.

The big race of the 1869 July meeting was again the Birmingham Handicap Stakes, which went to the four-year-old Ligurian, a 4 to 1 chance, carrying 7st 10lb. That year's autumn meeting, incidentally, was abandoned due to new turf being laid on the course.

In 1870 the £160 Birmingham Handicap Stakes was won by a three-year-old named Disturbance, carrying just six stone. Three years later Disturbance would carve his name in Aintree history by winning the 1873 Grand National. By coincidence, the last race at the following year's autumn fixture was won by Reugny who went on to win the 1874 running of the world's most famous steeplechase.

A tragic accident

The first day of the 1870 autumn fixture saw a dead heat between Witchcraft and Curio in the Birmingham Autumn Handicap. However, the meeting was overshadowed by the death of jockey Henry (Harry) Taylor on the second day.

The Longmoor Valley course staged predominantly Flat racing with the occasional hurdle event. Among the races on Wednesday 21st September was a one-mile hurdle race over three flights of hurdles, for which there were just three runners. Taylor's mount, Dean of York, was reputed to be a dangerous ride, and so it proved when, approaching the first jump, he swerved and collided with Walter White's mount, Marriage, the eventual winner, then pitched and fell heavily at the hurdle. Taylor landed on his back and his mount landed on top of him. Badly injured, Taylor lay prone on the course for some time before being carried unconscious on an improvised stretcher to nearby Bannersgate Cottage, where he "lingered in great agony" and died of "concussion of the brain" early the following morning.

An inquest was held on Taylor in the presence of the coroner, the Reverend E. H. Kittoe. The jury returned a verdict of accidental death. Mr James Cockin, who had identified the body, "suggested that in future the committee should cause gorse to be put on the hurdles. In running, the sight of horses frequently became defective, and they had difficulty in seeing bare hurdles." The Coroner promised to convey the suggestion to the race committee.

Taylor, 29, who left a wife and three children, had been a jockey for around fourteen years. He trained at Hednesford and had at one time given up riding but subsequently returned to the saddle. He had ridden Fan in that year's Grand National. Fan had finished second in the 1867 'National' but refused at the second fence in each of the next three runnings. Incidentally, that Aintree fence still bears her name today.

Archer and other celebrities

The 1872 Summer Meeting witnessed the Sutton Park debut of a racing legend, Fred Archer. He was unsuccessful at that particular fixture, but he put that right the very next year, with two winners on the first day and another on the second day. Archer then rode a treble on both days of the 1873 autumn meeting, when the crowd was entertained between races by the sound of Hardy and Wolverson's brass band.

Archer also made his presence felt at the 1874 autumn fixture. He was out of luck on that first day, finishing second twice and third on his three rides, including in the Birmingham Autumn Handicap, which was won by Raby Castle, beating the Archer-ridden favourite Hippias by a length. But it was a different story on the Wednesday when all four of his mounts won.

Fred Archer rode 21 winners at Sutton Park.

Mr Hardy's band played throughout both days of the following year's summer meeting, at which the races were started by Tommy Pickernell, rider of three Grand National winners. Sutton Park's race days had become incredibly popular and crowds of 20,000 were common.

On the first day of the 1875 autumn fixture – brought forward this year to the end of August - the ropes on both sides of the course were lined three deep with spectators. Its success was the best of all tributes to John Wiggan, whose death occurred later that year on 20th December at Park House, Sutton Park. As mentioned earlier, it was Wiggan who had founded the first 'proper' racecourse at Holly Knoll all those years ago.

Acrobat, ridden by leading amateur rider Sam Darling, won on both days of the 1876 summer meeting, the first victory being achieved despite a half-hour delay at the starting post due to a succession of false starts. Darling later became a successful trainer at Beckhampton and scaled the heights of his profession when training Galtee More to win the Triple Crown in 1897. Five years later he won a second Derby with Galtee More's half-brother Ard Patrick.

Fred Archer won the first three races on the card on the second day of that 1876 summer meeting. At the following year's fixture he rode one winner on the first day, then two more on the second. He was also in action at the 1878 August meeting, where he won three more races. They were to be the last of his total of twenty-one winners there. Champion jockey thirteen times, Archer is generally regarded as being the greatest jockey of the nineteenth century. He certainly enjoyed a big following at Sutton Park.

Some peculiar goings on

At Sutton Park's 1874 summer meeting, a mounted constable rode across the course causing three false starts for the Birmingham Handicap Stakes. When it eventually got under way, the race went to Bloomfield, who won easily by two lengths.

On the first day of the 1877 August meeting, during the Witton Hunters' Flat Race, Quicksilver, ridden by a Mr Blizzard, oddly attired in black trousers, jumped the rails after passing the stands, scattering the spectators. On the second day, Mr Fenwick, the owner-rider of Gaiety, who had finished second to Mr Spence's mount Huntingfield, was alleged to have 'pulled' his horse (i.e. stopped him from winning). The crowd was convinced that he'd cheated and he had to be kept in the weighing room for his own safety.

The second day of the 1878 August meeting saw an unusual incident in the first race, won by Kineton, gaining his fourth course victory. Following a false start, the starter, perhaps out of sheer frustration, resigned on the spot. The second race therefore had to be started by an "unofficial" starter. Guess what? It resulted in another false start!

The end of racing in Sutton Park

Drenching rain on the first morning of the 1879 summer meeting was no deterrent to 'course specialist' Bugle March, who won the Birmingham Plate for the third time, having also scored in 1876 and 1878. Despite heavy showers on the second day there was a large attendance, and also, it was observed, a large police presence.

Despite the sport's undoubted popularity, it was municipal opposition to racing that was to put an end to Sutton Park's Longmoor Valley course. The final meeting took place there on Thursday 19th and Wednesday 20th August 1879. It was the year of the Zulu War, which appeared to have some sort of influence on the youngsters of the district, for the local reporter complained about the "bad behaviour of begging children, half naked like Zulus, throwing Katherine wheels into the road."

Conditions were described as "dreadfully sticky" after heavy rain on the Sunday before the meeting and there was persistent drizzle during both race days. It was reported that John Sheldon, the clerk of the course, "did all that was possible in the way of planks and straw." The bad weather also played its part in ensuring that there was a low attendance for that last Sutton Park fixture.

Ironically, Sutton Park's own railway station had opened earlier that year despite considerable local opposition. It was on the line laid from Birmingham to Walsall by way of Castle Bromwich, Penns Sutton Park, Streetly and Aldridge. To construct it had entailed the disposal of

John Sheldon
Junior.

a two-mile strip of the Park to the Midland Railway Company for £6,500. Alas, it came too late to save horse racing at Longmoor Valley. The Sutton Park railway station continued but was eventually closed to passenger traffic in 1964.

In 1897, Sutton children danced around the newly erected maypole skirting Holly Knoll and Blackroot Pool, near to the site of the first "proper" racecourse, to commemorate Queen Victoria's Diamond Jubilee. But they were far too young to remember when racehorses once galloped round there. As for the racecourse in Longmoor Valley, Westwood Coppice (which adjoined the grandstand) is today a mixed wood of oak, mountain ash, Scots-pine, larch, sweet chestnut, holly and birch.

Subsequently...

By 1963, the land on which Birmingham's Bromford Bridge racecourse stood was wanted for housing, and there were serious suggestions by the then Birmingham and Wolverhampton Racecourse Company that a new track could be established in Sutton Park. The proposal would also involve the closure of Wolverhampton's Dunstall Park, the two courses to be replaced by one modern, brand new facility that would be the pride of the West Midlands. The directors of the Bromford Bridge Racecourse Company together with the Inspector of Courses visited the park with a view to siting the new Midland Racecourse project there. However, the Borough Council rejected the proposal outright, thus precluding the return of horse racing to its former home.

Then in February 1973 a retired minibus operator, Bob Burns, aged 71, of Lyndon Road, Sutton Coldfield, organised a petition for a new racecourse to be built in Sutton Park. Mr Burns told the *Birmingham Evening Mail*: "People have been paying hand over fist for the park and a racecourse would ease the burden on the rates." He added: "A racecourse could be laid on the Streetly and Bannersgate side of the park, without affecting Sutton Coldfield Golf Club's course. All it would affect is barren wasteland."

The following week, Mr Burns said: "I have had lots of people ring me up and not one of them has been an objector." He also announced that he would donate £1,000 to the Longmoor School for severely handicapped children at Banners Gate when the first race was run there.

The notion was given further credence by the fact that Aintree was experiencing ownership problems at the time. Its future was uncertain and there was even speculation in some quarters that Sutton Park could become the new home of the Grand National.

The racecourse plan could hardly have been expected to find favour with the Friends of the Park Association, Sutton Park's very own protection society, founded in 1950, and it was no surprise that they came out vehemently against it. Their secretary commented: "It is absolutely preposterous. We would come down on it like a ton of bricks. It would bring in crowds of people with cars and would devastate that part of the park. We would be dead against it."

Councillor Clive Wilkinson, leader of Birmingham District Council, told the *Mail*: "My first reaction is that a suggestion like this would be considered by Sutton people to be blasphemous." But he added: "If there is some sense and value in the idea and it increases the social life of the new district, I have no doubt we would be interested in looking at it. We want to promote more entertainment and more festivals in the new district."

He concluded: "The park is a particularly fine piece of public open space and I do not think we would want to put a racecourse there."

The council members weren't impressed either and the scheme never got off the ground. Undaunted, Mr Burns went elsewhere and focussed his attentions on a proposal to build a new super racecourse near Coleshill. Once again, however, the scheme was doomed to failure.

****

Some people swear that the ghost of Fred Archer has been seen riding his steed over the Heath at Newmarket. Perhaps, on moonlit nights in Sutton Park, the sound of horses' hooves and the cries of a whip-wielding Archer may occasionally be heard on the wind.

Or could it be Adamas, old Escott's three-year-old racer, trained right there in the grounds of Sutton Park, raising his game to the cheers of the crowd and gaining his revenge on the filly that never did beat him in Epsom's Derby. Maybe, at last, this was his year.

OLTON

(BIRMINGHAM STEEPLECHASES)

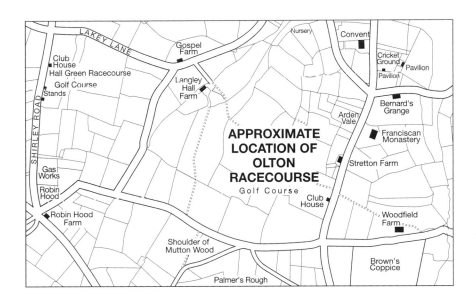

In 1875 a National Hunt racecourse was founded at Olton, on an estate owned by William Charles Alston, who was also a steward of the meeting. It was one and a half miles round with two water jumps, one of them being a brook in front of the stands. The clerk of the course was John Sheldon, who carefully juggled the job with a similar position at Sutton Park.

The course was situated about one mile from Olton Station and it held its inaugural meeting under the title "Birmingham Steeplechases" on Wednesday 10th and Thursday 11th February 1875, with seven races on both days.

The first day brought doubles for two jockeys. William Daniels won the Solihull Handicap Plate on Irene and the Selling Plate on Harbinger; while amateur rider John Goodwin landed the Red Coat Stakes on Maria and the Open Hunters' Plate on Lucy.

The equine star that year was Mrs Starr, who won the Erdington Plate on the first day, then reappeared the following afternoon to land the valuable Birmingham Grand Annual Steeplechase. She was ridden to both victories by John Jones, who scored a third success aboard Chilblain in the Craven Cup. Jones was to achieve his greatest success on Shifnal in the 1878 Grand National. He later trained at Epsom and was the father of Herbert Jones who rode two Derby winners, Diamond Jubilee in 1900 and Minoru in 1909.

Jimmy Adams was another jockey to ride three winners at that first Olton meeting, his second day hat-trick comprising the Scurry Plate and the Olton Selling Plate, both on Castaway, and the Hunt Cup on Revenge.

While the inaugural meeting itself passed without incident, Samuel Kimberley, aged 40, a police officer on duty at the races, was killed at Olton Station while running for a train after racing on the second day.

The next fixture took place on Tuesday 8th and Wednesday 9th February 1876. The layout of the track had been changed, with the stands having been moved to the opposite side of the course, placing them closer to the road and making it easier for racegoers to view the action.

Mrs Starr won the Birmingham Grand Annual for the second year running, but the day was overshadowed by the accident to the well-known amateur rider George Darby in the first race. Darby, aged 21, who had won the Maiden Plate on Pearl King at Olton the previous year, was riding that same horse in the Open Hunters' Chase but fell heavily at the second fence. He was carried to a nearby house by his father and a friend, Mr Coupland. Afterwards he returned home to Hillmorton, Rugby, where he died two days later of a punctured lung caused by broken ribs.

An inquest was held into Darby's death. Police-constable Acton, who was on duty at the second fence, where the accident happened, stated that, nearing the fence, Pearl King was just in front but he swerved to the right and cannoned into San Domingo who, in taking the jump, caught Darby with its forelegs. Both horses fell, with San Domingo landing on top of his rider, Mr Lloyd. Constable Acton rushed to the assistance of Lloyd, who was trapped underneath his horse, while Darby got to his feet, walked two yards and then collapsed.

There was much consternation regarding the coverage, for statements had appeared in the newspapers that Darby had been taken back to Rugby contrary to the advice of the doctor. This caused great annoyance to Darby's father and friend who claimed they had distinctly heard the doctor give orders that he should be taken home as soon as possible.

The verdict was returned that Darby had died "from injuries received while riding in a steeplechase." By a macabre coincidence, on his train journey to Birmingham for the race meeting, Darby mentioned that he had dreamt he would be killed.

The next Olton meeting, held on Tuesday 6th and Wednesday 7th February 1877, passed off without incident. An unknown writer paid tribute to John Sheldon's enthusiasm as follows: "For years Mr. Sheldon has worked the oracle and so long as the meeting was held over the old course at Sutton Coldfield, all went well, and most of the best horses of the day ran there; but suddenly the course was needed for more mercenary purposes. The next attempt to get a track was made in 1875 (Olton), when considering the short time at his disposal, Mr. Sheldon did wonders, and many improvements have been made since."

The 1878 fixture was held on Tuesday 12th and Wednesday 13th February. Rock Savage, ridden by "Mr St. James", the *nom de course* of Sir Reginald Greville-Nugent, won the Birmingham Grand Annual. Known as "The Limb", Mr St. James was the son of Lord Greville. Just two weeks after winning the Grand Annual, he was killed in a fall at Sandown Park.

Juggler, ridden by Mr Garrett Moore, won the Birmingham Grand Annual at the 1879 meeting, which on this occasion was held on a Friday and Saturday, 21st and 22nd February. The following month, Moore was to land an even more prestigious prize, winning the Grand National on The Liberator. Moore, who hailed from the Curragh in Ireland, was a top-class amateur rider and had already won the Irish Grand National twice on Scots Grey. However, standing well over six feet tall and being a "natural 12-stoner", he was forced to give up riding in the early 1880s and took up training. He died in Winchester in 1908.

In addition to the traditional February fixture, a second meeting was held in 1879. Called "Olton Hunt" rather than "Birmingham", it was run over the same racecourse on Saturday 22nd March.

The 1880 fixture was held on Thursday 12th and Friday 13th February. The *Birmingham Daily Globe* reported the events of the opening day: "A lovely spring morning succeeding a wet, cold night, ushered in the first day of the Olton Meeting, and from the large contingent of visitors overnight it became evident that the programme issued by the executive had found universal favour. The morning trains brought their full complement, and towards midday a continuous stream of vehicles and foot passengers set in towards the course.

"The beauty of the morning had encouraged in a majority of instances the discarding of great coats and wraps, and when just before the numbers were the hoisted for the first race, the clouds which had covered the blue sky discharged a heavy shower, a general stampede ensued to every available bit of shelter, and it looked any odds on a soaking wet afternoon; but happily the storm was soon spent, and the sun's welcome reappearance put everybody on good terms again. The attendance was one of the best ever seen, all the enclosures being filled, while the general public, mustering in force, crowded on to every spot from which a view of the sport could be obtained."

The first event of the opening day was the Hunters' Selling Flat Race, for which Abelard was made a warm 6 to 4 favourite. However, he failed to cope with Lady Shrewsbury, ridden by Mr Arthur Coventry, who won cleverly by half a length. Five faced the starter in the Erdington Chase, for which Gipsy looked the proverbial "good thing", but once again the favourite had to make do with second place, as

Quibble, partnered by Jimmy Adams, dominated the race, making all to win by ten lengths. The punters' luck was also out in the Selling Hurdle, as another hot favourite, Le Promeneur, was beaten by the veteran Prodigal, who won in a common canter, providing a second winner for Mr Coventry.

The Selling Chase produced only four runners but, at last, the favourite obliged, with even money Alstone, winning by six lengths from Royal Charlie. In the Elmdon Handicap Hurdle, Arthur Yates' Bird of Prey, ridden by John Childs, the evens favourite, held on to win by a length and a half despite a slow jump at the last flight. The Solihull Handicap Steeplechase, over two miles, went to Little Fawn, ridden by Mr Letheren, while Moorhen, the mount of Mr William Rippon Brockton, won the Hunt Cup Steeplechase.

Moorhen and Mr Brockton also won the second day's opening race, the Tally-Ho Hurdle. The feat was emulated by Neptune, who won the Selling Hurdle and the Olton Selling Steeplechase, ridden to both victories by Henry Davis. The main event, the Birmingham Grand Annual Steeplechase, went the way of Bugle March, partnered by Jimmy Adams.

Adams had been a successful jockey on the Flat, with the Cambridgeshire and the Royal Hunt Cup among his big race successes, before increasing weight forced him to switch to riding over fences. He became even more successful in that role, winning the Grand Metropolitan Steeplechase, the Scottish Grand National and Aintree's Grand Sefton, as well as three Birmingham Grand Annual Steeplechases. His Olton victory on Bugle March was his second Grand Annual, his first having been on Corfu at Sutton Coldfield in 1872.

Quibble was to provide Adams with his third Birmingham Grand Annual triumph in 1881. But this time it would be at yet another course, for that Olton meeting of 1880 marked the end of racing there.

Olton's golf course now occupies the place where horses once raced over the greensward during its brief flirtation with the Sport of Kings. And with Sutton Park racecourse having gone the year before, the energetic John Sheldon was on the look out for another Birmingham racing venue. In fact, he'd already found one. It was called Four Oaks Park.

FOUR OAKS PARK

First, a slice of history: Four Oaks Hall, with its formal gardens, was built in 1712 by Lord Ffolliott. It was subsequently owned by Simon Luttrell, later to become Lord Irnham, who sold the hall in 1778 to the Reverend Thomas Gresley, who died shortly afterwards. It was then bought by Sir Hugh Bateman, whose daughter married into the Scott family of Great Barr. (The name is still retained in the Scott Arms.)

Sir Edmund Cradock Hartopp purchased Four Oaks Hall from Sir Hugh in 1792. He also bought the adjoining land and expanded the Hall's grounds. In 1826 Sir Edmund reached an agreement with Sutton Corporation for an exchange of land, whereby he obtained 63 acres on the Ladywood part of Sutton Park and incorporated it within his Four Oaks estate. In return, as this transaction had alienated many Sutton people, Sir Edmund gave the Corporation 97 acres of land on the side nearest to the town, including the area that is now the main entrance to Sutton Park and land adjoining Powells Pool. As a result, the townspeople gained a much more convenient entrance to the Park by way of a new road, which duly became Park Road.

When Sir Edmund died in 1833, his second son, also named Edmund, inherited the hall. On his death in 1849, his brother, Sir William Hartopp, became the owner. He was succeeded by his son, Sir John Hartopp, a captain in the 17th Lancers.

The closure of Sutton Park racecourse in 1879 had failed to dampen the spirits of its indefatigable clerk of the course, John Sheldon. He went straight out and acquired the 246 acres Four Oaks Estate for £60,000 from Sir John Hartopp. It was all old pasture land, with a dry sub-soil, and thus ideal for a racecourse. A Racecourse Company was formed on 9th December 1879.

A further £40,000 was spent on laying out the course and building paddocks, stables, offices and grandstands, the work being carried out by Surman & Sons of Great Colmore Street, Birmingham. The course was about one and a half miles in circumference, 30 yards wide, with a straight five furlongs chute. It had five stands comprising a Club stand, Tattersalls stand, the main grandstand, which could hold 3,000 people, the open air Minor stand, plus one for the press and jockeys. They were designed on those at Kempton Park and the fashionable Parisian track of Auteuil.

Four Oaks Park was the first racecourse in Birmingham to cater equally for both Flat racing and National Hunt racing. Admission to the Course Enclosure cost a shilling; Grandstand 10s (Ladies 7s 6d); and Minor Stand 2s 6d. Sheldon's dream was to make it the premier racecourse venue in the Midlands, a place that would put Birmingham racing firmly on the map.

The magnificent grandstands at Four Oaks Park.

The first twelve months

Four Oaks Park commenced with a National Hunt fixture on Thursday 17th and Friday 18th March 1881, with an opening day crowd of between 15,000 and 20,000 attending in glorious weather and being entertained by an "excellent band" that played at intervals in front of the grandstands. The first race on the card was the Hunters' Selling Flat Race Plate, which had six runners and resulted in a one-length success for Troubadour II, ridden by Mr Arthur Coventry.

Mr Arthur Coventry.

The main event was the £250 Grand National Hunt Steeplechase. This race was a moveable feast, being staged at 25 different venues before finally finding a permanent home at Cheltenham's National Hunt Festival. It was for many years considered the most prestigious event of the meeting, outranking the Gold Cup itself. Its only visit to Four Oaks Park produced a field of eight, with victory going to Pride of Prussia, the mount of leading amateur rider E. P. 'Ted' Wilson.

The day's other big race was the prestigious Birmingham Grand Annual Chase, which also had eight runners. It was won by Quibble, the third triumph in this race for jockey Jimmy Adams, having previously scored when it was held at Sutton Coldfield and Olton. The second day of the meeting again saw fine weather and another huge crowd. It was a great start for the fledgling racecourse.

The 1881 Easter Monday fixture was a mixed meeting with four Flat races and the remainder under the Grand National Hunt Rules. Despite the cold weather, there was a crowd in excess of 20,000 and the band of the Staffordshire Yeomanry played in the Club stand. The richest race of the day was the one-mile Spring Welter Handicap Plate, worth £250, won by Herald, the evens favourite, carrying 10st 3lb. But there was no doubt about the day's most appropriate winner - the Lady Wood Two-year-old Plate was won by a filly named...Lady Wood!

Fred Archer dominated that year's Summer Meeting, held on 28th and 29th June, winning five races on the first day and three more on the second day. He also rode four winners from five rides on the opening day of the Autumn Meeting.

The big race at the final Flat fixture of 1881 was the Four Oaks November Handicap, worth £300. It went to Colonel Forester's Dreamland, the 4 to 1 favourite, ridden by Jack Watts. Watts was then only twenty and still two years away from riding the first of his nineteen English Classic winners. They included four Derbys on Merry Hampton, Sainfoin, Ladas and the great Persimmon.

The weather was fine and the ground was perfect for Four Oaks Park's Boxing Day fixture. Two amateur riders stole the show, Mr Gus Lowe winning three races while 'Mr Abington' - of whom, more in a moment - won two.

In contrast, fog lingered throughout the 1882 February meeting, at which the Birmingham Grand Annual Steeplechase went to Funny Eyes, ridden by Billy Sensier. The Four Oaks National Handicap Hurdle, over two miles and eight flights of hurdles, was worth a staggering £500, making it among the most valuable hurdle races run anywhere. The 8 to 1 chance Assegai won it by three lengths from May Queen. Notwithstanding the vagaries of the weather, it had been a satisfactory first twelve months.

The warning off of 'Mr Abington'

Easily the most infamous occurrence in Four Oaks Park's history was the warning off of the prominent amateur rider George Alexander Baird. He was the son of George Baird, a Glasgow ironmaster who had become rich in aftermath of the industrial revolution. When he died in 1870 he bequeathed a fortune of £200,000 to his only son, George Alexander Baird, who was then just nine years old.

Spoiled by an indulgent mother, young Baird endured brief spells at Eton and Cambridge and developed a passion for race riding. He rode under the *non-de-course* of 'Mr Abington' so that his trustees wouldn't get to know of his huge expenditure. Although only an amateur rider, he was widely acknowledged to be the equal of all but the very best professional jockeys.

He was, though, a thoroughly objectionable, disreputable man, an uncouth bully possessed of no manners whatsoever. And he rode like the character he was, with little or no regard for anyone else.

On Tuesday 11th April 1882, the second day of Four Oaks' Easter Meeting, he won the Hunters' Selling Flat race by eight lengths on his own horse Billy Banks, only to be disqualified, along with two others, for carrying the wrong weight. This was not in itself a warning off offence. Far more serious, however, was the complaint lodged by Lord Harrington, the rider of Gartmore. Besides making highly offensive remarks to him during the race, in the closing stages Baird had threatened to put him over the rails if he didn't let him past. When Harrington remonstrated with him after the race, Baird replied sulkily, "Beg pardon, I thought you were a bloody farmer."

Had Lord Harrington, an experienced race rider himself, received a more sincere apology, he might have left it at that. Instead, incensed by Baird's offhand response, Harrington reported him to the stewards of the meeting. All of the four acting stewards disliked Baird for his arrogance, and at least two were known to have personal grudges against him arising from his flirtations with their wives or mistresses. Baird's well-known lust for carnal desire overrode any romantic intentions.

As it would have been virtually impossible for Baird to receive a fair hearing, the Four Oaks stewards handed over the matter to the stewards of the National Hunt

Committee. Not that they were any more sympathetically disposed towards Baird; they had little time for him and had long been concerned about his flagrant contempt for racing's rules and his rough riding style which put the safety of other riders at risk. They duly warned him off for two years. The Jockey Club's stewards imposed an identical ban, thus extending the warning off to cover Flat racing as well as jumping.

Shunned by society, and convinced (probably rightly) that racing's 'establishment' was against him, Baird mixed with the lowest of low life from the racing and prize fighting fraternities. Human vultures of both sexes became his so called friends and were forever imploring him to 'lend' them money which they had no intention of repaying.

Baird resumed race riding when his licence was reinstated in 1884 but continued to drink heavily in the West End of London. His time out of racing had certainly not improved his demeanour towards those in authority. In 1887 he achieved what would normally represent the pinnacle of any owner's dream when his horse Merry Hampton won the Derby, but, with typical surliness, Baird flatly refused to lead his horse into the winner's enclosure.

In 1888 'Mr Abington' was back at Four Oaks, riding an Easter Monday double, supplemented by another double there on Whit Monday. Although he had lost none of his skill in the saddle, his hard drinking lifestyle had made it almost impossible to keep his weight down, meaning that he could hardly eat anything. By now the combination of starving himself and carousing late into the night meant that his health was deteriorating.

Baird was to die in New Orleans in March 1893, aged 31, the result of a severe chill caught while attending the fight between Jem Hall and Bob Fitzsimmons. He left behind just a small amount of the fortune that had been, to quote one obituarist, "squandered on horse-racing, prize fighting and harlotry."

Archer's dominance

Fred Archer continued to dominate racing at Four Oaks Park, as well as just about everywhere else. He rode four winners at the 1882 Summer Meeting, including the £1,000 Great Midland Foal Plate on hot favourite Rookery. There were four more winners for Archer at the Autumn Meeting, including the Portland Nursery Plate on the 11 to 10 favourite Keel-row. Jack Watts rode the winner of the Four Oaks November Handicap for the second year running, this time on Royal Prince, the 6 to 4 favourite.

Highland Mary, ridden by Tom Skelton, won the 1883 Birmingham Grand Annual Steeplechase at the February meeting. The £265 Four Oaks National Handicap Hurdle went to Ridotto, the mount of Arthur Barker.

Virtually all of the top jockeys were in action at that year's Summer Meeting. Charles Loates notched three winners on the second day, whereas Archer rode only on the first day and scored just a single victory. The Four Oaks Two Years Old Plate was won by a filly called Pibroch, who initiated a hat-trick for her jockey Charles Wood. The following day Wood won the Great Midland Foal Plate aboard Reprieve, the 7 to 4 favourite, trained by John Porter. Five weeks earlier, Wood had won the Derby for Porter on St. Blaise. Wood was subsequently warned off for ten years in 1887 but returned in triumph, aged 41, when winning the 1897 Triple Crown on Galtee More.

A train crash in Sutton on 12th February 1884 caused no serious injuries but many of the passengers decided not to go on to the races. Those that did saw Marplot, ridden by George Lambton, win the Birmingham Grand Annual Steeplechase.

There was seemingly no stopping Fred Archer, who won two more races at Four Oaks on 2nd June 1884. The second of these was the Corinthian Welter Handicap, in which his mount Redclyffe, despite carrying 11st 5lb, beat Student, ridden by the then restored 'Mr Abington', by half a length.

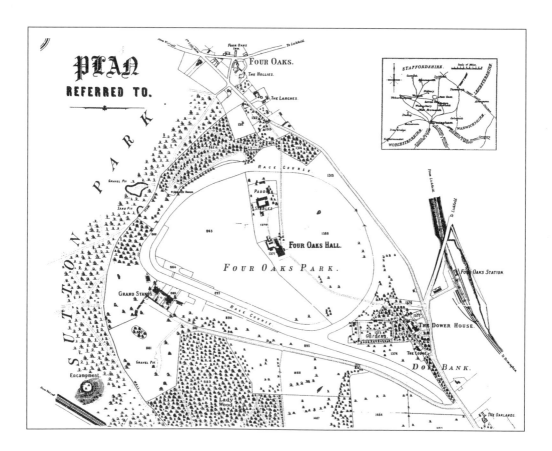

Although Four Oaks Park's early years had been successful, the 1884 financial report, which contained a statement of the company's affairs up to the last day of the previous year, showed a marked loss. The directors stated that they hoped that the new hare coursing grounds that had been laid out would, when the coursing meetings became more widely known about, prove a source of profitable income. Furthermore, with the new Four Oaks railway station having opened earlier that year, they anticipated a far greater number of visitors. A road was built soon after to allow the crowds to walk from the station to the course and grandstand. That road was called Bracebridge Road.

Meanwhile, the indomitable Fred Archer rode three winners and two seconds from five mounts at the 1885 Whit Monday fixture. At the July meeting he won the £400 Four Oaks Two Years Old Plate on Chatter, his only winner on the first day, but then rode a double on the second day. The October meeting brought more of the same, for he won the first three races on day one, then won another on day two. Archer was simply unstoppable. He finished that year as champion jockey for the twelfth year in succession, this time with a record score of 246 winners. The greatest jockey of the nineteenth century was at the height of his powers.

Troubled times

Whilst Archer may have been at his zenith, the same could not be said for Four Oaks Park. The 1885 financial statement for the previous year again showed a loss, which, the directors believed, was due to "the depressed state of trade". Despite attendances at the coursing meetings having failed to reach their expectations, they nonetheless had every confidence for the future.

It seems that their optimism was misplaced, for it was reported on 27th February 1886 that John Sheldon had resigned as Clerk of the Course and that a Mr Rudge of Nottingham had been appointed to replace him. Matters must have reached a nadir because nobody could ever excuse Sheldon of lack of enthusiasm. He did not limit his duties merely to those of a clerk of the course. He occasionally acted as starter and judge as well. No sooner had he started the horses on their first round of the course, than he would jump onto his horse and cart and make the best of his way – the last part with the runners closing at his heels – to the judge's box in time to call the result of the race!

Fred Archer rode a winner on both days of the 1886 September meeting, on his way to being crowned champion jockey for the thirteenth time. But they were to be his last at Four Oaks Park. Just a few short weeks later, Archer was dead, aged just 29, having taken his own life in a fit of delirium, shooting himself with the pistol he kept at his bedside as a precaution against burglars.

The 1886 financial report showed yet another loss. The directors expressed their disappointment with the poor attendances at the coursing meetings, which had now been discontinued, and were sorry to find that the sport had not been better supported.

Albert Cecil won the 1887 renewal of the Birmingham Grand Annual Steeplechase, held on Tuesday 8th February, but the day was overshadowed by the fall of John Sly on Coercion, one of six fallers in the Harrington Hunters' Steeplechase. Sly, 27, from Banbury, was the son of Bob Sly, who trained a string of chasers, including dual Grand National winner The Colonel. The fall came at a big open ditch, ominously referred to as 'The Grave'. The obstacle was said to consist of a fence and ditch, 8ft 6ins wide and 3ft deep, topped with holly. In attempting to get to his feet, Sly was mown down by following horses and sustained severe head and facial injuries. He was taken to the nearby Three Tuns Hotel where he died the next night.

At the inquest it was pointed out that the fence had been modified a few years earlier, having been deemed dangerous, and this was the first accident that had occurred there since. A verdict of accidental death was returned. Nonetheless, the jury expressed the opinion that "ditches should never be more than half the width of that where Sly met with his accident." Mr Sadler, representing the Four Oaks Park Company, promised to forward the jury's findings to the secretary of the Grand National Hunt Committee.

Pillery

Foaled in 1881, Mr Townley-Parker's Pillery became a standing dish at Four Oaks Park. On 6th August 1883 she won the King's Heath Two Years Old Plate, having finished second at the May and June fixtures. This was the first of her five course victories. The second came in a dead heat for the Alexandra Cup at the 1884 October meeting.

In 1887 Pillery won the Prince of Wales's Handicap at the Summer Meeting and the Montrose Handicap at the September fixture, ridden on both occasions by George Barrett. Then in 1888, she won the Prince of Wales's Handicap for the second year running. This was her fifth consecutive appearance in the race, having finished third on three occasions before winning it for the first time. Altogether her record at Four Oaks read: ran eighteen times; won five; second four times; third three times; fourth once.

From Four Oaks failures to Aintree triumphs

The final Four Oaks meeting of 1884 saw a five-year-old called Gamecock come home first in the Christmas Hunters' Steeplechase. Gamecock was destined to win the 1887 Grand National. However, a couple of other 'National' winners had tasted defeat at Four Oaks earlier in their careers.

On Whit Monday 1887, the two-year-old Father O'Flynn, with George Barrett up, started the 2 to 1 favourite for the Castle Bromwich Selling Plate, over five furlongs, but could finish only third in a thrilling finish in which just two necks separated the first three horses. In the circumstances it was a good performance by Father O'Flynn, given that he was hardly bred to be a precocious two-year-old. Steeplechasing was more his game, and five years later he won the Grand National.

At the Four Oaks meeting on 22nd March 1889, the five-year-old Ilex finished three-quarters of a length runner-up to Lown in the day's main event, the Four Oaks Spring Handicap Steeplechase. Twelve months later, Ilex, the 4 to 1 favourite, won the Grand National easily by twelve lengths to become the first of three winners of the race for his jockey Arthur Nightingall.

But by the time Ilex and Father O'Flynn won their respective Grand Nationals, Four Oaks racecourse had vanished from the fixture list.

The end of Four Oaks Park

A further sign of the parlous state of Four Oaks Park's finances was that the 1888 Birmingham Grand Annual Steeplechase, once ranked second only to the Grand National in terms of importance, was now worth a paltry £92.

That February meeting also produced another warning off, this time of the amateur rider Jonathan Riste. Following the running of the last race on the Tuesday, the Yarborough Hunters' Flat Race Plate, the *Racing Calendar* reported that: "Mr. Riste was called before the Stewards to explain the suspicious running and riding of West End, and, his explanation not being considered satisfactory, he was suspended from riding at the meeting, and the matter was ordered to be reported to the Stewards of the Grand National Hunt." They also deemed his explanation unsatisfactory and warned him off all National Hunt courses and reported him to the Stewards of the Jockey Club, who extended the sentence to cover all meetings held under the Rules of Racing. The Stewards of the Irish Turf Club and Irish National Hunt also extended the sentence to all meetings held under their rules.

On Wednesday 27th June 1888 the *Birmingham Daily Gazette* expressed the opinion: "Birmingham possesses one of the most picturesque racing parks in the country, which it does not support. Regular racegoers admit that Four Oaks, with its broad acres, will bear comparison with the finest racecourses in the country; yet how many Birmingham sportsmen rarely enter its gates."

By 1889 Four Oaks Park was struggling desperately to make ends meet. The formerly prestigious Birmingham Grand Annual Steeplechase was now reduced to a two-horse race and worth only £80. Purely for the record, Captain Sandeman's Flattery, ridden by William Stephens, beat the previous year's winner, Captain

Childe's Merry Maiden, by a length and a half. Even the Four Oaks National Hurdle was now only worth £150, this being won by Duke of Richmond, the mount of George Mawson.

Unfortunately, Four Oaks Park had failed to attract "either the best class of race-goer or the multitude." Financially, it had had not fulfilled its shareholders' expectations and in 1889 the Racecourse Company was summoned for non-payment of rates. An arrangement was reached between the Company and the authorities whereby payment was deferred for a while. A total of five meetings were held during that year, all of which lacked public support.

The final meeting took place on Thursday 22nd and Friday 23rd August 1889. The last race ever run at Four Oaks Park was the four-runner King's Heath Plate, won by Carronald, ridden by Charles Maidment.

The *Racing Calendar* announced in September that the accounts of that Four Oaks Park August fixture had not been settled in accordance with the Rules of Racing and until the money was paid it would not be able to hold any further race meetings. Its all too brief life was at an end.

The Racecourse Company was wound up in August 1890. The Four Oaks Park Estate and racecourse, together with all its buildings, furniture and equipment, was auctioned off the following month, the purchaser being the Marquis of Clanricarde who bought it for property development. The Club stand fetched £100, the main grandstand was sold for £110, the Tattersalls stand went for £100, the Minor stand for £75, and the Press and Jockeys' stand for £185. The refreshment and other rooms fetched £270.

Demolition began in September 1890. A fitting symbol of this disastrous enterprise was the crumbling condition of the foundation stone, recording the opening by Lady Berkeley Paget in June 1880.

The Royal Agricultural Show was held at Four Oaks Park in June 1898. The Prince Regent (later King Edward VII) was among those attending. As for Four Oaks Hall, it was left empty and became dilapidated before being demolished in 1908. The land on which it stood eventually became the site of Carhampton House in Luttrell Road.

The land on which the racecourse lay is now traversed by Hartopp, Bracebridge and Ladywood Roads, with Hartopp Road taking the line of the old racecourse past the Summer House. The site where the five impressive grandstands once stood is now occupied by Four Oaks Tennis Club.

Four Oaks Hall pictured in 1887.

WINNERS OF THE BIRMINGHAM GRAND ANNUAL STEEPLECHASE

The Birmingham Grand Annual Handicap Steeplechase was resurrected when Bromford Bridge opened. However, the race declined in quality, prestige and value with each consecutive running and was held for the last time in 1907.

Year	Location	Winner	Rider
1852	Knowle	Tipperary Boy	W Archer
1853	Knowle	Shinrone	C Boyce
1854	Knowle	Needwood	C Green
1855	Aston Park	Star of England	G Stevens
1856	Knowle	Franc Picard	H Lamplugh
1857	Sutton Coldfield	Sting	E Weever
1858	Sutton Coldfield	The Comet	G Stevens
1859	Sutton Coldfield	Franc Picard	H Lamplugh
1860	Sutton Coldfield	Joe Marley	G Waddington
1861	Sutton Coldfield	Doubtful	G Holman
1862	Sutton Coldfield	Penarth	G Holman
1863	Sutton Coldfield	Emblem	G Stevens
1864	Sutton Coldfield	Chamade	G Holman
1865	Sutton Coldfield	Sly Fox	J Monaghan
1866	Sutton Coldfield	Roadster	W White
1867	Sutton Coldfield	Tiger	Mr E P Wilson
1868	Sutton Coldfield	The Nun	J Wheeler
1869	Sutton Coldfield	Meanwood	Mr E P Wilson
1870	Sutton Coldfield	Hippolyte	J Wheeler
1871	Sutton Coldfield	Moose	J Page
1872	Sutton Coldfield	Corfu	James Adams
1873	Sutton Coldfield	Dodona	J Whiteley
1874	Sutton Coldfield	Morning Star	F Lynham
1875	Olton	Mrs Starr	J Jones
1876	Olton	Mrs Starr	J Jones
1877	Olton	Abdallah	Mr T Beasley
1878	Olton	Rock Savage	Mr St. James
1879	Olton	Juggler	Mr G Moore
1880	Olton	Bugle March	James Adams
1881	Four Oaks	Quibble	James Adams
1882	Four Oaks	Funny Eyes	W Sensier
1883	Four Oaks	Highland Mary	T Skelton
1884	Four Oaks	Marplot	Mr G Lambton
1885	Four Oaks	Struanite	W Nightingall
1886	Four Oaks	Cortolvin	W Dollery
1887	Four Oaks	Albert Cecil	J Childs
1888	Four Oaks	Merry Maiden	H Hewitt
1889	Four Oaks	Flattery	W E Stephens

(Known as the Grand Midland Steeplechase in 1852.)

FOUR OAKS COURSING

As mentioned in the Four Oaks Park chapter, horse racing wasn't the only sport to take place there. It also staged hare coursing.

The inaugural meeting was held on Thursday 11th and Friday 12th January 1883, with Mr J. Trevor, mine host of the Swan Hotel, in Lichfield, and Mr R. S. Sadler being the main organisers. The draw was conducted by Mr Hamar Bass at the Swan on the Wednesday afternoon, after which, all those present sat down to dinner, a feature of which, it was reported, "was a splendid baron of beef, done full justice to by most of those assembled."

Despite a lingering fog, a fair crowd populated the racecourse and the grandstands on that first day. The area over which the coursing took place was described as "a fan shaped piece of ground, slightly on the rise all the way, with the slipper standing in the narrow end." The meeting opened with the Doe Bank Stakes, for puppies, which was won by Mr J. Hinks' bitch Hetty Beard. The other events included the Four Oaks Park Stakes and the Sutton Coldfield Stakes, both being open to dogs of all ages.

The *Coursing Calendar's* reporter, writing under the pseudonym 'Allan-a-Dale', concluded: "The Four Oaks Park management may certainly be said to have scored a great success for their opening day's sport, and I am sure they will be among the first to give a great deal of the credit arising from this to Mr Case, so well-known in connection with the many successful ventures of this description of coursing."

After the second day's sport he confirmed: "The inaugural meeting at Four Oaks Park may certainly be said to have been a success in every way, and rarely has an opening fixture at any of the inclosed (sic) meetings promised so well for the future. It was a great point for the managers to have retained the services of Mr Case to see that the grounds and coverts were in proper order, and also to see that the right sort of hares were obtained."

The "Mr Case" referred to was Thomas Case, a farmer from Plumpton, in Sussex, who in 1877 conceived the idea of "park" coursing, otherwise known as "enclosed" coursing or "Plumpton" coursing, on his land. It differed from traditional "open" coursing in that two "parks" were enclosed at either end of a field. On the day before a meeting, the hares were driven into one end, then on the day itself were released one by one into a prepared coursing ground. At the other end of the field, about 600 yards away, was an escape fence, through which the hare could pass and elude its pursuers.

Although the concept was at first derided, "park" coursing quickly became the new craze and Case was in demand to build enclosed coursing venues elsewhere. Racecourses were ideal locations and Plumpton soon had plenty of imitators, notably at Kempton Park, Newcastle's High Gosforth Park, Haydock Park and Four Oaks Park (hence the term "park" coursing). Case was even invited to build "Plumpton" type courses in Russia, New Zealand, Australia and the United States. (There are towns called Plumpton in each of those last three countries.)

"Park" meetings offered far greater prize money, while the fact that the courses were uniform in length also made it more of a test of pace, rather than of stamina and agility. Even Altcar's Waterloo Cup felt the pinch for a while and came close to losing its status as the definitive coursing classic.

Four Oaks Park's 1883-84 coursing season began with a meeting on the last two days of October. Upwards of a thousand spectators were present on the first day, but the second day showed a marked falling off in attendance.

The next meeting was on 27th and 28th November. It was decided not to start the first day's coursing until 11.30 a.m. to enable people travelling by train from Birmingham and Worcester to see the early trials. Despite the second day's fine weather, there were fewer people in attendance than the previous day.

An ambitious three-day meeting took place on 8th, 9th and 10th January 1884. The *Coursing Calendar's* reporter noted on the first day: "To judge by the comparatively small number of persons present, and with no counter-attractions elsewhere, it would seem that the 'Brums' care little or nothing for coursing."

Four Oaks Park's 1884-85 season kicked off on Friday 17th and Saturday 18th November. Heavy showers on the Friday once again meant the attendance was limited, while Saturday's fine weather "tempted a much more numerous assemblage."

For the three-day January 1885 fixture, the London and North-Western Railway Company put on a special train each day to the newly-opened Four Oaks Station, leaving New Street Station at 11.35 a.m. and returning after the coursing. As the journey was only some twenty minutes, visitors would arrive in good time to see the first brace of dogs in slips. However, despite this convenience the crowds were still disappointing.

It was a similar story for the March meeting. The first day was conducted in a persistent drizzling rain, the few spectators present being only too glad for the shelter of the grandstand. The second and third days were better, although the *Coursing Calendar* reported that, while the Four Oaks Park meetings were well supported by owners, "the same cannot be said of the outside public, who, somehow or other, fail to patronise the sport shown in any great numbers."

Four Oaks Park held what was to be its final coursing meeting on Friday 26th and Saturday 27th March 1886. The *Coursing Calendar's* reporter lamented that, despite

Friday's fine weather, "the sport was carried on in the presence of very few spectators, and so little money was taken at the gates that the executive must have had a big balance on the wrong side."

After Saturday's coursing had been conducted in front of another meagre attendance, he concluded: "All season the Four Oaks Park Meetings have met with reverses of one kind or another; but the company's secretary, Mr R. H. Sadler, is not the sort of man to throw up the sponge in a hurry, and next autumn may bring about many changes."

Indeed it did. The committee cut its losses and opted not to hold any further meetings. Coursing at Four Oaks Park thus came to an end after little more than three years and only fourteen fixtures. Quite simply, coursing never caught on despite being adjacent to the new railway line and special trains being run for the benefit of spectators.

It appears that the *Coursing Calendar* reporter's words of two years earlier were prophetically true, that Brummies cared little or nothing for coursing. Perhaps Four Oaks Park missed the boat as other big enclosed meetings, such as Kempton, High Gosforth and Haydock, were already well established before it. Having said that, Birmingham had no local coursing tradition, unlike in the north-west or north-east of England.

As for "park" coursing, its popularity soon waned. It became too predictable for bookmakers and the dogs ran too cunningly for coursing purists. By 1889 Gosforth and Kempton had abandoned coursing altogether, and Haydock followed suit in 1893 when horse racing took over. The remains of Haydock's hare park still exist, thus accounting for the pronounced kink in the back straight.

FOUR OAKS PARK
OPEN COURSING MEETING,
SUTTON COLDFIELD.

PATRONS:
THE MOST NOBLE THE MARQUIS OF ANGLESEY. MAJOR-GEN.
GOODLAKE, V.C.
COMMITTEE OF MANAGEMENT:
THE DIRECTORS OF THE FOUR OAKS PARK COMPANY, LIMITED.
COURSING SECRETARY: MR. J. TREVOR, LICHFIELD.

THE FIRST MEETING
WILL TAKE PLACE
On TUESDAY and WEDNESDAY, OCT. 28 and 29, 1884.
JUDGE—MR. A. A. Steward.   SLIPPER—A. Luff.

SECOND MEETING, DEC. 4, 5, 6.
JUDGE—MR. Hedley.   SLIPPER—T. Wilkinson.

The Meeting to be governed by the National Coursing Rules.

PACKINGTON PARK

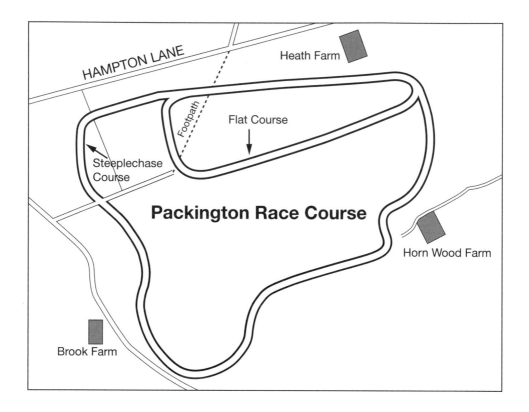

Richard Marsh, or Dick Marsh as he was popularly known, was, as the title of his autobiography confirms, "A Trainer to Two Kings". He was also one of Flat racing's greatest trainers, sending out thirteen Classics winners from his stables at Egerton House, Newmarket. Three of Marsh's four Derby victories were with horses owned by the Prince of Wales (later Edward VII), namely, Persimmon (1896); Triple Crown hero Diamond Jubilee (1900) and Minoru (1909).

The son of a Kentish hop farmer, Dick Marsh had been a successful steeplechase jockey in his youth. Among his many victories in the saddle were the 1870 Sefton Chase on The Nun – his first ride in a steeplechase – and Bristol's Grand Annual Chase in 1873 aboard Phryne. But he never forgot the day he rode at Packington Park – Saturday 11th April 1874.

The Packington Handicap Steeple Chase drew a field of eight, namely: Derviche (ridden by Jack Jones), Morning Star (Fred Lynham), Dainty (Mr Joseph Hathaway), Humble Bee (Dick Marsh), Peter Simple (Bill Daniels), The Admiral (Sam Daniels), Julien (John Deakin) and Glenarvon (Jem Adams). There was heavy betting on the race with Derviche the well-backed favourite at odds of 11 to 10. Humble Bee was backed down to 4 to 1, while there was plenty of money for both Dainty and Glenarvon at 7 to 1.

In the race itself, all the horses jumped well and there were no fallers as they approached the second last fence. By then The Admiral, Morning Star, Dainty and Humble Bee were in close company, this quartet being well clear of the rest. But having jumped the last, Humble Bee quickly drew well clear with only the long run-in to go. The riders of The Admiral and Morning Star both came to the conclusion that the leader was gone beyond recall and duly eased their mounts down. At that point, having looked round and been convinced that he had the race well in hand, Dick Marsh steadied Humble Bee to a virtual trot. But the real drama had not yet begun, as the *Licensed Victuallers Gazette and Hotel Courier* recalls under the headline: "A Sensational Steeplechase. Dick Marsh Caught Napping":

"Mr Hathaway, on Dainty, clapped spurs to his mare, and came pounding along under a wet sail, and he was close on the easy going leader before the yells from the ring caused Dick Marsh to look back and realise his danger. Naturally, he lost no time in setting Humble Bee going again; but, alas, it was too late, for Dainty under full pressure was on top of him a few strides from home, and amidst the wildest excitement, the old mare got up and snatched the race out of the fire by a head. Morning Star finished third, six lengths from the second, and the same distance in advance of The Admiral.

"As may be supposed, when the winner and second returned to scale, there was the deuce of a hullabaloo, and whereas Mr Hathaway was the recipient of a ringing ovation, the disappointed supporters of Humble Bee said all manner of unkind things to Richard. The latter had, of course, no one but himself to blame, and could therefore offer no excuse."

Dainty and Mr Hathaway were to come tantalisingly close to winning the following year's Grand National, being beaten just half a length by Pathfinder.

Racing at Packington Park had commenced with a two-day meeting on Friday 25th and Saturday 26th April 1873, having inherited the old Birmingham Hunt fixture previously held at Knowle. It took place on land belonging to Lord Aylesford, whose horses were trained in Packington Park by Joseph Cannon. A feature of the course was its challenging water jump, said to be about 11ft in length. A commodious grandstand was erected and there was a good attendance, although the cost of admission was considered rather expensive. Racegoers were kept entertained by the band of the Warwickshire Yeomanry Cavalry, who played on both days of the meeting. The first race ever run at Packington Park, the Yeomanry Cup, was won by a horse named Pluto, ridden by Captain Vernon.

The early meetings usually took place on the second Friday and Saturday of April. The report of the 1875 fixture, held on 9th and 10th April, stated that rain fell throughout the Friday and Mr Thomas "broke a rib or two" in a fall. "Mr Thomas" was the pseudonym of 41-year-old Tommy Pickernell, who just the previous month had gained his third victory in the Grand National, this time on Pathfinder. The winner of Saturday's Packington Handicap Steeplechase was Congress, ridden by Mr Ted Wilson. Congress had been last of eight finishers behind Pathfinder in that year's Grand National and was destined to finish second in both 1876 and 1877.

There was fine weather for the meeting held on Friday 13th and Saturday 14th April 1877, with the band of the Warwickshire Yeomanry again playing on both days. On the Saturday, a good crowd, including many from Birmingham, saw a horse called Richman win the Selling Hurdle and then reappear a couple of hours later to win the Farewell Hurdle in the capable hands of Mr Arthur Coventry.

There was much grumbling from the Packington racegoers on the Friday in 1880 when all three runners took the wrong course in the third race, causing it to be declared void. The Saturday of the 1882 meeting brought heavy rain during the morning and afternoon, resulting in a poor attendance.

All bar one of the races on the first day of the 1883 meeting, held on Monday 23rd and Tuesday 24th April, were run at a distance of two miles. The exception was the three-mile Diddington Hunt Cup Steeplechase, worth £46, which went to a horse named Johnny Longtail, who would later finish third in the 1887 Grand National.

Tuesday's feature race, the most valuable of the meeting, was the Packington Handicap Steeplechase, run over two miles and worth £131 17s, the winner being Bloom, ridden by a Mr Gilpin. Tom Skelton rode two winners that day, the Selling Hunters' Steeplechase on Ballet Girl and the Selling Handicap Hurdle on Denzil Place. Lichfield-born Skelton had been a leading apprentice on the Flat before becoming a jump jockey. He won the 1886 Grand National on Old Joe, plus the following year's Grand Sefton and Lancashire Chases on Savoyard. He was forced to retire in 1890 after losing his left eye in a shooting incident. He became the landlord of the Black Horse at Kidderminster and later trained, but died young, aged 44, in 1900.

William Stephens dominated the 1884 Packington meeting, riding four winners. Billy Sensier was the star of the following year's fixture, which took place on Monday 20th and Tuesday 21st April, winning three races, including two on Dear Bargain. Sensier had been crowned champion jockey in 1884 and was almost certainly champion on other occasions, accurate records for "cross country" jockeys being hard to come by in those days. He started life as a humble stable lad but rose to become first jockey to top trainer Arthur Yates. A quiet and unassuming man, Sensier was a stylish rider and an artist in the saddle but he lost his life when still in his prime, dying from multiple injuries sustained in a fall in a Plumpton selling hurdle in 1894.

Roddy Owen.

Packington's meetings continued to be held on a Monday and Tuesday in April, although prize money gradually dwindled. The Packington Handicap Steeplechase, which once boasted a three figure prize, was worth only £71 by 1886. The famous military rider Roddy Owen rode a double there that year. Owen was champion jockey over jumps in 1891 with 49 winners and achieved his biggest success on Father O'Flynn in the 1892 Grand National. He was to die of cholera in 1896 while involved in the Dongola campaign in Egypt. The Owen Falls, located on the Victoria Nile at Jinja in South East Uganda, is named after him, as was the steeplechaser Roddy Owen, winner of the 1959 Cheltenham Gold Cup.

The 1888 fixture, held on 30th April and 1st May, was officially called the "Packington and North Warwickshire Meeting" but Packington's association with the North Warwickshire Hunt did little to arrest the decline in its prestige. By 1890 the Packington Handicap Steeplechase had disappeared from the programme, the name having being prefixed to the humble Hunters' Flat Race Selling Plate worth a paltry £46.

Racing at Packington Park came to an end following Lord Aylesford's death. The final meeting took place on Monday 13th and Tuesday 14th April 1891, when three horses, North Kilworth, Lady Pat and Roger, each won twice during the two days.

Packington Park is now the site of North Warwickshire Golf Course. Its closure meant that John Sheldon, who officiated as Clerk of the Course, had now presided over the demise of Sutton Park, Olton, Four Oaks Park and Packington Park, all within the space of twelve years.

THE SMALL HEATH
LADIES' RACE

The first ever race under Jockey Club Rules for lady riders was run at Kempton Park on 6th May 1972. But there'd been one at Small Heath long before that!

Pony racing is said to have been held in Small Heath during the 1850s, though no trace can be found of any advertisement or report of these meetings. But the "Birmingham and Small Heath" races definitely took place in the 1860s at the back of the Small Heath Tavern, run by Henry Jones, on the Coventry Road. The course was three-quarters of a mile round and contained a cricket ground on the inside.

A two-day race meeting was held there on 29th and 30th July 1863, with between 10,000 and 12,000 racegoers attending on the second day.

A programme of pony, Galloway and trotting races were held at Small Heath on Monday 30th August 1880, on land owned by Joseph Barrows at Green(s) Lane. The various events included a race for lady riders. In those far off days, such an innovation would have provoked considerable interest.

It is thus surprising that the following day's *Birmingham Daily Gazette* chose not to elaborate on the result of the Stewards' Stakes, the third race on the card. There were only two runners and the names of the riders were not listed, in common with the rest of the races.

The day began with the Small Heath Plate, for ponies not exceeding 13 hands, won by Mr Wills' Spinaway. This was followed by a Match for £20, in which Mr Parker's Macready beat Captain Williams' Miss Nell by a length.

Then came the aforementioned Stewards' Stakes, worth £12. All we know of it is that both horses were ridden by ladies and carried 10st 7lb apiece, and that Mr Baker's mare Polly beat Mr Parker's Macready, who had just won the previous race.

The next event was a one-mile Trotting Match which resulted in Mr Baker's Steel Grey beating Mr C. Winckett's Old Wonder. The meeting concluded with a £5 race for Galloways not exceeding 15 hands high. Again there were only two runners, both carrying 11 stone, with Mr Grayworth's All Bones beating Mr Baker's Polly, who thus failed to add to her success in the ladies' race.

Pony and hack races were held on Small Heath Athletics Ground on 13th September 1886, which appears to be the last reference to racing in this area.

Nonetheless, Small Heath does have its own small niche in racing history as the place where a race for lady riders was held, 92 years before they became part of the British racing scene.

WORDSLEY

Race meetings for horses of all descriptions were staged at Wordsley, on a half-mile course at Belle Vue, beginning with a meeting on 24th and 25th September 1860. A two-day fixture during the second half of September became an annual event over the next few years.

The meeting held on 21st and 22nd September 1863 was reported by the *Birmingham Daily Post* as follows: "The first day of this year's Wordsley Races was yesterday, when a large number of the people of Wordsley and its surroundings mustered together to share in the excitement caused by these popular events. The weather was, on the whole, not unfavourable, though occasionally there came some sharp scuds of rain, which tended to increase the business in the refreshment booths. Proprietors of shows, swing boats, shooting galleries, and the like were present in some force, and contributed no little to the general bustle and to-do of the gathering."

The first race of the day was the Trial Stakes, restricted to ponies not exceeding 12 hands in height, both heats being won by Alfred the Great, beating five others. This was followed by the Wordsley District Glass Trade Handicap, for ponies not exceeding 13 hands, which went the way of Metty, the 6 to 4 on favourite. Then came a match race for £50 over one mile, in which Mr Cooper's Cream of the Valley, carrying 9st 6lb, beat Mr Hall's Compton Lass, 8st 6lb, by three lengths.

The day ended with the main event, the Wordsley Stakes, worth £25 added to a sweepstakes of £2 each. The race conditions stipulated the weight to be carried as: "three-year-olds, 7st 8lb; four, 8st 13lb; five, 9st 6lb; six and aged, 9st 10lb. Three times round and a distance." Only three runners started, Mr Cherrington's five-year-old mare Kitty being made the 3 to 2 on favourite, with Captain Knight and Idleness both at 2 to 1. Kitty made the running in the first heat "at a tremendous pace," but fell on the second circuit, leaving Captain Knight to beat Idleness. It was the same order in the second heat, Captain Knight winning by three lengths to take the spoils.

There was a fair sized crowd for the second day, "notwithstanding the slippery state of the ground, and the drizzle dropping from the clouds," and favourite backers got off to a good start when 5 to 4 on Metty added the Ladies' Purse to the previous day's victory. The Silver Cup, the second race, had identical conditions to the Wordsley Stakes but was worth only half as much. It was won easily by Mr Rickett's three-year-old filly Queen of Clubs, the 6 to 4 on favourite, ridden by Lomas.

The third race on the card was for a Plate worth £5, given by the tradesmen of Wordsley, added to a Sweepstake of 7s 6d each. It was restricted to ponies not exceeding 131/2 hands, being "bona fide the property of owners residing within 4 miles of Wordsley, for three months previous to the race." This somewhat parochial affair went to Mr Corbett's Chanticlear, the 2 to 1 on favourite, winning the first heat by two lengths and the second heat by three.

With odds-on favourites winning the first three races, the bookmakers on course must have been licking their wounds, but there was no respite in the final event, a hurdle race, of four times round and a distance. Kitty, ridden by Mr G. Richards, was made the 2 to 1 on favourite for the first heat and duly won by three lengths after Captain Knight refused to face the hurdles and was led back into the paddock. With only one opponent left to face in the second heat, Kitty was made 5 to 1 on to win and was gifted the race when Professor fell second time round. Fortunately, his rider, Mr Talboy, escaped injury.

The Wordsley fixture lapsed after 1867 but was revived in 1896 when a race meeting took place on 21st September. Meetings were then held during September for the next few years and took place for the final time on 8th September 1902. The following day's *Birmingham Gazette* published the results of that meeting.

The six-race card opened with the Seventh Revival Stakes, "for ponies and Galloways not exceeding 14.2; to carry 11st; 11/2m." This was won by Kilmorock, the evens favourite. The Kingswinford Hurdle, over about two miles and eight flights of hurdles, went to the 2 to 1 on favourite Royal George. Best Man, ridden by a jockey named Patrick, made all to beat Daisy and Pattie in the two-mile Wordsley Stakes, at 2 to 1 on, then turned out again later in the afternoon to win the Licensed Victuallers' Flat Race over the same distance, beating Kilmorock by two lengths, this time at odds of 5 to 2 on. Another odds-on winner was Lucy, who took the one-mile Kinver Flat Race, for ponies and Galloways not exceeding 13.2 hands, easily beating her two opponents, Country Girl and Nellie.

With hot favourites having won the first five races, the Wordsley bookmakers were once again on the ropes. Unfortunately for them, any hope of getting out of trouble in the last disappeared when the Wordsley Tradesmen's and Farmers' Hurdle Race, restricted to ponies and Galloways not exceeding 15.2 hands, ended up as a walk over, with Royal George being the beneficiary.

Maybe that's what marked the end of horse racing at Wordsley. You couldn't blame the poor old bookies for refusing to return!

EDGBASTON AND QUINTON

The *Birmingham Daily Gazette* of 8th November 1879 contains the following advert:

RESERVOIR GROUNDS, EDGBASTON, BIRMINGHAM.
THIS DAY (SATURDAY) NOVEMBER 8TH
AMATEUR BICYCLE RACE
WILL TAKE PLACE AT 2.30
BICYCLE v COB
AT FOUR O'CLOCK
ADMISSION – SIXPENCE EACH

The result of the bicycle race is unknown, as is the outcome of the match between the cyclist and the rider of the cob. Incidentally, as with the hunter and certain other members of the horse world, the Riding Cob is not a breed in itself. It is to an extent a chance-bred animal intended primarily for use as a hack.

Two days later, Monday 10th November 1879, the *Birmingham Daily Post* announced:

RESERVOIR GROUNDS
Edgbaston, Birmingham
GALLOWAY RACES THIS DAY (MONDAY) 1.30

'Galloways' were a breed of tough fast ponies which had originated in Scotland, hence the name. That day's *Birmingham Daily Gazette* listed the races and likely runners.

GALLOWAY RACES AT RESERVOIR GROUNDS
Order of running for this day
The Tradesmen's Plate...............1.30
Reservoir Hurdle Galloway Plate...2.15
Galloway Plate.........................3.00
Pony Race..............................3.45

Entries for the TRADESMEN'S PLATE. – Sugar Cone, Tommy, Flyaway Dick, Bob, Burkett, Polly, Miss Jenny, Spinaway, True Lass, Starlight, Hamlet, Morad.

Entries for the RESERVOIR HURDLE GALLOWAY PLATE. - Tommy, Miss Jenny, Spinaway, Polly, Flyaway Dick, Burkett, Hamlet, Leah, True Lass, Morad.

Entries for the GALLOWAY PLATE. - Leah, Fairy Queen, Umbrella, Erlazel, Maud, Starlight, True Lass.

Entries for the PONY RACE. – Joe, Zulu, Grimsel, Starlight, Maud, Russet Rose, Romeo.

The following day's *Daily Gazette* contains detailed results and entries for the

Thoroughbred race meeting at Shrewsbury but, alas, no report of the goings-on at Edgbaston.

Indeed, although Edgbaston Reservoir became a popular location for all manner of recreational and sporting events, there are no further references to any form of horse racing having taken place subsequently.

During the late nineteenth and early twentieth century, the Edgbaston Tally-Ho! Club held its annual point-to-points in Harborne, details of which can be found in the Harborne chapter. But in 1909 the Tally-Ho! Club moved to a new course at Quinton. The *Birmingham Daily Post* of Monday 12th April 1909 reported on the meeting that had taken place two days earlier:

"The course, which is a new one, was over a beautiful line of country of three miles of grass fields with thirty-two obstacles, including one large water-jump. The proceedings were associated with glorious weather, the sun shining brilliantly throughout, and a large assemblage of hunting and holiday folk witnessed some interesting racing."

The first event was for 13-stone hunters for a challenge cup, value 15 guineas, restricted to members of the Tally-Ho! Club. There were four competitors, and Mr F. W. Rudder's Pembroke, with Mr J. M. Thornicroft up, won easily from Mr W. Mathew's Dorothy, ridden by the owner.

A field of six contested the second event, for 14-stone hunters, open to members of the Harkaway and Tally-Ho! Clubs. The first prize of a silver cup, value three guineas, went to Mr T. E. Piper's Flint, ridden by Mr J. Rawlings.

The last event was for 12-stone hunters and was open to members of Midland Hunts. There were nine runners and the first prize of a silver cup and sweepstakes was won by Mr A. V. Negus's Bruree, the mount of Mr R. Thompson, who won a well-contested race by a length from Mr L. Leek's Gay Boy, partnered by the owner.

The report concluded by giving credit to Maurice Davis, the Treasurer, who did much to make the meeting a success.

Whether the Edgbaston Tally-Ho! Club's association with Quinton was restricted to this one-off fixture is unclear but we can trace no further records of horse racing in the vicinity.

HARBORNE

The manor of Harborne appears as 'Horeborne' in the Domesday Book of 1086. At that time it would have been no more than a hamlet situated in a clearing.

By 1841 the population of Harborne was 1,637 and the main settlement was clustered around the crossroads at the King's Arms Inn, the site of the original village green. It was at the King's Arms that entries were taken for a two-day meeting of trotting, Galloway and pony races, which took place in Harborne on 27th and 28th September 1852. This was Harborne's first association with the sport of horse racing. Pony racing was also staged there three years later, on 8th October 1855.

The Victorian period saw a steady growth in the population of Harborne. Its railway line opened in 1874 and, when Royal Assent was received in 1891, Harborne duly became a suburb of Birmingham. Even so, it retained its own 'village' identity and, in 1896, it staged the inaugural Harborne Private Point-to-Point races on Mr M. Pearman's land at Tennal Hall.

The races proved so popular that it was resolved to continue them the following year. They were held on Saturday 10th April 1897, when the *Birmingham Daily Post* reported that there was "a very large attendance, and the sport was excellent."

The course that year was over two miles and a half of natural country, with 26 fences. It was certainly a stiff one and there were falls in each of the three races, which were for hunters carrying 11 stone, 12 stone and 14 stone respectively, each horse having to be ridden by his or her owner.

The first race, for hunters carrying 11 stone, had six runners, namely: Mr J. Blakeway's Stella; Mr T. Turner's Tally-ho; Mr A. A. Howes' Rocket; Mr C. Nolan's Charlie; Mr J. Summer's Game Cock; and Mr A. W. Anster's unnamed brown horse.

The finish looked like being a close one between Stella and Tally-ho until the latter came down at the last fence. He was remounted but was unable to prevent Stella winning comfortably.

The second race, for hunters carrying 14 stone, was won "fairly easily" by Mr S. Cave Brown Cave's unnamed brown mare, beating five others.

The third and final race was the most exciting of the afternoon. Eight runners went to post, these being: Mr J. H. Betts' Paddy; Mr A. Millar's unnamed black horse; Mr J. Blakeway's Surprise; Mr E. Hague's Rosa; Mr H. S. Howes' Turpin; Mr H. Howes' Flower Girl, Mr Hodge's unnamed horse; and Mr T. Turner's Tally-ho.

Surprise made the running for three-quarters of the race but then refused, leaving Paddy in front. Paddy stayed on to win by "about a couple of lengths" from Mr

Millar's horse, with Surprise, having rejoined the race, a similar distance away in third.

The *Post's* report concluded: "In every respect the affair was successful, and credit is due to the committee, Messrs. M. Pearman, J. W. Benson, J. Blakeway, the well known veterinary surgeon, and Mr. Thomas Turner, the hon. secretary."

The annual Harborne Point-to-Point races were invariably well attended, even in 1899 when, despite poor weather, a large number of people braved the elements. Once again the races took place in the grounds of Mr Pearman's Tennal Hall. The meeting was organised by the Edgbaston Tally-Ho! Club and all competitors were members of the local hunt clubs. The course was one mile round and contained seven jumps. The races were all over three miles, entailing three circuits of the track.

Again, there were just three races, the first of which attracted six runners. This was soon reduced to five when Tally-ho fell at the second fence. For most of the race Mr A. J. Witton on Fragment looked to be in command, but Mr E. R. Carwardine's Red Pepper collared him in the closing stages and won cleverly.

This race was marred by an "unfortunate and at the same time a very sensational event," reported the local correspondent. Mr Nolan was thrown from his mount, Rebel, when endeavouring to avoid running over a child who had wandered on to the course. The horse then "proved himself to be a rebel in nature as well as in name, for he bolted in most determined fashion and eventually ran against the shaft of a pony trap with such violence that the poor brute's belly was ripped open and its entrails protruded from its body, besides which the occupiers of the trap (Mr. and Mrs. Wagstaff) were upset and thrown to the ground. Beyond a shock, however, they were not injured. The horse, which was a valuable animal, had to be shot."

Only three horses started for the second race, for hunters carrying 14 stone, but again, there was no lack of incident. On the first circuit, Mr A. Johnson was thrown from his mount, Sir Roger, and on the second circuit, Mr W. J. Benson suffered the same fate on Peter, though he pluckily remounted. The only other runner, Mr F. S. Arter's Margerine was left in splendid isolation by the misfortunes of his two rivals and finished first, but he was subsequently disqualified "for having fouled a flag near the winning post."

The point-to-point races continued to be held at Harborne into the early twentieth century. A meeting took place there on 5th April 1902, again organised by the Edgbaston Tally-Ho! Club, and there were also meetings in 1903 and 1904.

The 1905 fixture, held on 8th April, appears to have been the last at Harborne, with the Edgbaston Tally Ho! Club moving their annual point-to-point meeting to a new course at nearby Quinton.

HALL GREEN

Mention racing at Hall Green today and everyone thinks of dogs. As the home of competitions such as the Gimcrack Stakes and the Blue Ribband, it is one of the country's top greyhound stadiums. Yet less than one hundred years ago horses also raced within a mile of the York Road track.

There was indeed once a hall in Hall Green, although it was demolished in 1936. It was an open, half-timbered building, with a brick wing having been added in Victorian times. However, the name of Hall Green refers not to the hall itself but from the family who lived in it. Agnes Haw (or Hawe), known as "the Widow of the Hall", was living there in 1325, and it was either she or her descendants that gave their name to a small pasture which lay in front of their

moated house. The district was called Hawe Green in 1562 but was later corrupted to Hall Green and applied to a much larger area.

The inaugural Hall Green Steeplechases meeting took place on Friday 28th April 1871. The *Birmingham Morning News* reported the following day: "This quiet little cross-country meeting was brought off yesterday, over an enclosure of Mr. (Joseph) Page's, and although the affair was of a semi-private character, the road from Birmingham to Hall Green furnished abundant proof that something unusual was afloat; an immense number of breaks, whitechapels, gigs, and traps of every conceivable build lining the way, while more than one omnibus was pressed into service.

"The weather, though promising fair, turned out a 'fickle jade', and rain fell copiously after the first race. The course, nearly a mile in circumference, was very fair going, but with a deep 'dip' at the further end, including a water jump, that threatened to bring more than one horseman to grief. The arrangements for an opening attempt, were very fair, and the company, considering the private nature of the meeting, must have been very satisfactory to the promoters. The weighing room, though open to improvement, answered the purpose very well, but the scales showed a 'screw loose' on several occasions, and required continual adjustment."

Joseph Page, who owned Gospel Farm, the land on which the course was situated, ran the Bull's Head on Stratford Road and was the father of jump jockey Johnny Page. The course was a left-handed circuit, bounded to the west by Shirley Road, to the north by Lakey Lane, and to the east by Parish Road, leading to Gospel Farm. It had two grandstands and encompassed the Robin Hood Golf Course and Club House.

Mr Sankey's Red Knob was made the warm 6 to 4 favourite for the first of the four races at that inaugural meeting, the Birmingham Hunters' Handicap Steeplechase. However, it was Glenarvon, about whom 6 to 1 could have been had, who defeated the favourite by half a length. An objection by the runner-up's owner on account of Glenarvon running the wrong side of a post was subsequently withdrawn.

Five runners took part in the Pony Race but the favourite, Robin, was soon out of the contest, refusing at the very first fence. Victory went to Mr J. Whittington's Brandy following a protracted battle with the mare Alice Lee. The Hall Green Hunters' Steeplechase resulted in a one-length success for the "hot-pot" favourite Kemerton, "after a fine set-to with Red Skin, most resolutely ridden by Mr. Spafford."

A Scurry, run over two miles, was the last race on the card and drew eleven runners. Nonpareil, the odds-on favourite, was backed as if defeat was out of the question, and that looked to be the case as he went to the front coming into the dip and steadily drew clear. Unfortunately, with the race at his mercy, the favourite "bungled at the water jump", fell and broke his neck. This left Canny Boy and Little Widow in front, but they collided with each other close home, letting in Moonlight and Red Knight, who finished in that order.

In 1879 the course was altered slightly, moving further south of Lakey Lane and closer to Robin Hood Farm. The new circuit was described as being rather narrow. The six-way roundabout, still known today as Robin Hood Island, was then the location of Robin Hood Farm and a small inn that stood nearby in Shirley Road. Hood – no relation to his more famous counterpart of Sherwood Forest – was a local man with relatives living at Billesley. The story goes that he was surprised by the Sheriff's men while visiting there, but managed to escape and hid successfully near the Six Ways.

During its formative years there was a two-day meeting in May, supplemented by a November fixture in 1879 and a September one the following year. The 1881 fixture, scheduled for 17th and 18th May, was abandoned out of respect to Joseph Page, who had died the previous month. From then on it was held on just a single day, usually a Monday, in mid to late May.

The course was reconstructed and the fences secured in 1883, with the racing now being conducted under New Grand National Hunt Rules. That year's meeting comprised five races, all worth £28 bar for the 'Scurry', which was worth only £20. Despite the low level of prize money, there was rarely a shortage of runners taking part. In fact, it was by no means uncommon for horses to run in more than one race and, quite often, win them both. In 1885 for example, Johnny Longtail, ridden by Captain Hayhurst, won the King's Heath Steeplechase over three miles, then turned out again to win the two-mile Shirley Steeplechase Plate.

By now the annual Hall Green fixture was renowned as a "festival for the common people". Although the races were all steeplechases it was known locally as "Nailcasters' Derby Day", the reason being that it was common practice at that time for local denizens to have a small shed in their back gardens containing a furnace, at which they made their own nails.

In 1888, William Tyler, a former jockey of some fifty years earlier, took over the running of the course from Joseph Page's widow. That year's meeting attracted a crowd estimated at between 20,000 and 30,000. There was a tragic accident when one spectator, William Henry Garrish, aged 21, was caught on the left side of the jaw by one of the runners, Vagabond (the mount of Harry Justin), who jumped among the spectators. Garrish never recovered from his injuries and died later that year on 11th September.

That incident apart, the day passed off successfully. The Solihull Selling Steeplechase was won by M.C., the mount of Bill Daniels from Cradley Heath, who had won the previous year's Grand National on Gamecock. There was also a double for Fred Hassall, who won the Shirley Steeplechase Plate on Isabella and the Robin Hood Hunters' Scurry Steeplechase on Lady Kellie.

Hassall, from Whitchurch, Shropshire, enjoyed plenty of success at Hall Green. He rode one winner there in 1890 and then scored doubles at every Hall Green meeting for the next four years. He certainly was the jockey to follow. He struck up a fine rapport with the mare Cinderella, on whom he won the United Hunt Steeplechase three years running from 1890-92.

Hassall scored his twelfth and last victory at the course on Mistress Pru in the Hall Green Hunt Chase, the opening race at the 1897 fixture, held on Monday 17th May, when some 30,000 spectators were present. He became a successful trainer but died young in 1909, aged 44, following a fall on the gallops when exercising a horse.

Lady Gundrede

If it was horses for courses you wanted, they did not come hardier than Lady

Gundrede. She made her Hall Green debut in 1891, finishing second in the King's Heath Steeplechase. She again finished second in the race in 1893 but turned out again later the same afternoon to win the Shirley Steeplechase.

Running twice in a day held no fears for the gallant Lady Gundrede. In fact, she'd made her first two starts on the same day at Tanat Side Hunt in 1890. The following year she finished second to Father O'Flynn (who was destined to win the 1892 Grand National), at the V.W.H. Hunt fixture, then reappeared half an hour later to win the very next race on the card.

In 1894 Lady Gundrede again ran twice at Hall Green. She fell in the Shirley Steeplechase, the race being won by the four-year-old Grudon, ridden by Mr Morgan Bletsoe. (Grudon went on to win the Grand National in 1901, thanks largely to his innovative owner, who, realising that the race would be run in a snowstorm, packed the horse's feet with 2lb of butter to prevent the snow clinging to them.) None the worse for her fall, Lady Gundrede returned later that afternoon to win the Robin Hood Scurry Steeplechase, ridden by Fred Hassall.

In 1895 Lady Gundrede was back and this time she won the King's Heath Steeplechase and the Robin Hood Scurry Chase, ridden on both occasions by Mr E. H. Lord. Later that year, she and Mr Lord achieved their own small piece of racing history by winning the first steeplechase race ever held at Birmingham's new course at Bromford Bridge.

Lady Gundrede ran with the best during 1896. She finished second in the Birmingham Grand Annual Steeplechase, then fourth in the Champion Chase, run over three miles of Liverpool's Grand National course. In April she came home first at Ludlow, beating 1893 Grand National winner Cloister by five lengths, but was disqualified for having carried the wrong weight. Following that debacle she returned to Hall Green and won the King's Heath Steeplechase for the second year running, her fifth course victory.

Her record at Hall Green read: ran eight times, won five, twice second. During her career she won 24 races and finished in the frame in 51 of her 70 starts.

Unfortunately, the race in which she achieved her final Hall Green victory was marred by a fatal accident to a spectator. Charles Edgley, 21, a butcher, was standing in front of the water jump and evidently did not see or hear the horses approaching. He was knocked down and trampled on by Red Marley, the mount of Mr Harry Brown. The newspaper report stated that: "Edgley was at once attended to by Dr Benison of King's Heath, who, finding that he had sustained severe concussion of the brain,

Mr Harry Brown.

ordered his removal to the General Hospital, Birmingham. There he arrived in a still unconscious condition, and died shortly after his admission."

There was another accident that same afternoon. Mrs Fitter, the wife of a Birmingham solicitor, was shaken but otherwise unhurt when the horse pulling her trap bolted, throwing the coachman into the road and breaking his collarbone.

Lady Gundrede notwithstanding, the equine star of that 1896 meeting was Heyford, who, ridden by George Gazey, won both the Hall Green Hunt Chase and the Solihull Selling Chase, afterwards being sold to Mr J. Horton for 73 guineas. Heyford had been bought out of a Warwick selling race two years earlier for the nominal sum of seven guineas. Not a bad bit of speculation!

Into the twentieth century

Shortage of runners was never a problem at Hall Green. The 1902 meeting, held on Monday 2nd June, produced fields of 9, 10, 14, 6 and 10, well above average for such a minor fixture. Even F. H. Bayles grudgingly conceded in his *Racecourses of Great Britain* that "the meeting, though uninteresting, has much improved of late years."

The *Birmingham Daily Post* reported that year: "The entries were such as to satisfy the most exacting of executives, and with a brilliant day following a damp and disheartening eve, the spirits of the public rose with the barometer, and there was an enormous attendance. A happy holiday spirit, consequent on the peace rejoicings (two days earlier, the Treaty of Vereeniging had ended the Boer War), pervaded the whole proceedings, and backers and bookmakers, winners and losers, and the large section of every racing crowd whose only delight is to witness the kaleidoscope blending of colours which characterises every race for which a good field of horses turns out – all seemed to thoroughly enjoy themselves."

However, all did not go smoothly that day and the *Daily Post's* reporter was critical of the organisation. "It is a pity," he opined, "that with so many propitious elements favouring the meeting, certain of the officials should have been lacking in their duty to such an extent as to seriously peril the success of future meetings. An order of running was supplied to the press on Saturday evening in the usual course, but was subsequently altered, without any notification being given to the press. This caused much confusion and great annoyance to owners, many of whose horses were miles away from the course when they should have been in the paddock. This is a serious matter and one with which the local stewards should not fail to deal, and there should be some guarantee against such stupid blundering in the future. Racing, with the consent of the stewards, was put back fifteen minutes to allow, as far as possible, for the rectification of the blunder."

Nor was that the only problem. During the running of the first race, Deputy Chief-

Constable Wasley, of the Worcestershire Police, thinking all the runners had passed by, walked out onto the course and was knocked down and seriously injured by the tailed off Lough Arrow.

Minor changes were made to the programme when, in 1903, the Shirley Steeplechase was replaced by the Novices' Chase, then two years later the Selling Handicap Chase was added, making it a six-race card for the first time. This was good news for jockeys Alf Newey and William Pearce who rode two winners apiece. Newey rode two more winners at the 1906 Hall Green meeting but was to achieve a far greater victory the following year when winning the Grand National on Eremon, despite having to ride with only one stirrup iron for the last twelve fences.

The 1907 Hall Green meeting saw Barley-corn win the Robin Hood Scurry Chase for the second year running, then turn out again to win the Solihull Selling Chase. Surprisingly, there was no bid for him afterwards at the auction.

In 1908 Hall Green staged its first (and only) Saturday fixture, at which Barley-corn could only finish third in his attempt to win a third Robin Hood Scurry Chase. The report in the *Birmingham Gazette* on Tuesday 19th May revealed that four men had made off with the body of a horse that had been killed in a fall in the last race and sold it to a local slaughterhouse for five shillings. The villains were eventually brought to justice.

The Great Western Railway had opened its North Warwickshire line in 1907, giving Hall Green its own station beside the Stratford Road. Alas, the coming of the railway could not help the future of Hall Green Steeplechases, which staged its last day's racing on Wednesday 25th May 1910.

Alf Newey rode the last of his six winners there when landing the Hall Green Hunt Chase on Hackmount; and there was a double for another Grand National-winning rider, Bryan Bletsoe (he won on Rubio in 1908), aboard Lustre Jug in the Selling Handicap Chase and Islington Beau in the Kings Heath Chase.

The final race, the Novices' Chase, over two miles and worth £33 to the winner, went to S.S. Baltic, ridden by George Green, who won by two lengths from Vindicate, the mount of Bryan Bletsoe.

The sale of Hall Green Estate

Until 1911 Birmingham had stopped at Sparkbrook. Beyond that was Yardley Rural District, of which Hall Green formed part. Hall Green Parish extended as far as Shirley, bounded on the west by the River Cole Valley and on the east by the Rural District boundary. However, in 1912 Yardley Rural District was absorbed into the City of Birmingham.

That same year saw the sale by auction of the entire Hall Green Estate. Its 419 acres included the Bull's Head Hotel, Hall Green Hall, three farms, the Robin Hood

Golf Course and what remained of the racecourse.

The auction took place at the Grand Hotel, Birmingham, on Friday 7th June 1912, at 3.00p.m. prompt. The auctioneers were Messrs. Knight, Frank and Rutley.

Lot 1, Hall Green Hall, was sold for 1,425 guineas. Lot 3, the Bull's Head Hotel and farm buildings, fetched 5,000 guineas. Lot 9, Sparkhill Cricket Ground, went for 500 guineas.

Lot 16, "a valuable building estate of 77 acres, 1 rod, 24 poles", which formed Robin Hood Golf Course and the Hall Green Race Course, despite having been labelled "ripe for development," attracted no bid at the auction. Neither did the previous Lot, Gospel House Farm. Virtually everything else was sold. The land on which the racecourse stood was eventually sold for £7,150.

A brief resumption

During the summer of 1918, Britain was still at war with Germany. Horse racing was severely restricted, with very few meetings being held anywhere other than at Newmarket. On Monday 20th May, a race meeting was held on the Flat at Wolverhampton's Dunstall Park. Steve Donoghue rode a treble and Brownie Carslake landed a double. Curiously, on that very same day, pony racing took place at Hall Green.

Sandwiched between the results from Wolverhampton and a report of the Birmingham Police sports (athletics) at Villa Park, the next day's *Birmingham Post* contains the following report of an injury to a jockey:

"In one of the events at Hall Green races yesterday afternoon, a serious accident occurred to a jockey named Frank Mines (28), of the White Lion Hotel, Whittington, Oswestry. Mines, who is a well known jockey at this class of meeting, was riding Rose Garden. On turning a corner of the course the horse ran into some fencing, which had not been observed by the rider. The result was that the jockey was thrown violently onto his head. He was rendered unconscious, and was conveyed to the General Hospital by Police-constable Andrews and Special Constable Chance. There it was found that he was suffering severely from concussion. In the course of the evening Mines rallied, and at his own request was removed to the house of some friends."

We can find no further reference to this or to any subsequent meetings at Hall Green.

The golf course lasted until shortly after World War II before going the way of the racecourse. Now there are few memories of either, other than of the Hall Green Stud Farm, which is recalled in Studland Road.

Yes, there is still racing at Hall Green, but today it comes in canine form.

THE YARDLEY STUD

Said the *Birmingham Daily Gazette* on 27th June 1888: "Owners and trainers know that after Blankney and Hampton Court the finest stud farm in England is that at Yardley, owned by Messrs Graham; yet the statement causes the average Birmingham sportsman to open his eyes in amazement. That a prophet has no honour in his own country is very evident in the present case. Not four miles from the centre of Birmingham, the Yardley stables are seldom heard of."

The *Gazette* reported that the stud was located "about seven minutes walk from Stechford Station, which, being on the main line to London, affords most convenient means of transport to any part of the country."

The brothers George and Young Robertson Graham owned Yardley Stud Farm, the latter running his horses under the pseudonym of 'Mr Drummond'.

Members of an old Scottish family, the Grahams settled in Oxfordshire, where the youngest son, given the name Young Robertson, was born in December 1827. The family then moved to Birmingham, where they were corn merchants and agents for the brewers Bass in the purchase of barley. Shortly after learning "the ways of the thoroughbred" in Scotland, Young Graham joined his brother George and sister Isabella in founding Yardley Stud.

They purchased a mare named Honeydear, with a colt foal at foot by Birdcatcher, at a sale at the Birmingham Horse Repository in 1857 for around £50. Named Oxford, he had a successful turf career cut short when he was 'nobbled' prior to the 1860 Derby. He was retired to their stud in 1862, where he went on to sire the full-brothers Sterling (1868), Playfair (1869) and Standard (1874), the trio being out of the mare Whisper, a daughter of Flatcatcher.

Playfair was sold to a brewer named Frederick Gretton, for whom John Porter trained him to win the 1872 Cambridgeshire Handicap. Standard, though no world-beater as a racehorse, sired the 1885 Doncaster Cup winner Hambledon.

But the best of the three was Sterling, who finished second to Bothwell in the 1871 Two Thousand Guineas and was narrowly beaten in that year's Cambridgeshire. He was owned throughout his racing and stud career by Isabella Graham, who raced under the *nom de course* of 'Mr Blaydon' and took an active part in the management of the stud.

Sterling was leased to Gretton as a four-year-old and ended his career by carrying 9st 4lb to victory in the 1873 Liverpool Autumn Cup. Having been returned to Miss Graham, Sterling was retired to Yardley Stud in 1874, where he proved a successful and influential sire. He sired four Classic winners, namely Harvester, who dead heated with St Gatien for the Derby in 1884; and Paradox, Enterprise and Enthusiast (the latter being out of the Grahams' mare Cherry Duchess), who all won the Two Thousand Guineas.

The best of those three Guineas winners was Paradox, foaled at Yardley in 1882. He was purchased as a yearling by John Porter, who produced him to win the 1884 Dewhurst Stakes. As well as the Two Thousand Guineas, Paradox also won the Sussex Stakes, the Champion Stakes and the Grand Prix de Paris in 1885 and was second, beaten a head, to Melton for that year's Derby. He was retired to stud as a four-year-old but died at the age of eight, having become extremely savage.

Although not a Classic winner, Sterling's best son was Isonomy, bred by the Grahams out of the mare Isola Bella, by Stockwell. He was bought at Doncaster Sales for 360 guineas on behalf of Frederick Gretton and put into training with John Porter. His sole victory at two was a half-mile nursery at Newmarket. In his only outing as a three-year-old in 1878, he won the Cambridgeshire at 40 to 1 in a field of 38, winning Gretton more than £40,000 in bets.

But it was from four onwards that Isonomy really excelled, winning the Ascot Gold Cup and the Gold Vase on consecutive days, followed by the Goodwood Cup, the Brighton Cup, the Ebor Handicap with 9st 8lb (starting at 11 to 8 on!) and the Doncaster Cup. In 1880 he won the Manchester Cup carrying 9st 12lb and the Ascot Gold Cup for the second time.

Isonomy entered the stud in 1881 and went on to sire two Triple Crown winners in Isinglass and Common, as well as the 1888 Oaks and St Leger heroine Seabreeze, plus Gallinule, the sire of Pretty Polly.

Other good horses sired by Sterling at Yardley include Isonomy's full brother Fernandez (foaled in 1877), winner of the Craven Stakes; Esterling (1882), who also won the Craven Stakes; Beaudesert (1877), winner of the Middle Park Stakes; Geologist (1878), narrowly beaten by Iroquois in the 1881 St Leger; and Cherry Ripe, a full brother to Enthusiast, who sired the 1898 Grand National winner Drogheda and the 1903 Irish Derby victor Lord Rossmore.

Miss Graham twice refused offers of £10,000 for Sterling and reputedly stated in response to a purchase inquiry from Australia, "All the gold in Australia would not buy him." It proved a wise decision.

In addition to Sterling and Standard, the stud's other stallions at the time of the *Gazette's* 1888 report included Westbourne and Plebian. The article ends: "The Yardley Stud is the largest for breeding high-class racehorses, shorthorns and Shropshire sheep of A1 quality in England."

However, it appears that the stud's successes of the 1870s and 1880s declined following Sterling's death in 1891. In February 1897 the *Country Life* reported on the sale of some 42 of the Yardley Stud horses. There was "a lamentable absence of buyers" at the sale and consequently the horses realised poor prices.

The writer was somewhat critical of the way the stud was being run, opining that the Grahams expected "everything born in Yardley to win a Derby, or to be another Isonomy" and adding that for this reason they would never part with their yearlings "except at very big prices", nor would they geld any of the colts. The result of this policy, continued the writer, was that the paddocks "get filled up with troops of the most beautifully-bred colts and fillies of all ages, which have never learned to gallop, many of whom have never been broken and which, therefore, grow everyday more and more worthless as racehorses. The colts, too, being of the high-couraged Sterling blood, grow coltish and tricky, and by the time they are three or four years old, are very often worthless for any purpose whatsoever."

Young Robertson Graham, predeceased by his brother and sister, died in Edgbaston on 5th January 1905, leaving £8,830 in his will.

The stud had been sold in 1901, an auction of bloodstock taking place on 19th March. A total of 44 lots were sold, including broodmares, yearlings, two-year-olds and stallions, among them Farndale (foaled in 1891) by Sterling, a winner of six races, and MacMahon (1880, by Macgregor), winner of the York Cup at three and the Sandown Autumn Cup at four. The *Birmingham Daily Post* reported: "There was a good company of spectators round the ring, but buyers were either scarce or were shy at bidding, and the prices realised can only be described as moderate."

An interesting fact is that three of the stallions that were sold had all won on the same day – 1st May 1899 – at Shirley Hunt, with Sum Total (1895, by Pioneer) winning the two-mile May Day Maiden Hurdle; two races later Hardy (1894, by MacMahon) won the three-mile Scurry Hunt Chase, and in the last race, Kowloon (1895 by Endurance out of Cherry Duchess, and so a half-brother to Enthusiast) won the two-mile Monks Path Steeple Chase. All three were ridden by Mr Arthur Wood.

The *Birmingham Daily Gazette's* account of the auction noted, "It is upwards of 50 years since Mr. Graham started the stud, and his method of rearing has proved most successful in producing really useful horses." It adds: "The last sale of his bloodstock was in 1898, and since then Mr. Graham has made purchases of brood mares at Newmarket and elsewhere, and nearly all these traced back to the old Yardley blood of Sterling, who earned for the stud such a world wide reputation."

The following day, 20th March, saw a second auction at the stud which included select herds of Jersey and Shorthorn cattle, two carthorses, assorted agricultural implements and "100 lots of useful household furniture".

Thus the book was closed on Yardley Stud. All that remains as a reminder of this once famous Thoroughbred nursery is a street in the area named Stud Lane.

YARDLEY WOOD, BILLESLEY AND WARD END

While Yardley Stud remains far and away this area's richest horse racing legacy, there was another link with the sport. Yardley Racing Club, based around Yardley Wood, used to stage race meetings at Billesley Common.

Furthermore, the *Birmingham Evening Mail's* "Table Talk" column on 18th July 1908, comments on the North Warwickshire Polo Club, the president of which was the Earl of Aylesford; the vice president being George Graham of Yardley Stud fame. It stated that the club used to practice at "Mrs Lawley's farm at Billesley, near King's Heath", adding that this was also the venue for "an excellent steeplechase course last century." However, we have been unable to trace further references to this. It may possibly have been a point-to-point course.

What we do know for certain is that a race meeting took place on the "Flying Ground" at Billesley Common on Easter Monday 24th and Tuesday 25th April 1916, a time when the Great War was at its most fierce.

Under the headline "Big Holiday Crowd at Yardley Wood", the *Birmingham Gazette* reported on the Tuesday: "Thanks to the enterprise of the members of the Yardley Racing Club, the sportsmen of Birmingham and district were entertained to an afternoon's racing yesterday, and they will be similarly catered for to-day, when another 'card' is due. Considering that the meeting was hurriedly promoted it was particularly successful, and there was a large attendance."

There were six events on the opening day's programme. Only two runners started in each of the first two races, the Antwerp Plate Hurdle, over one mile six furlongs, and the Khaki Plate Hurdle, over two miles. Both ended in bloodless victories for Miss Lucy Latham's Taxi Boy, ridden by G. H. Brown. In the first race, sole rival Canterbury ran out and fell, while in the second contest, solitary opponent Tulip was pulled up half a mile from home. There were bigger fields for the other races, all of which were keenly contested. There was also a third winner for Miss Latham when White Socks won the seven-furlong Calais Plate by a length from Cassy, with the 5 to 4 favourite Limited a length and a half further away in third.

Tommy, a 10 to 1 outsider ridden by his owner, Mr A. Orton, carried 8st 10lb to victory in the six-furlong race for ponies of 14.2 hands and under, beating 5 to 4 favourite Dover by two lengths. Six runners went to post for the Verdun Stakes, over one and a half miles, and once again the favourite was turned over, with the 7 to 2 chance Arthur, ridden by G. Jackman, winning by four lengths from Coton. The last race, the Tradesmen's Pony Race for ponies of 13.2 hands or under, run over one mile, went to Grey Leg, the mount of W. Haddock.

The Gazette concluded: "Despite the big attendance there were no accidents or untoward incidents, and if to-day's is successful to a similar degree the enterprise of the Yardley Racing Club will be not only amply repaid, but will be highly appreciated."

The meeting was undoubtedly a much-needed morale booster, providing a few precious hours of relaxation and entertainment in troubled times. However, the haste with which it was arranged inevitably meant there were aspects in need of improvement, particularly in respect of the restricted viewing and the track itself. A new group of organisers duly came forward to plan a Whitsuntide meeting, again to be held at the Flying Ground, Billesley Common.

The Gazette, referring to their acknowledgement of the required improvements, reported: "They are men with wide experience of racing, and no scheme in connection with the sport would be too big for them to tackle. Unlike their predecessors, they have not been handicapped by lack of time. Their object is to ensure comfort for spectators and competitors, and it may be taken for granted that the proceedings on 12 and 13 June will be conducted on up-to-date lines.

"The course, which has been improved, will be kept clear while racing is in progress, and there will be much better accommodation for the public. The stakes, which are substantial, amounting to £270, have been deposited and it is confidently predicted that entries will be numerous. Details of the programme will be advertised as soon as they are completed."

However, at the start of June, Mr Jesse Brown, on behalf of the organisers, announced that the Whit Monday and Tuesday meeting had been postponed until the August Bank Holiday. *The Gazette* reported: "The sportsmen responsible for the arrangements have spent a lot of money in improving the course and there seemed every prospect of the meeting being a big success. They had no hesitation, however, in placing patriotism before profit, and their action, which means considerable loss, will meet with the approval of all sportsmen.

"All the people actively interested in the meeting are above military age and have sons or brothers at the front, and it is their unanimous opinion that racing in Birmingham would be out of place when workers are cheerfully sacrificing their holidays at the request of the Minister of Munitions. In August munition workers will have an extra day for recreation, and Mr. Brown and his colleagues will then endeavour to provide sport worthy of the occasion."

But while the Billesley Common fixture may have been postponed, Yardley Racing Club came up with a new venue, at Ward End, and arranged an alternative meeting around the Whitsuntide weekend, to be held on Saturday 10th June and on Whit Monday. The programme comprised four open horse races, six open pony races, and two pony races restricted to Birmingham tradesmen only.

The Ward End course was situated just half a mile from Bromford Bridge and was ten minutes walk from both Stechford and Saltley stations. The track itself measured about a lap and a half to a mile and a good view of the racing could be obtained from the surrounding high ground. It also had, the organisers claimed, "one of the prettiest enclosures and paddocks in England."

Mr T. Southall, manager of Yardley Racing Club, acknowledged that the Billesley Common meeting had been put back to August but defended the decision to race at Ward End. The *Birmingham Gazette* reported on Tuesday 6th June: "It is realised by the Executive of the Yardley Racing Club that there will not be many holiday-makers in Birmingham and district at Whitsuntide. They have decided, however, to hold the meeting arranged for Saturday and Monday next at Ward End, their programme being timed to suit the convenience of workers, who can enjoy a few hours sport when the day's labour is ended.

"On Saturday afternoon racing will not commence until 3.30, an arrangement which will meet the approval of all Midland sportsmen who leave work at one o'clock. It is proposed to start the first race on Monday at three o'clock, but this, we understand, is subject to revision."

The following day's *Gazette* reported that Mr Southall had informed them that excellent entries had been received. "It is satisfactory to learn," the *Gazette* added, "that it will be possible to witness the sport in comfort. Stands have been provided and the course will be kept clear by experienced officials when the races are being run. The executive having decided to pay the amusement tax, the prices of admission will be: - Course only, 1s; ring and paddock, 2s 6d; As sport does not commence until 3.30 on Saturday, a big attendance is expected."

By then there was even more pressure on munition workers' time, with a plethora of other sporting events having been cancelled. Immediately below that day's upbeat report for Ward End Races was an announcement that Windsor's race meeting, scheduled for Friday 9th and Saturday 10th June, had been abandoned in consequence of the death of Lord Kitchener.

That Saturday, the *Gazette* published a report headlined, "Race Meetings. New Powers for Minister of Munitions." Regulations had been put in place under the Defence of the Realm Act whereby, if there was reason to believe that any race meeting would impede the production of war materials or associated work, the Minister had the power to impose an order prohibiting it from taking place. In the case of race meetings to be held after 15th June 1916, seven days written notice had to be given to the Minister. Any person found to have taken part in organising any race meeting that had been prohibited by the order would be deemed guilty of an offence against the new regulations.

It wasn't just minor fixtures such as those organised by the Yardley Racing Club that were affected. The *Birmingham Gazette* reported in June 1916 that the Prime Minister, Mr Asquith, had received a deputation from the Jockey Club in reference to the government's prohibition of racing. The deputation was led by the Earl of Rosebery who, when interviewed afterwards, stated, "I don't think there is any immediate prospect of the resumption of racing." The Prime Minister stated that he hoped to be in a better position to review the situation and give a reply towards the end of June.

Contrary to Lord Rosebery's pessimism, racing under Jockey Club Rules resumed soon after, albeit on a much reduced scale. But sadly, despite all their enterprise and good intentions in terms of raising morale, it was the death knell for minor affairs like those at Yardley Wood, Billesley and Ward End.

THE MYSTERY OF HAY MILLS RACES

*A*ris's *Birmingham Gazette*, dated 22nd May 1920, contains an intriguing advert for the Saturday of that Whitsun weekend.

HAY MILLS RACES

TODAY (SATURDAY), 22nd
All races closed with capital entries.
Trains every two minutes to only entrance to course.
HAY MILLS BRIDGE PARK
Admission 2/-.   First Race 2.15.

It appears that this was horse racing of some form, presumably for ponies. However, we have been unable to unearth results or reports appertaining to the event. Hence, Hay Mills' association with the Sport of Kings remains a mystery!

SHIRLEY PARK

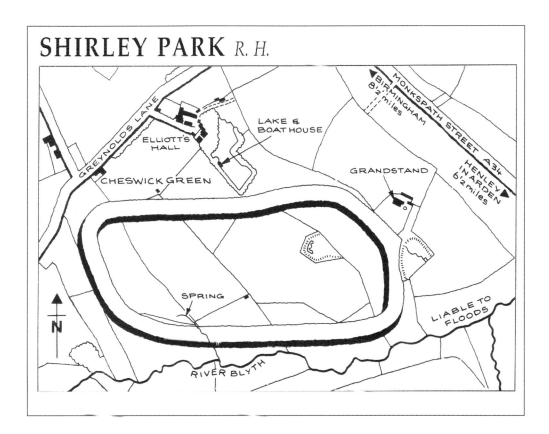

SHIRLEY PARK *R. H.*

Shirley was originally part of the Manor of Ulverlei, a large manor created in Anglo-Saxon times that stretched from what is now Olton across to Solihull in the east. Most of what was at first little more than a remote hamlet grew up alongside the Stratford Road, which became a turnpike in 1725 with a tollgate being erected in Shirley Street, close to where the Saracen's Head now stands.

At the start of the nineteenth century, Shirley – it's name has two possible derivations, either 'bright clearing' or 'boundary clearing' – was still an isolated farming community, but its population gradually increased during the course of the century. It was part of Solihull until Shirley Parish Council came into being in 1894.

On 16th September 1895 a race meeting was held in the meadows adjoining the Saracen's Head, comprising a mixture of steeplechases, galloway and pony races.

135

The crowd was said to have numbered several thousand and it was reported that the meeting was "much better than last year's", so racing had obviously taken place there before.

In fact, it appears that some form of private race meetings, perhaps pony racing, took place in the area as early as 1850. There is a report of a viewing platform being erected that year at the back of Elliot's Hall, which today is the site of Lloyds TSB Management College.

Racing's popularity subsequently influenced the Parish Council to approve a scheme for establishing a National Hunt racecourse in Shirley. The course was built at Monkspath Street (now forming part of the A34 Stratford Road), seven miles from Birmingham's city centre and three from the lesser known National Hunt track at Hall Green. The Shirley course was, according to F. H. Bayles' '*The Racecourses of Great Britain*', "11/2 miles round, over a good turf, running left-handed (it was later changed to right-handed). The fences are very easy to negotiate."

Locally, there were train services to Solihull (21/2 miles away), Knowle (2 miles) and Widney Manor (11/2 miles) stations, all on the Great Western line. The meetings were organised by John Horton of Elliot's Hall, while the experienced John Sheldon, who had previously been involved with Sutton Park, Olton and Four Oaks, officiated as Clerk of the Course.

Early years

The inaugural meeting at 'Shirley Hunt' took place on Monday 1st May 1899. The first race, the Henley Selling Hurdle Plate, run over two miles, was won by Kippur, the mount of Harry Iles. The second race, the May Day Maiden Hurdle, went to Sum Total, the first leg of a treble for Mr Arthur Wood, who then won the Scurry Hunt Chase on Hardy and the Monks Path Steeplechase on Kowloon.

Arthur 'Stosher' Wood was one of the foremost amateur riders of his day and had been champion jockey over jumps in 1898 with 50 winners. Four weeks before Shirley's first meeting he had won the Welsh Grand National on Nat Gould. He again dominated proceedings at Shirley Hunt's second fixture on Monday 13th November 1899, winning three of the four steeplechases on the six-race card. Wood retained his champion jockey's title that year with 59 winners.

Another top amateur rider was Herbert Sidney, the youngest son of Alderman Thomas Sidney, a former Lord Mayor of London. He, along with Wood, was one of the few amateurs to become champion National Hunt jockey, achieving that feat in 1900 with 53 winners, with Wood finishing runner-up. Both gentlemen rode winners at Shirley during its early years.

Shirley Hunt was granted four one-day fixtures in 1900, all Mondays, in March, April, September and December, although this was later reduced to just April and

September. Mondays became the recognised day for racing at Shirley and, apart from an occasional Wednesday, would remain so throughout its existence.

In 1902 a 15-year lease, backdated to 1901, was granted to Frederick Gowing, a builder from Balsall Heath, for the whole of the Elliot's Hall Estate, comprising some 189 acres, for an annual rent of £500. The lease stipulated that Mr Gowing could use the land to operate a racecourse, provided that he did not lose his licence to do so.

The lease also referred to "The Grandstand, Payboxes, and other wooden erections on the course, which belong to Frederick Gowing, insured against loss or damage by fire in the sum of One Thousand, Five Hundred and Fifty Pounds."

Course specialists included Dandolo, whose four victories at Shirley comprised the Greet Maiden Hurdle and the Tanworth-in-Arden Chase in 1902, and the following year's Knowle Handicap Chase and Shirley Handicap Chase. Another was Brantingham, who won the Foxhunters' Handicap Chase four years running, from 1908 to 1911. He didn't compete in the 1912 renewal of the race, which was won by Sergeant Buzfuz, named after a character in Dickens' 'Pickwick Papers'.

The inter-war period

Despite meagre prize money of £30 to £40 per race, Shirley's meetings were generally competitive with plenty of runners. However, when racing returned following the Great War with a fixture on 8th September 1919, only eighteen horses turned up for the six races, the first of which, the Monkspath Hurdle, was won by the twelve-year-old Last, ridden by Harry Atherton Brown. After Last had come first, he was reunited with Mr Brown for the last race, the Solihull Chase, where they faced just one rival, the four-year-old Robert Heath. Unfortunately, the race had to be declared void when both horses repeatedly refused to jump the fences.

There was another void race at the 1921 March meeting. Eight riders weighed out for the Tally-Ho Hunters' Handicap Chase, but it was declared void on account of part of the fence at the open ditch having been damaged beyond repair in the previous race. In those days, racing's inflexible rules did not give officials authority to omit a fence from a race. If the fence couldn't be jumped, the race couldn't take place.

At that year's May meeting, Drifter, ridden by "Tich" Mason, finished alone in the three-runner Consolation Chase after both his rivals had fallen. It was no surprise that Drifter was able to jump round, for this was a safe-as-houses conveyance who the following year would finish second to Music Hall in the Grand National, then fifth in 1923, fourth in 1924 and ninth in 1925.

Prize money ranged between £80 and £100 per race by 1925, the last year that they raced under the title 'Shirley Hunt'. Afterwards it was known either as just plain Shirley or Shirley Park.

On 8th March 1926, jockey Roy Philip, aged 23, from Cheltenham, was badly hurt when his mount Tranga fell at the third hurdle in Shirley's opening race, the Novices' Hurdle. He was taken to the Queen's Hospital where he died two days later of spinal cord injuries and a broken neck.

Jockey brothers Keith and Victor Piggott, father and uncle, respectively, of Lester, both rode a winner at the 1927 May meeting. But punters had a nasty shock when odds-on favourite Melleray's Belle fell in the Hunters' Handicap Chase. Three years later, Melleray's Belle came within a neck of winning the Grand National, being beaten by Shaun Goilin.

Carfax, who had failed to complete the course in the 1929 Grand National and Welsh National on his previous two starts, found easier pickings at Shirley when he was the beneficiary of a walkover for that year's Plodders' Chase. The 1926 Cheltenham Gold Cup winner Koko turned up at Shirley for the 1930 Plodders' Chase. Ridden by Eric Foster, he won easily by thirty lengths.

While not quite good enough to win a National or a Gold Cup, Shirley Park did have its own course specialist during those years. Her name was…

Royal Toy

Royal Toy is one of the forgotten equine heroines from the inter-war period, and it is well worth scrutinising her remarkable record. Foaled in 1918, by Ardoon out of Santoi's Queen, the bay mare made her debut when unplaced in a Ludlow maiden hurdle on 13th October 1922.

At Shirley Park's 1925 September meeting, Royal Toy scored her first course

Taking the water jump in the Shirley Selling Handicap Chase, 30th May 1927.

victory in the Earlswood Handicap Chase, over two miles and fifty yards, ridden by "Tich" Mason. In 1926, she won the Solihull Handicap Chase at the May meeting, then returned in September to win the Earlswood Handicap Chase for the second year running, her third course and distance victory. Later that year, Royal Toy finished fourth to future Gold Cup winner Easter Hero in the Molyneux Handicap Chase over the Grand National fences at Liverpool.

Billy Stott – rode 13 winners at Shirley Park.

In September 1927, Royal Toy won the Earlswood Handicap Chase for the third year running to record her fourth course and distance success. On her next appearance at Shirley, on the last day of April 1928, she suffered a surprising four-length defeat at the hands of Jargoon, the mount of champion jockey Billy Stott, in the Solihull Handicap Chase. However, she then bounced back to form, winning her next five races, including the Earlswood Handicap Chase for the fourth successive year. She won the Earlswood Handicap Chase for the fifth time in 1929, but that was to be her last race for nearly two years.

Thirteen-year-old Royal Toy finished unplaced in the Wood End Selling Handicap Chase at Shirley in September 1931. It looked as though age had finally caught up with her. But the game old mare still had plenty of leap left in her, as she proved on 'Leap Year's Day', 29th February 1932. Despite carrying 10lbs of overweight, she won the Shirley Selling Handicap Chase at 20 to 1. It was her seventh course and distance success.

She ran at each of the other three Shirley Park fixtures that year, finishing fifth in the Dorridge Selling Handicap Chase, third in the Shirley Selling Handicap Chase, and second in the Wood End Selling Handicap Chase. And she was back in 1933 when, ridden by Lord Somerton, she again finished fifth in the Dorridge Selling Handicap Chase. Remarkably, the fifteen-year-old won six races that year and also finished sixth in the Molyneux Chase at Liverpool.

Royal Toy made her last appearance at Shirley, aged sixteen, in the Shirley Selling Handicap Chase on 5th March 1934. Ridden this time by Lord Normanton, she for once let her supporters down by falling for the only time at Shirley. Nonetheless, she won another four races during the year and was in the frame on fifteen of her twenty starts. She continued to race until June 1935, when, at the grand old age of seventeen, she finished second in her last race, a selling chase at Huntingdon.

In a career spanning four months short of thirteen years, Royal Toy ran in a total of 137 races, winning 34; finishing second 17 times, third 26 times, and 14 times fourth. Her most valuable victories were achieved in the 1927 and 1929 runnings of the Wetherby Handicap Chase, worth £492 to the winner, which in those days was a very big prize indeed for a National Hunt race. She also finished third, fourth, and sixth in three runnings of the Molyneux Chase, run over part of the fearsome Grand National course.

Her record at Shirley reads: ran 15; won seven; second three times, third once. There was surely no more game and consistent performer than Royal Toy.

Racecourse improvements

Part of the far side of the course was out of sight to most racegoers, which led to various stories of bumping, barging, interference and other such irregularities among the horses and riders. This section of the circuit also ran alongside the River Blythe, which involved a sharp, almost right-angled turn. It again created perfect conditions for the skulduggery that was alleged to have taken place.

Considerable improvements were made to the course during 1931. The *Solihull News* of Saturday 5th September reported: "The new layout of the entrance to the course consists of a central turnstile building for admittance of the general public, with a gateway for vehicular traffic on either side, and a further group of entrance gates to the road itself.

"Other work consists of the raising of a portion of the track at the commencement of the finishing straight for a length of about 150 yards. During the coming winter it is proposed to raise a further section of this finishing straight, and thus complete another work of improvement as far as actual racing is concerned. At the present time the view across the course from the public enclosures is somewhat obscured by an intervening hummock. In order to facilitate the view of the general public the directors are considering a scheme whereby the summit of the hill itself shall be removed and remoulded – a large and somewhat difficult undertaking, which, however, it is hoped will be carried out and completed in time for next year's fixtures.

"The fencing round the far side of the track itself has been considerably extended and improved. A new iron fence has also been erected to enclose the roadway from the loose boxes to Tattersalls enclosure. New catering arrangements have been entered into and will be considerably extended. Arrangements have been made with the British Betting Control Board for a totalisator to be in operation in future, to be placed between Tattersalls and the public enclosure, easily accessible from both sides."

Totalisator betting had made its debut in 1929 and all racecourses were now adopting this alternative method of placing a bet. The Tote soon began publishing its own 'Racing Annual', the 1934 edition of which revealed that admission charges at Shirley were: Tattersalls 14s (7s 6d for Ladies); Course 2s. There was no Race Club membership at Shirley, although ladies received free badges.

A telegraph office was available underneath the main grandstand and racing at Shirley Park became ever more popular during the 1930s. On race days, the 6.00pm express train from Birmingham's Snow Hill Station to Paddington made a special stop at Knowle and Dorridge Station, some three miles from the course, to pick up racegoers returning to London. Crowds were large and the greatly increased traffic on race days prompted many anxious parents to keep their children at home.

National Hunt race card, 1934.

The end of National Hunt racing

The vagaries of the British weather were occasionally prone to disrupt racing at Shirley Park. In 1937 the March meeting was abandoned due to snow and the waterlogged state of the course, and then, ironically, the September meeting was abandoned due to the hard state of the ground. Hard ground also caused the abandonment of the 1938 April meeting. More ominously, however, the meeting scheduled for Monday 4th September 1939 was among the first fixtures to be called off owing to the state of emergency, with war having been declared with Germany.

The Second World War would take its toll on racing and a host of minor National Hunt courses were lost forever, many of them being ploughed up to assist the war effort. Midland casualties included Bridgnorth, Wenlock, Pershore and Colwall Park, although the last-mentioned would later reappear in another guise.

What was to be the final National Hunt meeting at Shirley Park took place on Monday 11th March 1940. It attracted 111 runners for the six races, only one of which had less than sixteen starters. Fred Rimell, who was later to train four Grand National winners, rode a double, while the last race on the card, the Novices' Chase over two miles and fifty yards, was won by Harlequin, the 5 to 2 favourite, ridden by Jack Dowdeswell.

During the war years, various events were held there, including a performance by a troupe of Cossack riders and the Midland Counties Cross Country athletic meetings. But while the war saw the demise of many racecourses, it did not see off Shirley Park.

The pony racing era

After the war and with the loss of Northolt Park to Ealing Council in May 1946,

Berkshire's Hawthorn Hill, like Shirley a former National Hunt course, became the new headquarters for racing under Pony Turf Club Rules. It was also in 1946 that the Kirkby Mallory Racecourse Company Ltd. from Leicestershire took out a lease on Shirley Park from the freehold owners, South Midlands Estates, and it duly became pony racing's second venue.

Seven summer dates were allotted for 1947, between 2nd July and 27th August, with *The Racegoer* magazine advising its readers: "Racegoers can be assured that at Shirley, racing will be presented with imagination and showmanship. Its energetic and enterprising managing director, Mr J. S. Sail, has a wide experience of racing in Canada, USA and the Argentine, and at Shirley, and later on at Mallory Park, the best ideas to be found in these countries will be grafted on to the English way of doing things. With the large population of Birmingham to draw on, the success of Shirley is assured."

Jack Sail, as he liked to be called, was a demon for hard work and brimmed over with infectious enthusiasm. In *The Racegoer* he pledged: "I want to cater for ALL racegoers, especially the working man and his family, who patronise the cheaper enclosures. The 'average man' – the general public – is the backbone of sport, includ-

Putting the finishing touches prior to the launch of pony racing in 1947.

Shirley Park – a view of the straight in 1947.

ing racing, and I never intend to lose sight of that fact! At Shirley Park – and at Mallory, too, later in the year – I shall endeavour to stage Pony Racing with all amenities to meet the pockets of everyone at reasonable prices."

In a promotional flyer advertising the post-war revival of racing at Shirley Park under PTC Rules, Sail stated: "It is the intention of the management to rebuild at Shirley and to give 100% racing efficiency, but this cannot be done as yet until restrictions are eased. Houses come first."

Shirley Park reopened for business as planned on 2nd July 1947. Racegoers attending that first meeting were pleasantly surprised to find the "Ponyform", giving details of the last two outings of each runner, contained in the official race card. Though widely used overseas, this innovation had been ignored by the myopic officials responsible for running the major racecourses. There was also a running commentary on each race, another area in which 'proper' racecourses were dragging their feet. The first race on the card was the Coventry Juvenile Plate, worth £100, over five furlongs, which was won by Peter's Pride, the 13 to 8 second favourite. May Wood won the second race, ridden by Maurice Harrison, who completed a double when Highland Flour landed the day's last race.

Jack Sail's policy of catering for all racegoers reaped swift rewards, with the second meeting, held on Monday 14th July (when, incidentally, there were no Jockey Club Flat fixtures) drawing a crowd of between 14,000 and 15,000.

On 1st August the Racecourse Executive issued a bulletin to owners and trainers saying that, providing there was sufficient support, they were considering introducing hurdle races for its later autumn meetings. However, there was a proviso in that they were only prepared to stage hurdling if the ponies had been sufficiently well schooled and were ridden by experienced jockeys.

Pony racing had a big following in the immediate post-war years, particularly at Shirley Park. Buses ran from the Bull Ring in Birmingham direct to the course, with additional services being run from Redditch, Coventry and Wolverhampton. By the start of 1949 there were fifteen meetings allocated to Shirley Park, scheduled between early April and the beginning of November.

Four former National Hunt tracks – Colwall Park, Shirley, Newport and Hawthorn Hill – had fixtures scheduled for 1949, as did the newly constructed left-handed track at Kirkby Mallory, situated between Hinckley and Leicester. Mallory Park, in the grounds of Mallory Hall, had been modelled on Woodbine racecourse in Toronto and its "almost saucer-like layout" would give racegoers an unimpaired view of the racing without the need for binoculars. Mallory Park's actual starting date had not yet been finalised and its fixtures had been left open, with Shirley having an option to take them over.

However, matters were not quite so healthy as they appeared. Both Newport and Colwall had short-lived second careers, while the Kirkby Mallory course never opened. Indeed, in May 1949 Kirkby Mallory Racecourse Company Ltd. was

Racegoers brave the rain to cheer home the winner of a pony race.

Shirley Park's main grandstand.

declared bankrupt and went into liquidation. Racing at Shirley Park was immediately suspended. The Shirley Park Racecourse Company Ltd. was hastily formed and took over the lease from the liquidator but, even so, no fixtures were to be allocated to Shirley Park for the whole of 1950.

Enter Mr Featherstone

With the Kirkby Mallory Company having been declared bankrupt, George Featherstone, a well-known Midland sportsman, immediately submitted an application to Solihull Urban District Council to convert Shirley Racecourse into an amusement park and build a large indoor arena, incorporating a swimming pool and a riding school. The new venue would be capable of hosting various sporting events, including athletics, boxing, swimming and show jumping, plus agricultural shows.

The plans also included, controversially, the construction of a motor and motor cycle racing circuit. It was intended that the track should be just over a mile long and constructed of concrete. The application had the enthusiastic support of the Solihull Motor Cycle Club. The Council approved Featherstone's proposal in principle but decided to defer sanction of the motor racing circuit to a later date.

Featherstone asked the Council to reconsider its decision, as his intention was to hold six motor racing and twenty motor cycle racing meetings during each year, and without support for this it could mean that the whole project would fall through. He also talked initially of a speedway track, though this aspect was subsequently withdrawn, and in certain other respects appeared unclear as to exactly what he wanted. The Council therefore asked him to provide full details of his proposals, on receipt of which "the matter would receive further consideration." Featherstone duly pressed on with his preparation of detailed plans.

The proposed scheme immediately met local resistance, with the Shirley Residents Association firmly opposing the application. They deplored the approval that had already been granted to use the site as an amusement ground, and submitted a petition to the Parish Council protesting against the use of the racecourse "for any purpose likely to create disturbance." The Association cited the problems of increased traffic and the possibility of "undesirables" being attracted to the area. They were supported by the Reverend J. S. Billings, vicar of Shirley, and the Shirley Chamber of Trade, both of whom put forward their own representations calling for the scheme to be rejected in its entirety.

It was pointed out that, "112 acres – a considerable slice of the district's rural zone – would be taken up by the arena," and that it would be "detrimental to the amenities of one of the most beautiful parts of the district." The amusement park was branded as a "vulgar presence". The residents informed their local councillor that if the scheme went through, "the site would, in due course, become a second Donington," (referring to Donington Park motor racing circuit). The Council and the residents were clearly on opposite sides of a very large fence.

The matter was discussed at a meeting of the Urban Council on 15th November 1949. The following night's *Evening Despatch* reported: "After receiving three petitions and numerous letters concerning the proposal to convert Shirley Park racecourse into a sports arena, Solihull Urban Council last night approved a recommendation from its Building Plans and Town Planning Committee that the scheme should be sanctioned subject to car and motor-cycle racing being excluded. The County Council will be recommended to endorse this decision."

This was in effect a reiteration of the Council's original decision and was far from what Featherstone wanted. He told an *Evening Despatch* reporter that he intended to lodge an appeal with the Ministry of Town and Country Planning in an effort to secure sanction for his complete original proposal.

Meanwhile, all of these goings-on, allied to the fact that Featherstone was describing himself as the "prospective lessee", caused considerable irritation and head-scratching among the Shirley Park Racecourse Company, who declared: "We have nothing whatsoever to do with Featherstone, he is not a shareholder or a director, we are not in negotiation with him, nor are we ever likely to be. As for the assignment of the lease, we took it over because we want to start National Hunt racing there, and

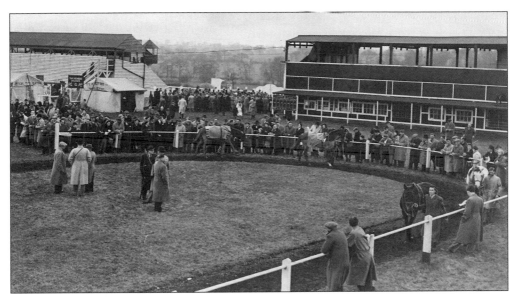

A panorama view of the paddock and stands in 1951.

if we cannot, then we shall carry on with pony racing. We have got a reversion of the lease for twelve years and we intend to keep it."

Solihull Council thus notified the Ministry to the effect that, even if the appeal was allowed, Featherstone would be unable to carry out any part of his scheme because he didn't own or lease the land. This meant that Featherstone's project had no chance whatsoever of succeeding.

However, a confidential Solihull Council memo regarding Featherstone's planning application makes for interesting reading. The Clerk to the Council remarked that his opinion, "off the record, not guaranteed, and not to be quoted" was that "if Featherstone had put in his application in the first instance without being so vague (which caused delay while what he wanted was checked), and without bringing in speedway (which is highly unpopular locally on grounds of noise nuisance, and had brought forth a petition with hundreds of signatures), then it would have been granted and he would have got the lease before Shirley Racecourse Company came in."

Racing's short-lived return

During 1951, 26 days of pony racing were held at Shirley Park, six of which were evening meetings. Evening racing proved a big success and the enthusiastic Racecourse Executive, led by Wally Miller and his two sons, made every effort to ensure that the catering, betting and viewing facilities were as good as could be achieved. The most valuable race run at Shirley Park that year was the Banbury Cup, a two-mile handicap worth £225. There were six runners and the winner was Lady Burnham's consistent mare Roseblush, trained by Jack Ward and the mount of Fred Payne. Roseblush gave 27lb and a short head beating to Tudor Green, with Mullion, the 1948 Pony Turf Club Derby winner, only a length away in third.

By this time, all but one of the other pony racecourses had been forced to close down. When Hawthorn Hill went the same way at the end of 1951, Shirley was left as the only course in the country still staging pony racing. Because of this, a great many ponies, particularly those based in the south of England, were taken out of training.

A further 28 meetings were staged in 1952, with another allocated 23 for 1953. The problem was that, because of the shortage of ponies

Race card for Shirley Park's final meeting.

left in training, the same ones were appearing time and again. It became a case of familiarity breeding contempt and, gradually, the public began to lose interest.

Shirley Park staged its last fixture of 1953 on Wednesday 4th November. The organisers applied to the Pony Turf Club for 20 fixtures the following year, but in January 1954, the PTC stewards announced that there would be no further meetings.

A Shirley Park official said: "With only one course operating (in the country), the meetings at Shirley were too frequent and with insufficient ponies and support not forthcoming from the public, we had a difficult time at Shirley last year…. It is hoped that National Hunt racing, which was a feature before the war, will be resumed."

Alas, it wasn't. Racing at Shirley Park was over. Local trainer Jack Lea used the course to exercise his string, the riders including jump jockeys Jim Edmunds, Sammy McComb and Bernard Wells. But they were the last racehorses to gallop over its turf.

The end of the racecourse

During June 1954, the year in which Solihull became a municipal borough (it was to become a county borough eight years later), auctions were held at Shirley Park to dispose of the racecourse's equipment. Over 300 lots were offered, including weighing scales, starting gates and a mile and a half of railings. The buyers were mainly farmers, scrap merchants and racecourse representatives.

There was plenty of interest in the actual racecourse, including from a local bookmaker who was keen to continue its use for racing. But it was eventually sold by auction on Tuesday 17th May 1955 to the Birmingham Jewish Golfing Society for £19,500. The sale comprised all of the course's buildings, including 85 stable boxes and two grandstands. The main grandstand housed a number of offices, such as the old telegraph office.

The stewards' box – a convenient "lovers' nest" for golfers!

The racecourse was transformed into Shirley Golf Club. The tea room and the jockeys' weighing room, a long timber building with numerous entrances, became familiar to golf club members as the professional's shop. Subsequently painted in broad black and white stripes, it contrasted sharply with the surrounding greens and fairways until it was burned down in 1975.

What used to be the Tattersalls enclosure lay just behind where the eighteenth green now stands. There also stood the stewards' box, a watchtower accessed by steps on the outside of the structure. If some sources are to be believed, the watchtower later made a convenient lovers' nest for some of the Birmingham Jewish golfers!

An ironwork archway that once marked the entrance to the racecourse from the Stratford Road, bearing the legend 'Shirley Racecourse', along with part of the entrance buildings, remained in place for a number of years. As for what remained of the racecourse itself, the last vestige disappeared with the removal in 1992 of the old running rails bordering the field alongside the fifteenth fairway, these being replaced by gorse and broom.

The Clubhouse windows look out to where the winning post once stood. But as today's golfers drive down the fairways or chip their way out of bunkers, few of them will realise that, but for Shirley Park Racecourse Company, whose dreams of reviving National Hunt racing failed to materialise, and the steadfast opposition of the Shirley Residents Association, the site might well have been Shirley's answer to Wembley Arena.

BROMFORD BRIDGE

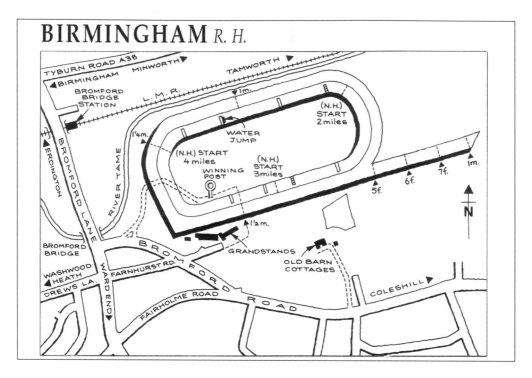

In 1894, the brothers John and Stanley Ford, with the backing of a new company, of which the Earl of Aylesford was chairman, secured a 42-year lease of land on the Earl of Bradford's estate at Bromford Bridge. Given the history of failure and ill luck that had befallen so many racecourses in and around Birmingham during the nineteenth century, it was a brave move.

This new site, on the flat river meadows bordered by the River Tame to the north and west, was located in an area then unspoilt by urban development. It lay between the village of Castle Bromwich and the city of Birmingham, which at that time was still a mile or more away.

There had been steeplechasing in the Castle Bromwich area during the mid-nineteenth century. A Castle Bromwich Steeplechase, over about three miles, took place on Friday 27th March 1846. Mr Richards' horse Sarsfield, ridden by the owner, won the race, beating four others. Four years later, 28th March 1850, a "Birmingham Garrison" fixture was held "for officers on full pay". It comprised just one race, the Castle Bromwich Military Steeplechase, again over about three miles, and offered a silver claret jug to the winner. The runners had to jump the River Cole, which varied in width between 8-12ft. It attracted nine runners and was won by Dunroe, carrying 11st 12lb, owned and ridden by Captain Prime.

The word Bromwich means the dwelling or farm where the broom grows, broom being a shrub with yellow flowers, once common in the area. That area was called Bramewice in 1168, but by the late thirteenth century was known as Castlebromwic to differentiate it from another nearby Bromwich that eventually became Little Bromwich. For centuries the manor of Castle Bromwich belonged to the Devereux family, but in 1657 Anne Devereux sold the land to the Bridgeman family, which later became the family of the Earl of Bradford.

The old boundary between Little Bromwich and Castle Bromwich ran from Bromford Bridge on the River Tame along Bromford Lane and Stechford Lane to Stechford Bridge on the River Cole. Thus Bromford, the broom ford, lay within the manor of Castle Bromwich. However, Bromford Mill was on the north bank of the Tame and fell within the manor of Erdington.

Before the new racecourse was built, Bromford Bridge was farmland and belonged to an area called the Five Fields, which stretched from St Margaret's Road across to the present Bromford Bridge estate and up to the Fox and Goose pub.

Initially it appeared as though the misfortunes of the past would continue to dog this latest enterprise. The first day's racing was originally scheduled for Easter Monday 1895 but the long harsh frosts of the preceding winter meant that the track couldn't be made ready in time and the fixture had to be abandoned. However, the project was in the capable hands of ambitious men with vision and influence, for John and Stanley Ford had already made a big impact on racing in the Midlands. They were responsible for the success of Nottingham's racecourse at Colwick Park and had breathed new life into a decaying Lincoln. Furthermore, the Bromford Bridge venture was financially sound.

The growing public interest in horse racing also meant that it stood a better chance than its predecessors. The working man's average wage had risen steadily and the population level in the manufacturing areas of the Midlands had virtually doubled between 1850 and 1900. When free education for the masses was introduced in 1891 it brought a consequent rise in reading capabilities, while the emergence of daily newspapers carrying the lists of probable runners enabled racing to reach the eyes of the majority.

Stanley Ford – one of the founders of Bromford Bridge.

In addition, one of the main reasons for the failure of

earlier courses was their distance from the heart of Birmingham, making them difficult to get to by public transport. With Bromford Bridge there were no such problems. Situated just four miles from the city centre, the course sat between two Midland Railway stations, namely Saltley and Castle Bromwich, and was within reasonable walking distance of Gravelly and Stechford railway stations, and of Saltley, Nechells and Gravelly Hill tramway termini.

One scribe in *Baily's Magazine* referred to the opening of the new track as follows: "When Birmingham some time ago wanted a Bishop, the *profanum vulgus* scouted the idea and said they preferred a racecourse! They had one given in the unfortunate Four Oaks Park, and now have got a new one with a natural grandstand for the masses, and an erected one for the classes. The Brums neglected Four Oaks, which was a little too far off, but Castle Bromwich is much more accessible, and should be a profitable concern."

The new Birmingham racecourse was a good galloping right-handed circuit of slightly more than one mile three furlongs, with easy turns and a run in of just over half a mile. The ten-furlong National Hunt track was on the inside of the Flat course and had a run-in of 300 yards from the last fence. There was also a straight mile course, about which *Ruff's Guide to the Turf* remarked, "after Newmarket, it is undoubtedly the best straight course in the United Kingdom."

Charles Richardson wrote in *The English Turf* a year or two after it opened: "The new Birmingham course has been laid out on very sensible lines and as regards placing the stands, it is a perfect model of what a racecourse ought to be. Those who were responsible for the job evidently took note of the mistakes which had been made with regard to several comparatively recently built enclosures, and profited by them. The result is that the racing, and in particular the finishes, can be seen better at Birmingham than at many places, and it may be added that the course is a good one."

Richardson continued: "Birmingham has its stands on raised ground; it has a hill

Bromford Bridge racecourse in 1896.

Jockeys returning to the weighing room in 1896.

– an admiral coign of vantage – from which the 'bob a nob' gentry can view the racing…it lies midway between two stations of the Midland Railway, and horses can be unboxed a few hundred yards from the stables. Were it situated close to London it would do big things, but being where it is, it is likely to remain the scene of fair second-class racing and nothing more."

The inaugural meeting

The inaugural meeting eventually took place on Friday 14th and Saturday 15th June 1895. Thursday's *Birmingham Daily Post* previewed the opening day: "If the weather is fine tomorrow there is sure to be a very large attendance at Castle Bromwich. No effort has been spared to get the course in good order and considering the lack of rain, the going is in every way satisfactory. The straight mile has been watered daily by means of hydrants, and the rain which fell on Tuesday was exceedingly welcome. There is sure to be a big field for the Birmingham Handicap and an interesting race should result."

Only three runners went to post for the first race on the card, the Midland Welter Handicap over a mile and a quarter. It was won by Mr G. F. Fawcett's Philology, ridden by Fred Finlay, beating Polish by two lengths with the 13 to 8 on favourite Knocklayd a further four lengths back. The day's feature race, the one-mile Birmingham Handicap, worth £1,000, attracted ten runners and went the to 10 to 1 shot Sardis, the mount of Seth Chandley, who led virtually throughout and won by a length and a half from the favourite, El Diablo.

The *Post* reported: "Any doubts that might have been entertained respecting the success of the new racecourse at Birmingham were fully set at rest today, when over

15,000 spectators assembled to witness the sport. One does not expect everything to work smoothly on the first day of a new meeting, and yet it is pleasing to chronicle the fact that everything passed off without the slightest hitch.

"The main road which leads to the course was by no means large enough for the traffic today, and with a scarcity of vehicular accommodation (which would have been more keenly felt had the weather been unpropitious) it was made manifest that if the meeting is to prove a lasting success a railway station will have to be constructed by the side of the course, for the means of reaching and returning from the course by road will not do for such large crowds as assembled today.

"Everyone seemed pleased with the arrangements, and such a goodly number of members have already been enrolled for the club enclosure that their subscriptions alone should ensure the venture proving a success."

The *Birmingham Daily Mail* reported: "Today the new racecourse at Bromford Bridge near Castle Bromwich, was thrown open to the public for the first time. Although the enthusiasm of the multitude for racing is such that its regular patrons are undaunted by showers, yet the complete success of the meeting much depends on good weather, and the promoters could scarcely have had a more favourable day...the attendance was very large.

"At an early hour this morning it was evident that the Birmingham public had made up its mind to go racing...at eleven o'clock there was not a vehicle of any size to be had in the city...men in racing attire were visible on every hand. The scene to be witnessed in the thoroughfares leading to the course defied description. From 11 o'clock a strong force of police from the city guarded the highways and lanes within the borough, while a large number of county officers from Aston and elsewhere were on duty at other points. For fully three hours a long and almost unbroken string of vehicles was to be seen slowly travelling from the centre of the city to the course. This string was made up of vehicles of every description, and when after two o'clock they had taken up their position outside the course, the sight was really an interesting one. Four Oaks, even at the zenith of its fame, never produced anything like such a collection of conveyances."

At the rear of the main grandstand, the telegraph office handled messages to and from Birmingham, Manchester, Liverpool and London. Twenty-five operators and officials plus a large staff of messengers were kept busily employed, dealing with some 2,400 messages during the afternoon.

Beyond the stands, a timber fence formed the racecourse boundary. Unfortunately, an area of rising ground made it easy to negotiate from the road outside. A large number of people climbed over the fence and got in to the course for free. The police were quickly on the spot and ejected as many interlopers as they could find.

The main event on the second day was the £500 Bradford Handicap, this being won by Ranald M'Eagh, ridden by Charles Loates. The *Birmingham Daily Mail* reported: "Bright pleasant weather again favoured the inaugural meeting today. The sun was brilliant, but not too hot, and a light breeze tempered the heat. Crowds teemed out of the city to the racecourse. Trains were crowded, cabs were at a premium, and brake followed brake from Dale End, all filled directly they appeared. The course was a picture of bustling life, from the stables at one end where the horses were paced about on the turf, to the noisy half-crown ring before the Grandstand. The spectators were crowded on each other's heels in a hurry to perform their business and to get to a good position for a sight of the racing."

Early years

Two more Flat meetings were staged during that first year, on Friday 14th and Saturday 15th August, and a one-day fixture on Saturday 2nd November. The first National Hunt meeting followed on Friday 20th and Saturday 21st December, with the opening race, the three-mile Walsall Handicap Steeplechase, going to Lady Gundrede, ridden by Mr E. H. Lord. The most valuable race on Saturday's card was the Great Warwickshire Handicap Steeplechase, worth £355 to the winner, this being won by Emin, the mount of George Mawson.

Emin and Mawson followed up by winning the Birmingham Grand Annual Handicap Steeplechase at the 1896 February meeting. Lady Gundrede finished third, while future Grand National winner Grudon was among the fallers. Grudon made amends for his lapse when returning to Bromford Bridge later that year to win the King's Norton Handicap Chase.

Summer Lightning won the Great Warwickshire Chase in 1899 from Ford of Fyne and Barsac. Both the second and third ran well in the following month's Grand National, Ford of Fyne finishing second to Manifesto with Barsac fifth.

It was clear that the Birmingham Racecourse Company spared no effort to make their venture a success. The Company's minute book records no less than thirty-seven board meetings during the first three years of its existence, held in a variety of locations including Nottingham, London, Derby and Newmarket, as well as Birmingham itself. Once they even met on Rugby Railway Station where the secretary divulged the takings from the inaugural race meeting. Unfortunately, the amount is not recorded in the minutes.

Bromford Bridge's Easter Monday meeting, first held in 1896, quickly became a firm favourite with the public and would continue right until the course's demise. Otto Madden certainly liked it. He rode four winners on the first day of the 1898 Easter meeting, then added two more on the second day. It was the start of a great season for Madden, for not only did he win that year's Derby on Jeddah, he was also crowned champion jockey for the first time. He rode seven winners at the 1901 Easter meeting, the year in which he was champion jockey for the second time. Madden went on to win two more jockeys' titles in 1903 and '04.

Another champion was Sam Loates, one of four jockey brothers, who won his title in 1899. He rode four winners at that year's Birmingham September meeting, including the September Plate on Perthshire and the Great Midland Handicap on Lexicon. He dominated the 1900 August fixture, winning nine of the thirteen races, four on the first day and five on the second.

Around that time, a number of crack American jockeys were plying their trade in Britain with conspicuous success. Among the best were Tod Sloan, who rode four winners at the 1899 September meeting, and John Reiff, whose seven winners at the corresponding fixture in 1900 included a five-timer on the second day. His wins in the September Plate and the Great Midland Handicap were both achieved on the same horse, Escurial.

The year 1904 brought the first running of the Warwickshire Breeders' Foal Plate for two-year-olds, a race that would be perpetuated throughout the course's existence. It was won by Sweet Clover, the mount of the royal jockey Herbert Jones. Jones had already ridden the Prince of Wales's Diamond Jubilee to win the 1900 Triple Crown, and would go on to win the 1909 Derby on Minoru for the same owner, who had by then ascended the throne as King Edward VII.

There was no shortage of exciting finishes at Birmingham. The second day of the 1910 Autumn Meeting saw three dead-heats in the first four races, with jockeys Frank Wootton and Charles Trigg being involved in two of them. The introduction of the photo finish camera was still nearly 40 years away.

The camera would not have been required to determine the result of the two-mile Birmingham Handicap Steeplechase on Tuesday 10th January 1911, but it was a close call nonetheless. Bill Payne, riding Golden Ray, was unseated at the first open ditch. Undaunted, he ran alongside his horse for several yards and then vaulted into the saddle with all the agility of a circus rider. Golden Ray went on to win the race by three-parts of a length, much to the delight of his supporters. No doubt a few celebratory glasses were raised that night to toast the achievements of young Payne!

The emergence of Donoghue

Easter Monday 1909 had seen the first Birmingham winner for the great Steve Donoghue, on Tres Moutarde in the Coventry Plate. That year also saw the first running of the Great Midland Breeders' Foal Plate for three-year-olds over a mile and a quarter, won by Major, the mount of George McCall. This was followed two years later by the inaugural Guernsey Stud Produce Stakes for two-year-olds, which Donoghue won on River Song. Both of these new races would enjoy long histories.

It was at Birmingham on Tuesday 26th November 1912 that Donoghue achieved his only victory over hurdles. It came about as the result of a £50 bet with fellow jockey Albert "Snowy" Whalley as to which of them could be the first to ride a winner under National Hunt Rules. Steve persuaded trainer Fred Hunt to let him ride Lady Diane in the Sutton Handicap Hurdle. With the exception of Grand National-winning jockey "Tich" Mason, all in the weighing room accepted Donoghue's presence for what it was, namely a bit of fun. Mason, however, made his views about well-healed Flat jockeys depriving him of part of his livelihood abundantly

Steve Donoghue
champion jockey.

clear. Unperturbed by this or by the blinding snowstorm which began just as the race started, Steve won the race by a length to land the bet. And that was that; he never rode over hurdles again.

Donoghue became champion jockey for the first time in 1914, his 129 victories including Snoot in the Guernsey Stud Produce Stakes. That was also the year in which the Club and Tattersalls stands were burned down by the Suffragettes. It was one of many such incidents up and down the country at the time when the votes for women campaign was at its height. It was, perhaps, a blessing in disguise for it gave the Racecourse Company the opportunity to rebuild the stands on more modern lines.

But by then there were much darker clouds on the horizon. The 1915 Easter meeting was to be the last at Birmingham for three years due to the Great War. With hostilities nearing an end, a one-off meeting was held on Easter Monday 1918. Donoghue naturally rode a winner, while the Birmingham Spring Handicap went to Chapel Brampton, the mount of Freddy Fox.

Between the wars

Following the Great War, racing at Birmingham was re-established on the pre-war pattern. Although it may have lacked "the influence of social patronage", it was an undoubted financial success and its investors were well pleased with their returns. During the 1920s and 1930s the Racecourse Company's affairs continued to prosper.

Racing resumed in earnest at Birmingham in 1919 with its traditional two-day Easter fixture. The return of National Hunt racing came in November, when Turkey Buzzard, ridden by the aforementioned Bill Payne, won the Tamworth Handicap Chase. Turkey Buzzard and Payne followed up that victory by winning the two-mile Birmingham Handicap Chase at the 1920 January meeting, at which a future Grand National winner, Music Hall, won the Packington Chase.

On Monday 7th June 1920 the Birmingham Handicap, for three-year-olds and run over the straight mile, became the first £1,000 race ever held at Bromford Bridge. Out of that £1,000, the winning owner received £830. The Packington Handicap, a late season five furlong sprint, became the second £1,000 race in 1921, being worth £865 to the winner. Steve Donoghue won it on Francis Joseph at the two-day October fixture in 1923. Of greater significance, however, was the fact that young Gordon Richards scored his first Birmingham victory at that same meeting, winning the Sutton Handicap on Miwani.

The Stayers' Handicap Chase

It wasn't just the Flat racing that received a welcome cash injection. The winner's prize for the Stayers' Handicap Chase, run at the February meeting, had been increased to £264 when it resumed in 1920, then raised again to £442 in 1921, making it the most valuable National Hunt race then held at Birmingham.

The race had started life in 1899 as the Liverpool Trial Handicap Steeplechase, over three and a half miles. Though regarded as a Grand National trial, in the early days it was only worth around £70 to the winner and by and large its winners cut little ice at Liverpool, although the 1905 winner Ranunculus did finish fourth to Kirkland in that year's 'National'. However, the boost in prize money, a change of name to the Stayers' Handicap Chase and a change of distance to three miles and three furlongs elevated the race to a new status.

General Saxham, ridden by Bill Payne, won that first running, beating the 1915 Grand National winner Ally Sloper by four lengths. General Saxham fell in the 1920 Grand National and got no further than the first fence the following year. Forewarned, the mount of Jack Anthony, was the 1921 winner, beating Wavebeam and Any Time. All three took their chances in that year's 'National' but none of them completed the course.

But things got better after Conjuror II, trained by Tom Coulthwaite and ridden by the owner's son, Mr Cecil Dewhurst, won it in 1923. The following month he finished third behind Sergeant Murphy and Shaun Spadah in the Grand National.

Ruddyglow won the 1925 running, ridden by his owner, Mr Billy Filmer-Sankey. They started favourite for the following year's Cheltenham Gold Cup but could finish only third. Also in 1925, Jack Horner won the Saltley Chase at Birmingham. He was destined to win the next year's Grand National.

The one-eyed ex-hunter Bovril III, runner up at 100 to 1 in the 1927 Grand National, won the 1928 Stayers' Chase in the hands of his owner, Mr G. W. 'Bobby' Pennington,

Jack Anthony.

158

beating Patron Saint by a length. Patron Saint had won the Highfield Handicap Chase at the January meeting and was to win that year's Cheltenham Gold Cup, ridden by Dick Rees. At the 1928 November fixture, Gregalach finished second in the Coleshill Chase. The following March he carved his name in Aintree folklore by winning the Grand National at 100 to 1.

Great Span, so unlucky in the 1928 Grand National when a slipping saddle caused him to unseat his rider two out, won the 1930 Stayers' Chase, ridden by Ted Leader. Shaun Goilin could only finish third but he went on to land that year's Grand National. The following year saw Apostasy, ridden by Fred Brookes, win from Don Sancho and Grakle. In the following month's Grand National, Apostasy failed to get beyond the first fence, whereas Grakle won it at the starting price of 100 to 6. Grakle returned to Birmingham to win the 1932 Stayers' Chase, ridden by Jack Fawcus.

Waterlogging and frost caused the abandonment of the next two runnings but it was back in 1935, when Broadwas, ridden by Eric Brown, beat Lazy Boots. The runner-up finished fourth behind Reynoldstown in that year's Grand National.

Probably the best renewal of the Stayers' Chase was in 1936. The top-class seven-year-old Avenger, ridden by Fred Rimell, beat Reynoldstown (Fulke Walwyn up) by a length and a half, with Stars and Stripes third and Lazy Boots fourth. Among the 'also rans' were the previous year's winner Broadwas plus two Grand National runner-ups in Really True and Blue Prince. On his next start Avenger won the National Hunt Handicap Chase at Cheltenham. He lined up as the 100 to 30 favourite for the Grand National but was killed when falling at the seventeenth fence, leaving Reynoldstown to land a second 'National' triumph.

Reynoldstown surprisingly fell in the 1937 Stayers' Chase, which was won by Norman Glory. The Amateur Riders' Handicap Chase at that same meeting produced a battle of the joint favourites, with Beriberi just beating Pucka Belle by a neck. On her next start, Pucka Belle finished third to Royal Mail in the Grand National. Royal Mail himself came to Birmingham in November to win the Aston Handicap Chase, ridden by his Aintree pilot Evan Williams.

Didoric, ridden by Don Butchers, won the Stayers' Chase in 1938 by a length from Rockquilla. Former Grand National winner Kellsboro' Jack fell, along with Blue Prince. Both the winner and the second took their place in that year's Grand National line-up but neither completed the course, although Rockquilla was close up when falling at Becher's second time round.

Teme Willow, the mount of Fred Rimell, won what was to be the final running of the Stayers' Handicap Chase on Tuesday 28th February 1939 but was to get no further than the first fence in the Grand National. Nobody at Bromford Bridge that day realised it at the time but this would be the last day's National Hunt racing there for more than seven years.

The Tote comes to Birmingham

The Racecourse Betting Control Board (RBCB), a statutory body responsible to the Home Office, was responsible for introducing Totalisator betting. The Tote made its debut on a British racecourse at the Newmarket and Carlisle meetings on 2nd July 1929.

Notes from the RBCB's annual reports reveal that four brick Totalisator buildings were erected at Birmingham racecourse in 1930, one situated in the paddock serving the Members and Tattersalls enclosures, one in the Silver Ring, one in the Public Enclosure and one on the infield of the course. Hand selling operations were carried out for the first time at the meeting held on 2nd September 1930 and at all subsequent meetings during that year, giving a total of six days' racing. The total pools handled on those six days amounted to over £53,000. Blackboard indicators were used to provide information on the approximate odds of each horse, these being replaced by electrical Totalisator apparatus, which was installed the following year.

A proposal to install six automatic ticket issuing machines at Newbury in 1931, with costs being met by the manufacturer, British Automatic Totalisators Ltd., was delayed by a dispute over patents with Bell Punch Printing. Once the dispute had been settled, Newbury decided not to go ahead with the trials and so the test was switched to Birmingham. The trial duly took place at Birmingham's two-day fixture on 1st and 2nd August 1932 using the Bell Punch machines. The purchaser turned a dial to the chosen horse number for which a ticket was required, then inserted a two-shilling piece in either the 'Win' or 'Place' slot. The machine printed and issued the ticket and at the same time registered the bet on its central mechanism. It was noted in the RBCB's 1932 annual report that: "The machines created interest, in particular in the cheaper enclosures." However, concern was expressed about the "continuance of unfavourable economic conditions throughout the country, and particularly in the Midlands and the North."

The death of Mr Norris

Throughout its existence only one rider suffered a fatal injury at Bromford Bridge. It happened on the second day of the 1933 November meeting, when the amateur rider Graham Norris, aged 28, fell on White Bridge in the King's Norton Handicap Chase. Seemingly unharmed, he rode in two later races but collapsed while driving home and was rushed to hospital. He initially appeared to be recovering well but then suffered a relapse and died on 6th December from internal injuries incurred in the fall at Bromford. Eton-educated Mr Norris had also been a first class cricketer and had played for Northamptonshire in 1926.

On the first day of that same Birmingham meeting, the Sutton Handicap Hurdle had been won by Tibere, ridden by Murtagh Keogh. Little more than a month later,

Keogh, who had scored his biggest victory on Shaun Goilin in the 1929 Grand Sefton Chase, was killed in a fall at Manchester.

'The Miller'

In 1925, Thrown In won Birmingham's Highfield Handicap Chase. He was destined to win the Cheltenham Gold Cup two years later. By contrast, former Gold Cup winners didn't generally have a great record round Bromford Bridge. Red Splash, winner of the inaugural Cheltenham Gold Cup, could only trail in last of four in the Coleshill Chase in 1927. Another Gold Cup winner, Koko, fared no better in the same race in 1929.

But five-time Cheltenham Gold Cup hero Golden Miller had no such problems. Dorothy Paget's great champion turned up at Birmingham on Monday 22nd February 1937 and won the Optional Selling Chase easily by fifteen lengths in the hands of "Frenchie" Nicholson at odds of 9 to 2 on, prompting the following day's *Sporting Life* headline: 'Golden Miller Is Still Best Fencer in the Kingdom.' That's as maybe but even The Miller couldn't fix the weather and he was denied a sixth consecutive Gold Cup by a combination of snow and a flooded course which caused the second and third days of Cheltenham's 1937 National Hunt Meeting to be abandoned.

Golden Miller returned to Birmingham in 1938 to win the Optional Selling Chase for the second year running, again ridden by Nicholson. This was to be the last victory of Golden Miller's illustrious career. Strongly fancied to win his sixth Gold Cup, he was again denied, not this time by the weather but by Morse Code and Danny Morgan, who beat him by two lengths.

But as The Miller lost his crown, a new Cheltenham Gold Cup winner was to be seen in action at Birmingham later that year. A big, plain-looking, raw-boned individual named Roman Hackle, ridden by Fulke Walwyn, won the Burton Handicap Hurdle at the November meeting. Miss Paget soon acquired him and he would win the 1940 Gold Cup for her. Some spoke of him as a second Golden Miller, though he was never to attain such eminence.

An era of great jockeys

The strength in depth of jockeyship on the Flat during the inter-war period has probably never been equalled. Besides Steve Donoghue and Gordon Richards there were a dozen or more top-class riders, including Harry Wragg, Fred Fox, Tommy Weston, Charlie Elliott, Michael Beary, Charlie Smirke, Dick Perryman and Doug and Eph Smith.

By the mid-thirties Donoghue had long since been dethroned as champion jockey and was nearing the end of his career, though Bromford's Easter Monday racegoers would never have guessed it in 1933 when he rode three winners and three seconds

R.A. "Bobby" Jones.

from six rides. Gordon Richards, who rode five winners at that year's May meeting, was by now the undisputed champion. He notched a Birmingham treble on the second day of the 1934 Easter Meeting. And what a finish he and Donoghue provided when dead-heating for that year's Guernsey Stud Produce Stakes, with Donoghue on Red Biddy and Richards on Winandermere inseparable as they flashed past the winning post.

In 1935, "Bobby" Jones scored his third Midland Breeders' Foal Plate success, this time on Pampas Grass, trained at Malton by Captain Charles Elsey. Jones had won the race previously on Wraf in 1926 and Sea Rover in 1930. But it was Gordon Richards who was in the saddle when Pampas Grass made his next start, in the Rous Memorial Stakes at Royal Ascot three weeks later. A fine race he ran, too, finishing second to the previous year's Derby winner, Windsor Lad, beaten only half a length.

Birmingham's two most valuable juvenile races of the season produced a lupine coincidence double in 1936, with Barking Fox winning the Warwickshire Breeders' Foal Plate and Dark Vixen landing the Guernsey Stud Produce Stakes. There was plenty of sibling rivalry on display at that meeting with two sets of brothers, Doug and Eph Smith and Gordon and Cliff Richards, all among the winners. There was more brotherly competition at that year's August fixture. Sam Wragg won the August Handicap on 10 to 1 shot Star Comedian, but the best elder brother Harry could do that day was finish second to Donoghue in the last race.

On 8th June 1937, jockey Pat 'Rufus' Beasley won the Midland Breeders' Foal Plate on Santayana and the Guernsey Stud Produce Stakes on Betty Fay. The latter race was the first at Birmingham ever to have a winner's prize of over £1,000, being worth £1,080 to the successful owner.

Dick Perryman rode a treble on the second day of the 1938 August meeting. Michael Beary did likewise on Easter Monday 1939. Charlie Smirke rode the Aga Khan's Stardust to victory in that year's Guernsey Stud Produce Stakes, while Gordon Richards landed the Midland Breeders' Foal Plate aboard Lord Astor's Pigling Bland.

The two-day meeting on Monday 28th and Tuesday 29th August 1939 went ahead as normal, with Richards riding four winners and Sam Wragg having three, but within a week all racing had been cancelled owing to the state of emergency.

Despite the war, the traditional Easter Monday meeting took place in 1940. So did the two-day June meeting, at which the Smith brothers captured two of the feature races, Eph Smith winning the Warwickshire Breeders' Foal Plate on Lord Rosebery's

Proof that Gordon Richards could win on a donkey! Here he is (on right) riding at a charity Donkey Derby in Wolverhampton in the early 1930s.

Mercy, and Doug landing the Midland Breeders' Foal Plate on the Frank Butters-trained Desert Sunset. But that was to be the last racing at Birmingham before the end of the war.

During the war Birmingham's racecourse was taken over by the military authorities, firstly for use as a barrage balloon and an AA gun site, and then for accommodating large numbers of soldiers and an army stores depot. It was heavily bombed on three separate occasions by enemy aircraft seeking the war industries nearby. Eight bombs were dropped on the course - four of them landing on the straight mile - causing considerable damage to the track, stands and stables.

Post-war activity

The immediate post-war period was one of great activity to improve the racecourse itself and the quality of its Flat racing. Some £150,000 was spent giving all enclosures a face-lift of one sort or another. Birmingham became the first course after Newmarket to be equipped with a photo finish camera, and a determined effort was made to create opportunities for better-class horses.

*Easter Monday 1948 – Bromford Bridge
racegoers make their way home.*

When racing returned to Bromford Bridge after a gap of six years on Monday 5th and Tuesday 6th August 1946, Gordon Richards dominated the two-day fixture with seven winners, three second place finishes and a third from eleven rides. The world may have been a different place by then but Richards still reigned supreme.

Mind you, he had plenty of top-class rivals, not least the Smith brothers. Doug Smith bagged five winners at Birmingham on the first two days of September 1947, while Eph Smith – who had won the last inter-war Derby at Epsom on Blue Peter in 1939 - rode two.

Whereas winners for the Smith brothers were commonplace, the same could not be said for George Bowen who rode his first winner for twenty-two years when landing the Warwick Castle Stakes at Birmingham on Craigy Llin on 3rd May 1948. Bowen was head man for trainer John Waugh and only got the ride because he got on so well with the horse on the gallops.

The City of Birmingham Cup

Gordon Richards' seven-winner haul at that first post-war meeting of August 1946 had included the Warwickshire Breeders' Foal Plate on the odds-on favourite Marriage Day and the inaugural running of the City of Birmingham Cup on Lord Willoughby de Broke's Arromanches.

The City of Birmingham Cup, a handicap for three year olds over ten furlongs, was thereafter run on Whit Monday and, with its four figure winner's prize, quickly became a Bank Holiday favourite with the crowds. Local lad Ken Gethin, born in Balsall Heath, won the 1947 running on 5 to 1 shot Early Harvest.

Ridge Wood, ridden by Gordon Richards, looked to be an above-average winner of the race in 1949. He returned to Birmingham in August for the Midlands St. Leger Trial Stakes, where his only rival was Courier, the mount of Tommy Lowrey. It was one of the most farcical races ever run – if 'run' is the right word - for both Richards and Lowrey had been given strict instructions not to make the running. Consequently, when the starting tape went up, neither horse made a move. Eventually they condescended to start and proceeded at a virtual walk to the accompaniment of catcalls and booing from the stands. Only when the pair reached the home straight did the race began in earnest, with Ridge Wood drawing clear to win by three lengths, but the one mile five furlong journey had taken almost 5 minutes 15 seconds, more than twice the standard time. Nonetheless, Ridge Wood proved to be one of the best horses ever to race at Bromford Bridge, for the very next month he won the St. Leger, ridden on that occasion by Michael Beary.

Gordon won the City of Birmingham Cup twice more, on Highcrest in 1951 and Pearl Stud in 1953. Sandwiched between those victories, Norooz won it in 1952, the first of three winners that day for jockey "Snowy" Fawdon. Norooz progressed to win the following year's Ebor Handicap, again with Fawdon in the saddle.

The longest priced winner of the City of Birmingham Cup was Trent Bridge, a 25 to 1 shot, in a three-horse photo finish in 1956, ridden by Eph Smith. The race was worth £1,968 to the winner in 1958, making it the most valuable race so far run at Birmingham. It went to the Dick Perryman-trained Kabale, who completed a double on the day for jockey Tony Rawlinson.

Sir Malcolm McAlpine's Decree, the mount of Bill Rickaby, won the Warwickshire Stakes on the second day of the 1959 Easter meeting, returning the following month to win the City of Birmingham Cup. Decree came from the yard of veteran Newmarket trainer Reg Day, who won a second City of Birmingham Cup when Authorise, ridden by Paul Tulk, scored a 20 to 1 upset in 1962. Way back at the start of his career, Day had trained a horse called Pistol, runner up to the mighty Sceptre in the 1902 Two Thousand Guineas. Fifty-nine years later he

Trent Bridge, 1956 City of Birmingham Cup winner.

produced Sweet Solera, with Rickaby on board, to win the One Thousand Guineas and Oaks. Day was 85 when he finally retired at the end of 1968.

The most valuable running of the City of Birmingham Cup, worth £3,117, was in 1963 when it went to Lady Halifax's Saltarello, trained by John Oxley and ridden by apprentice David "Flapper" Yates.

The final running of the race in 1965 resulted in a decent winner, this being Dites, trained at Newmarket by Harvey Leader and the mount of Brian Taylor. Dites was to win the following year's Cambridgeshire Handicap.

The 'Autumn Double'

As well as the City of Birmingham Cup, 1946 also saw the inaugural runnings of the Midland Cambridgeshire, over the straight mile, and the Midland Cesarewitch, at two miles, both at the autumn meeting. They often proved consolation targets for the Newmarket also-rans.

Doug Smith won both of the autumn handicaps in 1947, the Midland Cesarewitch on Avon Prince and the Midland Cambridgeshire on Solfax. Fidonia, ridden by Harry Carr, won the 1949 Midland Cesarewitch before going on to win that year's Manchester November Handicap, again with Carr on board.

In 1950, Valdeso, beaten only a neck and a head in the Cambridgeshire Handicap six days earlier, gained a measure of consolation when winning the Midland Cambridgeshire, ridden by local boy Ken Gethin. Up and coming youngster Joe Mercer landed both legs of Birmingham's 'autumn double' in 1952, winning the Midland Cesarewitch on Misty Light and the Midland Cambridgeshire on Capsize, both trained by Major Fred Sneyd.

Sir Gordon Richards - he had been knighted earlier that year - won the 1953 Midland Cambridgeshire on Dumbarnie, who had finished fourth in the Cambridgeshire itself the previous week. The Queen's Opera Score won it in 1955, trained by Cecil Boyd-Rochfort and ridden by Eph Smith.

Top Australian jockey Scobie Breasley won the 1956 Midland Cambridgeshire on Herbert Blagrave's Variety King. Breasley won it again in 1957 aboard Nicholas Nickleby, who the year before had produced a 50 to 1 shock victory in the Royal Hunt Cup at Royal Ascot.

Grecian Granite, ridden by diminutive apprentice Ronnie Singer, won the 1959 Midland Cesarewitch. Singer's career was brought to a premature end just four

Ronnie Singer – won 1959 Midland Cesarewitch.

months later when he suffered serious head injuries after his mount slipped up in the Liverpool Spring Cup.

Sam Hall's Mustavon, a former Lincolnshire Handicap winner, scored his fourth win in a row when landing the 1962 Midland Cambridgeshire in the hands of Lester Piggott. Tropical Sky, owned and trained by Herbert Blagrave, won that year's Midland Cesarewitch under another leading Australian rider, Ron Hutchinson.

In 1964, Ruby Wedding won the last running of the Midland Cambridgeshire, ridden by the apprentice 'find' of the season, Paul Cook, while the final Midland Cesarewitch went the way of Peter Easterby's French Patrol, the mount of yet another top-class Antipodean pilot, Bill Williamson.

Other new races

More new races were created in 1947. They included the one-mile Midland Spring Handicap on the Easter Monday card, and the Union Stakes, run over six furlongs, the latter being won by the French challenger Vagabond II, ridden by Australian Rae Johnstone. This was the first French-trained winner at Bromford Bridge. In 1949, despite being worth £1,247 to the winner, the Union Stakes had only two runners, with Luminary, ridden by Charlie Elliott, defeating his sole opponent Sartorial at odds of 4 to 1 on. Gordon Richards won it the following year on Abadan, scoring an easy victory to follow up his recent Royal Ascot success in the Cork and Orrery Stakes.

The Shakespeare Stakes, over one mile five furlongs, was held for the first time in 1949. The first two runnings were won by a horse named Vic Day, owned and trained by Herbert Blagrave and ridden by Charlie Elliott. But Elliott was obliged to share the spoils in the 1951 Shakespeare Stakes, when, riding Chinese Cracker, he dead-heated with Strathspey, the mount of Scobie Breasley.

Strathspey was a tough and consistent stayer. Owned and bred by Mr James V. Rank and trained by Noel Cannon, he had already won the two-mile Bournville Stakes at Birmingham in 1949, the year in which he also won Newmarket's Cesarewitch. Strathspey won eleven races altogether during his career, his other victories including the Goodwood Stakes and Royal Ascot's Queen Alexandra Stakes.

The Jumping Game

The return of National Hunt racing to Bromford Bridge, for the first time since February 1939, came on Monday 25th November 1946. The best horse on view that day was Coloured School Boy, who Fred Rimell trained and rode to win the Novices' Chase by fifteen lengths. They followed up by winning the Four Counties Chase at the December meeting, then looked certain to win at a third successive Birmingham fixture in January 1947 but fell at the last fence when well clear. That winter of 1947

Jumping the last with a circuit to go – a competitive Bromford Bridge steeplechase in the early 1950s.

was a vicious one. Both days of the February meeting were abandoned as frost and snow wreaked havoc across the country.

New races were introduced over jumps as well as on the Flat, with 1948 witnessing the inaugural runnings of the Gold Cup Trial Chase, the Champion Trial Hurdle and the Grand National Trial Handicap Chase. The latter was the natural successor to the pre-war Stayers' Chase, run over three miles and three furlongs. That first running was won by Freebooter, destined to win the Grand National itself two years later. Although the distance remained the same, the name of this race was changed the following year when it became known simply as the Birmingham Handicap Chase.

Birmingham's 1948-49 season had quite an influence on the Grand National. Russian Hero, ridden by Leo McMorrow, won the Ashby Handicap Chase at the December meeting, while on the first day of the February meeting, Roimond won the Gold Cup Trial Chase from Happy Home. The following day, Bricett

Advert for Bromford's 1947 November meeting.

won the Birmingham Handicap Chase, beating Gallery and Magnetic Fin. At Aintree the next month, Russian Hero and McMorrow brought off a 66 to 1 shock Grand National victory. Roimond finished third and Happy Home sixth. Bricett also completed the course but Magnetic Fin fell at Becher's first time round, while Gallery was brought down three out.

Martin Molony.

The Gold Cup Trial Chase

The Gold Cup Trial Chase lasted only four years, from 1948 to 1951. The first running went to Dorothy Paget's Happy Home, ridden by Martin Molony. Happy Home went on to finish second to Cottage Rake in that year's Cheltenham Gold Cup. In the 1949 Gold Cup Trial, Lord Bicester's Roimond, the mount of Tim Molony, brother of Martin, beat Happy Home (ridden this time by Bryan Marshall) by three lengths.

Lord Bicester's colours of "black, gold sleeves, red cap" were among the best known in the jumping game at that time. Besides Roimond, his string of top-class chasers included Finnure, who, with Martin Molony up, won the Packwood Chase at Birmingham's 1949 December meeting by five lengths from Rowland Roy. Two months later Finnure was back at Birmingham and starting at the prohibitive odds of 8 to 1 on, enjoyed what amounted to a solo round to win the Gold Cup Trial Chase, after his only opponent, Nagara, had fallen at the third fence. The following month, Finnure went on to finish second to three-time winner Cottage Rake in the Cheltenham Gold Cup.

Lord Bicester's Silver Fame won what was to be the final running of the Gold Cup Trial in 1951, beating sole rival Bruno II easily at odds of 7 to 1 on before going on to win that year's Cheltenham Gold Cup. With both the last two runnings of the race having attracted only two runners and been little more than walkovers for Lord Bicester's top chasers, it was hardly surprising that Birmingham's organisers opted to discontinue the race in favour of something more competitive.

The Champion Hurdlers

The Champion Trial Hurdle, run at the February meeting, enjoyed a far longer existence than the Gold Cup Trial. In fact, it continued right up until the course's closure. The first running in 1948 was won by D.U.K.W. who went on to Cheltenham and finished second to National Spirit in the Champion Hurdle itself.

In addition to the Champion Trial Hurdle, Birmingham also staged the Nuneaton Hurdle at the November fixture. This conditions race was another opportunity for top

Sir Ken (Bryan Marshall up) leads Bachus (Johnny Gilbert)
over the last flight to win the Five Ways Handicap Hurdle,
on 15th January 1952.

grade hurdlers and rising stars to compete without having to give lumps of weight away in handicaps. The Vincent O'Brien-trained Knock Hard, partnered by Tim Molony, looked a potential star when winning the 1951 Nuneaton Hurdle by five lengths from Crudwell. And so it proved. Knock Hard was destined to win the 1953 Cheltenham Gold Cup.

Equally as impressive was Willie Stephenson's five-year-old Sir Ken, who carried 12st 7lb to victory in the Five Ways Handicap Hurdle at the 1952 January meeting. The following month Sir Ken returned to Birmingham to win the Champion Trial Hurdle. Then in March, ridden as before by Tim Molony in owner Maurice Kingsley's black and pink quartered colours, he landed the first of his three Champion Hurdles.

Sir Ken and Tim Molony were back at Birmingham in November 1952, winning the Nuneaton Hurdle at odds of 5 to 1 on. Three months later, this time starting at 4 to 1 on, he easily won his second Champion Trial Hurdle on the way to winning his second Champion Hurdle. Sir Ken returned to Birmingham in November 1953, winning the Nuneaton Hurdle for the second year running, ridden by Tim Molony. He duly won his third Champion Trial Hurdle en route to his third Champion Hurdle triumph.

Surprisingly, Sir Ken was beaten by Noholme (receiving 7lb) in his quest for a third successive Nuneaton Hurdle in 1954. That was his final appearance at Birmingham and he was to lose his Champion Hurdle crown in 1955, finishing only fourth behind Clair Soleil. Sir Ken made a fine start to his chasing career the following season, winning the Cotswold Chase at Cheltenham and the Mildmay Chase at Liverpool, but never reached the same level of greatness over fences to match his sparkling hurdling career.

Grenville Underwood.

A combination of snow and frost resulted in three of the four Champion Trial Hurdles being lost between 1955 and 1958. There was an upset in the one that survived, with the 100 to 7 chance Wayward Bird, ridden by Derek Ancil, defeating Bandalore and odds-on Flame Royal in 1957.

Bandalore, trained by Stan Wright at Leintwardine in Shropshire, had dead-heated for the Moseley Handicap Hurdle and won the Stoneleigh Handicap Hurdle at Birmingham in 1956. He was back for the 1957 running of the Nuneaton Hurdle, in which he fought out the finish with reigning champion hurdler Merry Deal, trained near Oswestry by Arthur Jones and the mount of Sutton Coldfield-based Grenville Underwood. Merry Deal beat Bandalore by a length and a half that day, but Bandalore was to get his revenge at Cheltenham four months later, leading virtually throughout under George Slack to win the 1958 Champion Hurdle at 20 to 1, beating Tokoroa and Retour de Flamme with Merry Deal back in fourth.

In November 1958, in what was virtually a carbon copy of the previous year's race, those same two Shropshire-trained Champion Hurdle winners fought out the finish of the Nuneaton Hurdle. Once again Merry Deal beat Bandalore, but this time only by a short head.

The 1959 Champion Trial Hurdle went to Fred Rimell's Tokoroa, runner up to Bandalore in the previous year's Champion Hurdle. Tokoroa started favourite for the 1959 Champion Hurdle but finished unplaced, having slipped on landing when leading at the third last flight. Tokoroa was back at Birmingham for the Nuneaton Hurdle in November, winning comfortably in the hands of Tim Brookshaw.

Saffron Tartan, a future Cheltenham Gold Cup hero, won the 1960 Champion Trial Hurdle, ridden by Tommy (TP) Burns. He scored by a neck from Retour de Flamme, with Laird o' Montrose third. In November that year there was an Irish-trained winner at Birmingham when Sparkling Flame, trained by Paddy Sleator and ridden by Bobby Beasley, beat the previous year's winner Tokoroa in the Nuneaton Hurdle. Tokoroa was then put over fences and won the Packington Novices' Chase at Birmingham's 1961 January meeting, a race in which former champion hurdler

Bandalore finished tailed off in fourth.

There was a shock for punters in the 1961 Champion Trial Hurdle when the odds-on favourite Eborneezer, the mount of Fred Winter, was turned over by 100 to 6 shot Costa Brava. Eborneezer duly shrugged off that defeat and went on to win the Champion Hurdle a fortnight later. Fulke Walwyn's grey Anzio, with Bobby Beasley up, destined to win the next year's Champion Hurdle, won his first race over jumps at that same Birmingham 1961 February fixture when landing the Graveley Maiden Hurdle.

At the 1961 November meeting, Quelle Chance, trained by Jack Fawcus and ridden by Jumbo Wilkinson, won the Nuneaton Hurdle, beating Tyson and Irish challenger Ferry Boat. Quelle Chance was to finish second to Anzio in that season's Champion Hurdle. Anzio himself, ridden by Willie Robinson, won the 1962 Nuneaton Hurdle impressively by four lengths. The 1963 running was won just as decisively by Rupununi, officially trained by Arthur Thomas at Guy's Cliffe, Warwick, but in reality prepared by Paddy Sleator in Ireland.

Snow and frost had wiped out three successive February meetings (1962-64), but thankfully it survived when held for the final time in 1965. The second day saw two Champion Hurdle winners oblige at short odds within half an hour of each other. Reigning champion Magic Court, at 11 to 4 on and ridden by Jimmy FitzGerald, landed the most valuable running (£1,042 16s) of the Champion Trial Hurdle; and the 1962 champion Anzio, partnered as usual by Willie Robinson, won division one of the Elmdon Hurdle at the prohibitive odds of 9 to 1 on.

Running the racecourse

In 1949 Birmingham Racecourse Company bought the Bromford Bridge course (it had up to then been leased) for £81,855. The panel of stewards included Lord

Lord Willoughby de Broke.

Willoughby de Broke, Mr Fred Withington, Major Macdonald-Buchanan, and Lord Leight, while the Clerk of the Course was Stanley B. Ford of Nottingham, a son of the family firm that had built the course. Mr Withington, who had taken over as chairman of the Racecourse Company in 1935, died in 1951 and was succeeded by Lord Willoughby de Broke, who was to be the last chairman of the company.

Among Bromford Bridge's non-racing activities, used car auctions were conducted each week in one of the car parks. Other events there included cross country racing. In 1949 the English Cross Country Championship was held on the racecourse, and the 1952 International Cross

Country Championship followed the same route. For the last ten years of its life, Birmingham Education Department used some 30 acres as playing fields for local schools.

Throughout its existence, the Bromford Bridge site was used for rearing and fattening cattle. Quite unknowingly, many a Birmingham resident dined on roast beef and milk from animals nurtured on the racecourse's grasslands.

Into the fifties

As the war-ravaged decade of the 1940s approached its end, many of the old guard of jockeys had hung up their boots. Donoghue had gone, so had Harry Wragg, but there were plenty of promising youngsters coming along to take their place. And none was more promising than thirteen-year-old Lester Piggott, who on Monday 26th September 1949 rode his first Birmingham winner (and only the fourth of his career) on Gold Sandal in the Chesterton Apprentice Plate. Lester would go on to ride a total of 78 winners at Birmingham.

Gordon Richards continued to dominate at Bromford Bridge as the forties turned into the fifties. He rode five winners at Birmingham's two-day meeting at the start of August 1950 and finished the month there with a four-timer.

Richards and Doug Smith went through the six-race card between them on 14th May 1951, both jockeys riding trebles. The following month Smith was back in the Bromford winner's enclosure after Sir Malcolm McAlpine's two-year-old filly Zabara had won the Guernsey Stud Produce Stakes impressively by five lengths on her racecourse debut. Zabara was rated the second-best juvenile at the end of that year and went on to win the 1952 One Thousand Guineas, ridden by Ken Gethin.

Ken Gethin

As mentioned earlier, Gethin was born in the Balsall Heath district of Birmingham. He was apprenticed to Epsom trainer Stanley Wootton and rode his first winner on Sea Monarch at Gatwick in 1929. He gained his first important success when winning the 1931 Northumberland Plate on Blue Vision. On completion of his apprenticeship, Gethin was appointed stable jockey to Atty Persse. He later rode for Peter Thrale and married that trainer's daughter, Peggy.

During the war Gethin served in the Royal Engineers for four years, being invalided out with a damaged spine and fractured pelvis after being knocked down by a lorry in the blackout. Despite those injuries he made a suc-

Ken Gethin.

cessful riding comeback after the war, winning the Victoria Cup and the Eclipse Stakes on Sir Alfred Butt's Petition.

Though numerically he enjoyed his best season in 1947 with 81 winners, it was during the 1950s that Gethin reached the front rank of jockeys. Zabara was his only Classic winner but he was always in demand in the big handicaps, his many such victories including the Cambridgeshire, the Cesarewitch and two more Victoria Cups. His highest placing in the jockeys' table was fifth in 1954, when his big race winners included a second Eclipse Stakes on King of the Tudors and the Yorkshire Oaks on Feevagh.

Gethin scored his last major victory in the 1959 Manchester November Handicap on Operatic Society. He retired the following year after more than thirty years in the saddle and trained with moderate success for six years at Epsom. He died there in 1989, aged 78.

Incidentally, Zabara wasn't the only future Classic winner to win at Birmingham in 1951. The Kineton Nursery Stakes wouldn't normally be the place to look for next year's Derby winner but that was the case on the first day of October. The Aga Khan's Tulyar, trained by Marcus Marsh and ridden by Charlie Smirke, came with a strong run to win "cleverly", according to the form book. After he had won the 1952 Derby, Tulyar progressed from strength to strength, winning in succession the Eclipse, the King George VI and Queen Elizabeth Stakes and the St. Leger.

More top chasers

Workboy, trained by Alec Kilpatrick and ridden by Tim Molony, won the Aston Handicap Chase at the 1950 November meeting, beating River Trout and future Grand National winner E.S.B. Twelve months later, Workboy won the race for the second time, ridden on that occasion by Bert Morrow. By the time of his retirement Workboy had won thirteen steeplechases and been placed a further sixteen times from 46 races. Not bad, but the best was yet to come because he was then, comparatively late in life, trained for a show jumping career.

Owned and ridden by Brigadier C. H. 'Monkey' Blacker, he eventually reached the top in his new sphere. Blacker and Workboy were members of the winning British Nations Cup Team in Madrid in 1959. They also represented Britain in Lisbon in 1959 and in Rome in 1961. At the International Horse Show at the White City they won the Imperial Cup in 1959 and finished second in the George V Gold Cup.

Meanwhile, E.S.B., ridden by Johnny Bullock, won the Highfield Chase easily on the second day of Birmingham's 1952 January meeting. The February fixture saw an impressive performance by the Neville Crump-trained Teal, who won the Birmingham Handicap Chase in the hands of Arthur Thompson. So fresh was Teal at the end of the race that Thompson struggled hard to pull him up. As a result of that

E.S.B., with Johnny Bullock up, leads Wigby (Tommy Cusack) over the last fence to win the Highfeld Chase on 15th January 1952.

win his odds for the Grand National tumbled from 50 to 1 down to 100 to 8. And no wonder, for the following month saw Teal gallop to a clear-cut Grand National victory.

Despite the loss of the Gold Cup Trial Chase, Birmingham continued to attract top-class jumpers. Monday 16th February 1953 saw the inaugural running of the Withington Handicap Chase, over four miles and a few yards. The race was won by Glen Fire, trained locally by Syd Mercer at Knowle and ridden by Michael Scudamore.

At the 1953 November meeting, smart chaser Galloway Braes, ridden by his regular pilot Bert Morrow, humped 12st 7lb to victory over Glen Fire in the Kenilworth Handicap Chase. Galloway Braes defied 12st 9lb when winning the Ashby Handicap Chase the following season. Morrow rode another high-class chaser to victory at Birmingham, this being Pointsman, who won the Droitwich Handicap Chase in December 1953.

Crudwell, ridden by Dick Francis, won the 1954 running of the Withington Handicap Chase, beating Gay Fox and Bar Point. At the November 1954 fixture, Crudwell, again ridden by Francis, won the Kenilworth Handicap Chase, while future Gold Cup winner Limber Hill took the Charlecote Novices' Chase. Crudwell was to add another Birmingham victory to his rapidly growing tally of wins in November 1956. He finished his career the winner of no less than fifty races.

In November 1955, E.S.B., destined to win the Grand National in dramatic circumstances later that season, beat former Cheltenham Gold Cup winner Four Ten by a head in a thrilling finish to the Kenilworth Handicap Chase. At the 1956 January meeting, Kerstin, ridden by George Milburn, proved too good for her rivals in the Highfield Handicap Chase. She was to win the Cheltenham Gold Cup in 1958.

The Bill Wightman-trained Oscar Wilde won the 1959 Withington Handicap Chase in the hands of "Taffy" Jenkins, beating the previous year's winner Mr Gay, with Badanloch third. Oscar Wilde had scored the first victory of his career on the Flat at Birmingham.

R. E. 'Taffy' Jenkins.

The Festival and the Stanley Ford Stakes

In addition to the Union Stakes, inaugurated in 1947, a new six-furlong conditions event was introduced in 1951. It was called the Festival Stakes. Held at the Whitsun meeting, the day after the City of Birmingham Cup, it provided a perfect stepping stone to Royal Ascot and offered a decent four-figure prize to the winner. The race was an instant success and attracted the same type of sprinters that would return to compete for the Union Stakes in September.

The first winner of the Festival Stakes was Lord Sefton's Bob Cherry, ridden by Australian jockey Neville Sellwood. Four weeks later that same combination won Royal Ascot's Cork and Orrery Stakes.

In 1952 Grey Sovereign, a three-parts brother to Derby winner Nimbus, won the Festival Stakes on a tight rein. Grey Sovereign returned to Birmingham later that season to win the Union Stakes 'comfortably' by half a length. At stud, Grey Sovereign became a notable sire, his progeny including French 2,000 Guineas winners Don II and Zaddaan, plus top notch sprinters Matatina, Raffingora and Young Emperor.

In 1953 Set Fair, ridden by Eph Smith, won a high-class Coronation Festival Stakes, beating Dumbarnie, Easter Bride and Vilmoray. The 1954 running, while perhaps not up to the standard of previous renewals, was won by a decent horse in King Bruce, trained by Peter Hastings-Bass and ridden by Frankie Durr. King Bruce, who started the 6 to 4 favourite in a field of four, went on to win the Stewards' Cup at Goodwood the following year.

The Union Stakes was renamed the Stanley Ford Stakes in 1954 to commemorate one of the course's founders. That year produced a good renewal of the race, with Dumbarnie, ridden by Frank Barlow, winning from March Past, Vilmoray and Set Fair.

Top-class sprinter Pappa Fourway was the middle leg of a Harry Carr treble when winning the 1955 Festival Stakes easily by three lengths from Dumbarnie. This was the third successive victory for Pappa Fourway, who ended up unbeaten in eight starts that season, including the July Cup, King's Stand Stakes, Diadem Stakes and Gosforth Park Cup.

In 1956, Matador, having won the July Cup, the Stewards' Cup and finished runner-up in the Nunthorpe Stakes on his last three starts, beat three lesser rivals in the Stanley Ford Stakes with the minimum of effort.

Vigo and Lester Piggott beat Matador by three-quarters of a length in the 1957 Festival Stakes prior to landing Newmarket's July Cup, but they could finish only third in the Nunthorpe Stakes. Vigo was then beaten a neck in the Stanley Ford Stakes by Arcandy, with Tommy Gosling up. Arcandy was winning for the fifth time in a row that season, among those victories being the Stewards' Cup.

The prize money for the 1957 Stanley Ford Stakes was almost half that of the previous year, which was a shame because 1958 would see its most brilliant winner. His name was ...

Right Boy

On Whit Monday 1956, a grey colt called Right Boy, ridden by Lester Piggott, won the Burton Two-year-old Plate at Bromford Bridge. His owner, Birmingham bookmaker Geoff Gilbert, had paid just 575 guineas for him as a yearling. Few people thought much about it at the time, yet, despite his unfashionable breeding, Right Boy was to become one of Britain's best post-war sprinters.

After winning four races at two, including the Exeter Stakes at Newmarket, Right Boy won the King's Stand at Royal Ascot as a three-year-old. At four in 1958, he returned to Birmingham as the 7 to 2 outsider of four in what was another high-class renewal of the Festival Stakes. Ridden by Frankie Durr, Right Boy led after a furlong and ran on strongly to win by two lengths. Second was Ennis, who later finished third to Right Boy in Goodwood's King George Stakes. The third horse, Drum Beat, went on to win the King's Stand Stakes at Royal Ascot. Last of the four home was the favourite, Welsh Abbot, who later in the season won Doncaster's Portland Handicap.

Following his Festival Stakes victory, Right Boy notched up a remarkable four-timer in Royal Ascot's Cork and Orrery Stakes, Newmarket's July Cup, Goodwood's King George Stakes and York's Nunthorpe Stakes. He was back at Birmingham in September to land the Stanley Ford Stakes.

Starting at odds of 7 to 2 on, Right Boy was surprisingly beaten by Capuchon in the 1959 Festival Stakes, but it was only a temporary setback, as he then completed back-to-back wins in the Cork and Orrery, July Cup, King George and Nunthorpe. Right Boy was certainly one of the fastest horses ever to grace Bromford Bridge.

Farewell to Gordon

It was hats off to Sir Gordon Richards on 31st August 1953, when he rode the Frank Cundell-trained Barbara Louise, his first Birmingham winner since being knighted in June of that year. Doug Smith upstaged him the following day by winning on all five of his rides, but you couldn't keep the great man down for long, for Sir Gordon rode the last two winners on Bromford's card on 28th September.

On Monday 21st June 1954, Dorothy Paget's Constable won the Warwickshire Breeders' Foal Stakes to give Sir Gordon the last of his 157 winners at Bromford Bridge (the first was in 1923) over a period of 31 years. He had already decided to retire at the end of that season but his career came to a premature end at Sandown in July when a filly he was riding reared over backwards on leaving the paddock, breaking Sir Gordon's pelvis in the process. He recovered perfectly well but decided to give up riding there and then rather than making what would have been the briefest of comebacks.

The young tyros

Sir Gordon's magnificent career would be near impossible to emulate but there were plenty of young pretenders willing to give it a try. Several of them had Bromford Bridge to thank for giving them their start on horse racing's ladder.

Thirteen-year-old Edward Hide, 4ft 6ins tall and weighing just over four stone, had his first ride in public at Birmingham on 29th August 1950, riding Copper Wire in the Ward End Handicap. It was a true baptism of fire because, besides Gordon Richards, the other jockeys in the race included Doug and Eph Smith, Scobie Breasley and Lester Piggott. The distance was a marathon two miles five furlongs, a long way for a young lad having his first ride. Copper Wire pulled herself to the front, collided with the rails after six furlongs as her jockey vainly tried to restrain her, before gradually dropping back and finishing last. It was hardly the most promising start but young Edward was undaunted. He went on to ride over 2,500 winners in a career spanning 35 years, including the 1973 Derby on Morston.

On 22nd June 1953, Peter Robinson rode his first winner when Harry Wragg's Prince Yaky won the Elmdon Apprentice Maiden Plate. He became champion apprentice the following year with 55 winners, including the Ebor Handicap on Hyperion Kid and the Cambridgeshire on Retrial. The next year he won the Chester Cup on Golovine and went on to ride a host of major handicap winners, including the Lincolnshire three times and the 1964 Ayr Gold Cup on Compensation. Robinson began training in 1969 and sent out Prince de Galles to win that year's Cambridgeshire and to score a repeat victory the next year. Robinson died suddenly when returning from Salisbury races in 1978. His son Philip is one of today's most successful international jockeys.

*Peter Robinson wins the Coombe Selling Plate on
Port o' Christo on 30th October 1961.*

Still four days short of his fifteenth birthday, Josh Gifford rode his first ever winner on Dorsal for Syd Mercer at Birmingham on 20th July 1956. He notched his second winner there the following day, on Gaiety Lady for his boss, Cliff Beechener.

Gifford rode 51 winners on the Flat, including the 1957 Chester Cup on Curry, but soon became too heavy and switched to riding under National Hunt Rules. He was champion four times over jumps and rode as first jockey to the powerful Ryan Price stable. He retired in 1970 and began training, proving successful in that sphere, too. His name will forever be linked with those of Aldaniti and Bob Champion, for it was Gifford that trained the horse to win that unforgettable 1981 Grand National.

Josh may have ridden his first two winners at Birmingham but not all his memories of the place are as happy. He had a frightening moment there in the Bromford Novices' Hurdle on 14th November 1961. Riding a horse named Timber he appeared to have the race at his mercy when cruising past Tim Brookshaw on Joss Merlin at the second last flight. To really rub salt into the wounds he cheekily turned round to make some caustic comment to Brookshaw and give him a cheery smile as he swept majestically by. Unfortunately, as he did so he overdid the grin and his false teeth slid to the back of his throat. As the choking Gifford desperately tried to cope with almost swallowing the teeth while riding towards the final hurdle, Brookshaw regained the lead and to went on to win. Gifford always rode without his teeth after that!

On Tuesday 8th April 1958 the Harry Wragg-trained Pinky gave apprentice Peter Boothman the first winner of his career in the Warwickshire Handicap. It began a rapid climb up the ladder for Boothman, who became that year's champion apprentice with 37 winners. He rode successfully in Ireland for many years.

Another apprentice to enjoy a successful career away from Britain was Chris Cordrey, who rode his first winner on Arthur Budgett's Jules in the Kenilworth Castle Handicap at Birmingham on 6th June 1960. Cordrey went on to become a leading jockey and trainer in Scandinavia.

Bruce Raymond rode his first winner on Willie Stephenson's Arctic Bar in the one-mile Elmdon Apprentice Maiden Plate at Birmingham on 19th June 1961. Raymond become champion apprentice the following season and was to enjoy a long and successful career in the saddle, retiring in 1994 with a clutch of Group 1 victories to his name at home and abroad.

Apprentice Terry Sturrock rode his first winner at Birmingham when Doug Marks' Chu-Teh won the Charlecote Handicap on 4th June 1963. His biggest success came on Sky Diver in the 1968 Stewards' Cup.

Stars of the Flat 1955-59

Flat trainers were now sending their better-class horses to Birmingham, and not just those based in Britain. In 1955 leading Irish trainer Paddy Prendergast made a surprise Easter Monday raid on Birmingham, winning with both runners. He did so again in 1956 and won with his only runner, then repeated the feat for the third Easter Monday running in 1957.

Lord Porchester's colt Tamerlane, beaten only a neck by Our Babu in the Two Thousand Guineas on his previous start, won a high-class 1955 Midland Breeders' Foal Stakes from Nucleus. Trained by Norman Bertie and the mount of Scobie Breasley, Tamerlane won the St. James's Palace Stakes at Royal Ascot (held that year in July on account of a railway strike) on his next start. Nucleus also went to Royal Ascot where he landed the King Edward VII Stakes. He later finished runner-up to Meld in the St. Leger and followed that by winning Newmarket's Jockey Club Cup.

The next year's Midland Breeders' Foal Stakes was won by Rustam, trained by Geoffrey Brooke. Rustam had been unbeaten as a two-year-old in 1955, his victories including the Champagne Stakes at Doncaster. However, he proved disappointing at three and that Birmingham victory under Doug Smith was his only success in four runs. At stud he sired three top-class juveniles in Display, who won the Cheveley Park Stakes and was second in the One Thousand Guineas; Talahasse, winner of the Gimcrack Stakes and Champagne Stakes; and Double Jump, who won the National Stakes, Prix Robert Papin and Gimcrack Stakes.

Lord Astor's Hornbeam, ridden by Eph Smith, won the one-mile Bromsgrove Nursery Handicap in 1955. The following year he won York's Voltigeur Stakes and the Ormonde Stakes at Newbury, finished runner-up in both the St. Leger and the King Edward VII Stakes and fourth in the Derby. Hornbeam was back at

Birmingham in 1957, landing the Water Orton Plate under Joe Mercer. Later that season he won the Victor Wild Stakes at Kempton and the Winston Churchill Stakes at Hurst Park, besides finishing a close second in three major races, beaten a head in the Yorkshire Cup, half a length in the Ebor Handicap and a short head in the Doncaster Cup.

On Easter Monday 1958, Hornbeam, again ridden by Joe Mercer, won the Water Orton Plate for the second year running. He went on to win twice more that season but was again unlucky, being beaten a short-head in the Yorkshire Cup and finishing second to Gladness in the Ascot Gold Cup.

The policy of staging high quality Flat racing at Birmingham to attract good horses appeared to be paying dividends. The main drawback, however, was the ground, which tended to get hard in a dry summer, resulting in small fields. At the 1955 August meeting, none of the twelve races had more than seven runners. Three of them, including both feature events, the Shakespeare Stakes and the Stanley Ford Stakes, ended up as two-horse matches. The latter event provided an upset, with the odds-on King Bruce being outpointed by Live Spirit, but there were no such problems in the Shakespeare Stakes, in which Manchester Cup winner Chatsworth started at 33-1 on (the shortest priced winner ever at Birmingham) and beat sole opponent Fair Ellen by ten lengths with the minimum of fuss.

The Birmingham Water Department, struggling to cope with the ever increasing demands of industrial and domestic users, could not offer the racecourse any help when water was most needed in periods of low rainfall or drought. They suggested that the Racecourse Company sink a borehole and, after much wrangling, a licence was duly obtained to do so. Unfortunately, it was on one condition, namely that the Company put the water in before taking it out!

Besides the state of the ground, it was often the presence of top grade horses that frightened off the opposition. In 1956, for example, Zarathrustra, trained by Cecil Boyd-Rochfort and ridden by stable jockey Harry Carr, won the Shakespeare Stakes easily from his two opponents at odds of 9 to 2 on. Zarathrustra, a former Irish Derby and Irish St. Leger winner, had on his previous start won the Ascot Stakes by five lengths carrying 9 stone. The following year he was to win the Ascot Gold Cup.

Notwithstanding the paucity of runners, the big events sometimes produced thrilling finishes. In June 1957, all three of Birmingham's long established feature races resulted in photo finishes. Pebble Ridge (Joe Mercer) beat General Pil (Bill Rickaby) by a short-head in the Warwickshire Breeders' Foal Stakes; Medina (Scobie Breasley) beat Quaver (Willie Snaith) and Casse Noisette (Rickaby) by a head and a short-head in the Guernsey Stud Produce Stakes; and London Cry (Breasley) beat Veleta (Mercer) by a short-head in the Midland Breeders' Foal Stakes, a race in which the first four were split by less than three-quarters of a length.

Watering the course – the sprinklers are used
to moisten the ground.

The dry summer of 1959 once again delivered firm ground and small fields. The Warwickshire Breeders' Stakes, the Guernsey Stud Produce Stakes and the Midland Breeders' Foal Stakes could muster only eleven runners between them. At least the latter had a decent winner, with Lady Zia Wernher's Dickens, trained by Cecil Boyd-Rochfort, sandwiching in the Midland Breeders' Foal Stakes between his victories in York's Dante Stakes and the Goodwood Cup.

Come to Daddy, ridden by Alec Russell, won the three-runner Shakespeare Stakes on the last day of August 1959, beating the odds-on Supreme Courage. (Come to Daddy was to win the Cesarewitch in the hands of Doug Smith next time out.) There was another blow for punters the next day when the long odds-on favourite Title Deed whipped round at the start of the Stanley Ford Stakes and was hopelessly left. Sole rival Marsh Meadow had covered a furlong and a half before Title Deed even got into stride and maintained his advantage to win by a distance. Marsh Meadow was actually no forlorn hope, having won the previous year's Warwickshire Breeders' Foal Plate.

The last race on that day's card, the Coleorton Maiden Plate, over a mile and five furlongs, went to a Syd Mercer-trained horse that would become one of the most popular stayers of all time. His name was Trelawny. He won the Chester Cup for Mercer as a four-year-old in 1960, but it was after he joined George Todd's Manton stable that he really blossomed. Partnered by Scobie Breasley, Trelawny achieved a notable double at Royal Ascot in 1962, winning the Ascot Stakes over two and a half miles carrying 9st 8lb and the two and three-quarter miles Queen Alexandra Stakes three days later. He completed the double again in 1963, this time shouldering 10 stone in the Ascot Stakes. He also won that year's Goodwood Cup.

Moving with the times

Under the chairmanship of Lord Willoughby de Broke the effort to retain and increase attendances never ceased. Some things worked; others didn't.

On Monday 12th July 1954 Birmingham broke new ground with its first evening meeting. The first race started at 7.00pm and was won by Doug Smith on First Flake.

Birmingham held its first mixed meeting, a combination of Flat and National Hunt racing, on Monday 5th, Tuesday 6th and Wednesday 7th November 1956. Each day contained four Flat races, a hurdle and a steeplechase. The steeplechase victors included four-year-old Taxidermist, winner of the Guy Fawkes Handicap Chase. Trained by Fulke Walwyn, "Taxi" would develop into one of Britain's most popular post-war steeplechasers, his victories including the Whitbread Gold Cup and the Hennessy Gold Cup, both in 1958

It was a mixed affair once again in November 1957, when by far the most appropriate winner was a horse named The Fosse. Already a winner on the Flat and over hurdles at Birmingham, The Fosse completed the set when winning the Burford Novices' Chase. On the second day of the meeting, Pointsman, with Fred Winter up, carried top weight of 12st 3lb to victory in the November Handicap Chase.

On Tuesday 4th November 1958 Birmingham staged what would turn out to be the most valuable National Hunt race ever held there. This was a one-off running of the Tote Investors' Handicap Chase, over two and a half miles and worth £2,414 12s 6d to the winner. The big prize

Part of the world's longest bar, in the centre of the course.

183

attracted an enormous field of 31. Amazingly, there were only two fallers in the whole race. It was won by Mr Clifford Nicholson's Casamba, trained in Yorkshire by Charlie Hall and ridden by Paddy Farrell.

During the winter of 1958-59 a giant refreshment bar, costing £35,000, was built in the cheap enclosure in the centre of the racecourse. In addition to improving the facilities for its patrons, it also set a new record for the longest bar in the world, its 334 feet continuous run beating the previous record holder – a working men's club in Victoria, Australia – by 49 feet.

Whereas the evening fixtures were a great success, the mixed meetings met with little public support and were not all that popular with racing's professionals. Following a five-year trial, Birmingham gave them up after 1960.

By then the warning bells were already beginning to toll for Bromford Bridge. Evenings and Bank Holidays excepted, Birmingham's average crowd had fallen steadily as racegoers opted for the more rural meetings of Warwick or Stratford. Not even Birmingham's most ardent admirer could have claimed that it was a scenic course. Just beyond the back straight was the railway, alongside the giant industrial Fort Dunlop works, and adjacent to that lay the Bromford Wire Mills.

By the end of the 1950s, Castle Bromwich Golf Course – for many years the green neighbour of Bromford Bridge – had been engulfed as a housing estate. The course was surrounded on all sides. With attendances dwindling, many people wondered how long would it be before the racecourse went the same way as the golf course.

It wasn't only falling attendances that threatened the racecourse. The weather did all it could to disrupt Birmingham's National Hunt season. When both days of the 1959 January meeting were abandoned, it meant that a combination of fog, snow and frost had been responsible for the loss of eight of its last twelve jumping cards.

No racing... no wonder! The 1959 January meeting is lost.

Into the sixties

For the third year running, Birmingham's (1960) January fixture had to be abandoned due to snow and frost. Luckily, February's survived and the Atherstone Maiden Hunters' Chase produced a finish between two young amateur rider brothers. Terry Biddlecombe on Not a Link beat Tony Biddlecombe on Kingsley Road by four lengths. Both were shortly to turn professional. While Tony's career was a brief one, Terry went on to become one of our very best National Hunt jockeys.

On the Flat in 1960, the problem of small fields in condition races continued. Jim Joel's Red Gauntlet, with Bobby Elliott up, was gifted a walk over in the £1,092 Festival Stakes. (Red Gauntlet then won the following week's Jersey Stakes at Royal Ascot, ridden by Eph Smith.) Not surprisingly, the conditions of the race were changed the next year to make it a maiden race. That very thing had already happened to the Stanley Ford Stakes after the farcical two-horse affair of 1959; and the same fate awaited the Shakespeare Stakes following the bloodless 1960 triumph of the Sir Gordon Richards-trained Induna, who beat his two moderate rivals at the unbackable odds of 8 to 1 on. If you think that was bad, it was even worse in the Midland Breeders' Stakes, in which Peter Walwyn's filly Saint Anne (Lester Piggott up) beat her sole rival Nerium at a ludicrous 25 to 1 on. Uncompetitive racing such as this was hardly helping to bring in the crowds.

There were no such problems on Monday 26th September 1960 when Birmingham staged what was by far the richest race in its history, the Triumph Herald Handicap, over two miles and worth £4,784 12s 6d. It was won by the Irish challenger Farrney Fox, the 3 to 1 favourite, trained by Charlie Weld and ridden by Tommy (TP) Burns, beating Fourth of June and Poetic Licence, with Spartan Green fourth. Although there were twenty-two runners in a competitive handicap, the first four home were also the first four in the betting. Unfortunately, this race turned out to be another 'one-off' affair and was not repeated.

Nobody thought too much about the winner of the modest Burton Two-year-old Plate on 22nd May 1961. The horse was named Privy Councillor, trained by Tom Waugh and ridden by Tommy Masters. The following year, however, Privy Councillor won the Two Thousand Guineas at 100 to 6, ridden on that occasion by Bill Rickaby.

But eyebrows were most definitely raised when Irish trainer Mick Connolly sent Star Charmer over to run in a humble £257 two-year-old selling race on 24th July 1961, with top Irish jockey Burns on board. Star Charmer, despite drifting in the betting from 6 to 4 favourite out to 5 to 2, got up to win by a length and a half. At the auction, Birmingham bookmaker Jack Woolf bought the horse for 725gns.

By 1962, most of the jockeys from the inter-war period had long since retired, but the Smith brothers, Doug and Eph, were still going strong. On 12th June 1962, Eph landed a double, initiated by Jim Joel's Spring Wheat, beating brother Doug on the Queen's colt Step On It, and completed by Commander in Chief, who was destined to win the following year's Cambridgeshire Handicap. A fortnight later it was Doug's turn. He landed a hat-trick, completed by Geoffrey Brooke's Valentine in the Midland Breeders' Stakes. On his previous start Valentine had finished unplaced in that year's Derby. In his next race he finished second to Henry the Seventh in the Eclipse Stakes.

The Queen Mother's horses

When Jaipur, ridden by Bill Rees, won division one of the Bonfire Novices' Hurdle on 31st October 1960, it marked the Queen Mother's first winner at Birmingham. Classiebaun, ridden by Arthur Freeman, had been her first runner there in November 1957 but he could finish only fourth.

Birmingham's racegoers had to wait until November 1964 to cheer another of the Queen Mother's horses home, this being Mel in the Charlecote Novices' Chase, but they didn't have to wait long for the next two. In February 1965, the third division of the Graveley Maiden Hurdle went to Ballykine, trained by Peter Cazalet and the mount of Dave Dick. The very next day, Worcran, ridden by Bobby Beasley, became the Queen Mother's fourth and final winner at the course when winning the Elmdon Hurdle. On his next start at Cheltenham two weeks later, Worcran finished third behind Kirriemuir and Spartan General in the Champion Hurdle.

The Queen Mother at Bromford Bridge in 1963.

More jumping stars

The finish of division one of the Bromford Novices' Hurdle at the 1961 November meeting was fought out between two horses who would go on to make their mark over fences. Bob Turnell's Rondetto won it, beating Honey End by three lengths. Rondetto became a top-class steeplechaser whose victories included the 1967 Hennessy Gold Cup, while Honey End is best remembered as the horse that finished second in Foinavon's sensational Grand National.

Another useful recruit turned up at Birmingham's 1962 January meeting. The Four-Year-Old Hurdle was won by Ryan Price's Beaver II, ridden by Josh Gifford. Two months later, Beaver II landed the Triumph Hurdle, run that year for the last time at Hurst Park. Nobody knew it at the time but this was the final occasion on which Birmingham's January meeting would take place.

Lynn and Lynn's Own

Birmingham factory worker Lynn Taylor made the front page of the *Daily Mirror* in December 1962. Teenager Lynn bought a race-horse for £60 and called it Lynn's Own. Unraced on the Flat, Lynn's Own was a chestnut filly by the virtually unknown sire Glendrostan out of a mare named Copper Penny. She was put into training with John Power, whose stables were at Elvers Green, Knowle.

Me and my horse – Lynn Taylor with Lynn's Own.

The story of the factory girl and her £60 horse caught the attention of the *Mirror* and their photo appeared on the front page shortly before the filly was to have her first race. The race chosen was the Leamington Juvenile Hurdle at Birmingham on Monday 10th December 1962. She was partnered by 7lb claiming amateur rider Bob Woolley. The *Mirror* was on hand, photographing Lynn's mother placing a bet with the bookmakers. Could this be a fairytale come true for the nineteen-year-old working girl and her plebeian-bred horse?

Hope springs eternal with an unraced horse. It could be anything. The reality, however, is usually far different, and so it proved with Lynn's Own. The *Daily Mirror* cameraman caught Lynn's moment of disappointment as she watched her filly race up to the winning post – a long way behind the twenty other finishers. Lynn's Own had finished last.

Unfortunately, that was as good as it got. Lynn's Own ran in three more races and was pulled up each time. The day after Lynn's Own's Birmingham flop, 11th December 1962, top Flat jockey Greville Starkey rode his first winner over jumps there, this being Michael Pope's Starliner in the Warwick Handicap Hurdle. Another leading Flat jockey to score over jumps at Birmingham was Brian Taylor, who won a division of the Graveley Maiden Hurdle on Harvey Leader's All of a Kind in February 1964.

Happenings in '63

It was a bad start to 1963 with the January and February fixtures both being abandoned because of snow and frost as the worst winter since 1947 continued to wreak havoc across Britain.

Both of the feature races at the Easter meeting had been doubled in value, now being worth £1,390 to the winner. Blandford won Easter Monday's Midland Spring Handicap, one of three winners that day for jockey Denis Ryan. The Lowther Barratt-trained Strebor Gem, ridden by Jimmy Mullane, sprang a 33 to 1 shock in Tuesday's Warwickshire Handicap.

There was a great battle for the 1963 jockeys' championship between Lester Piggott and Scobie Breasley. Both were in action at Birmingham on the last day of September. Scobie finished the day still two up, 159 versus 157, after each rode a winner. On the final day of October there were two more Birmingham winners for Lester and one for Scobie as the fight for the jockeys' title continued. It ended up in Scobie's favour, but only just – 176 winners against Lester's 175. It doesn't get any closer than that.

The 1963 November meeting saw Tim Brookshaw ride what would be his last winner at Birmingham, Bold Biri in the Coleshill Handicap Chase. Brookshaw won on Bold Biri again at Leicester two weeks later and once more at Nottingham on 3rd December. That proved to be Brookshaw's last winner, for the following day he broke his back when his mount, Lucky Dora, crashed through the wing of a hurdle at Liverpool.

Also at that 1963 November meeting, the great Fred Winter, in his last season as a jockey, rode future Cheltenham Gold Cup winner What a Myth to victory in the Kenilworth Handicap Chase. Winter was due to retire in April 1964 and set up as a trainer, a sphere in which he became equally as successful.

Another popular victory at that same November meeting came in the Ragley Juvenile Hurdle, for it was won by Sir Winston Churchill's Sun Hat, trained by Peter Cazalet and ridden by David Mould.

Course specialists

Horses didn't have to be top class to earn a following at Birmingham. Several of a humbler order achieved recognition through their performances in handicaps. Two of the most popular were the versatile Black Diamond and the sprinter Selly Oak.

Black Diamond

On 10th July 1961 Black Diamond, with Doug Smith up, won the mile-and-a-quarter Guys Cliff Maiden Handicap. It was the first of his eight course victories.

Black Diamond was a brown gelding by Black Tarquin out of Six of Diamonds. Trained by Arthur "Fiddler" Goodwill, he was a true stayer and a real Birmingham specialist, with five of his seven victories on the Flat being achieved there. At the peak of his powers in the summer of 1962 he won twice over two miles and once at two miles five furlongs, humping weights of 9st 10lb and 10 stone.

At the end of that year he was bought by Norfolk farmer and permit holder Walter Wales and was thereafter ridden by his son David. Black Diamond proved a useful recruit to the winter game, winning three times over hurdles at Birmingham between November 1963 and February 1964. In the second of those wins he beat Fred Rimell's highly promising Spartan General by three lengths. Black Diamond ran in that season's Champion Hurdle but was a genuine 100 to1 shot in top class company and finished twentieth of the twenty-four finishers.

Between September 1961 and February 1964 Black Diamond ran in seven races at Birmingham and won every time. No wonder the racegoers loved him!

Selly Oak

On Monday 9th May 1960 a three-year-old horse named Selly Oak, ridden by Sammy Millbanks, won the six-furlong Warwick Castle Handicap to record his first win. He was to become a real favourite with the Birmingham racegoers.

Foaled in 1957, Selly Oak was a sprinter by March Past out of Gin Rummy and was trained by Frank Cundell at Aston Tirrold, Berkshire. He won a total of fifteen races during eight consecutive seasons between 1960 and 1967. Five of those victories were gained at Birmingham, including back-to-back wins in the six-furlong Fillongley Handicap in 1963-64, ridden on the first occasion by Lester Piggott and on the second by 7lb claimer Paul Cook. Three of them were at Birmingham's Monday night meetings, including when scoring at the finale meeting in June 1965.

Selly Oak was a genuine, unpretentious sprint handicapper. The nearest he got to winning a 'big one' was when finishing fifth in the 1961 Wokingham at Royal Ascot. But he adored Birmingham, as his five victories there amply testify.

And it might so easily have been six. On 13th July 1964 Selly Oak, again partnered by Lester, came within inches of another course victory in the Alcester Handicap. It was the closest finish in Birmingham's history, as the photo-finish revealed a dead-heat between Sylvan Ash and Balmoral Fair, with Selly Oak just a short-head away in third place. It was the nearest Bromford Bridge ever came to a triple dead-heat!

*The Bournville Handicap, 28th July 1958. Neargoli (Doug Smith up)
scores easily by six lengths from Fur Bonnet.*

*The groundsman tests the course in vain, as another winter fixture
falls victim to snow and frost.*

A Bank Holiday Monday scene in the betting ring.

*The Sutton Two-Year-Old Selling Stakes, 25th July 1960. Port o'Christo,
with Harry Carr up, wins by five lengths from Llandovery Star.*

Firsts and lasts of '64

It was another bad start to the year when 1964's January meeting was abandoned because of snow. The first day of February's meeting went ahead and Popham Down won the Withington Handicap Chase in the hands of Willie Robinson. Popham Down was destined to win the Scottish Grand National two months later but is forever remembered as the horse that helped create the chaos at Aintree in Foinavon's 1967 Grand National. The second day of the February meeting was abandoned because of snow, meaning that the Champion Trial Hurdle was lost for the third year running.

Willie Robinson.

Lester Piggott rode the hot favourites in the first two races on the Easter Monday card, but was narrowly beaten in each by jockey Bobby Elliott, who won on Proxy and Canadian Currency. Piggott did not leave empty-handed, however, for he won the three-year-old maiden race on Persinglass.

Fighting Charlie, ridden by Ron Sheather, was a well above average winner of Birmingham's Lord Leycester Maiden Plate over a mile and five furlongs on 18th May. Although failing to win another race all that season, Fighting Charlie went on to win the Ascot Gold Cup in 1965 (when ridden by Lester Piggott) and again in 1966 (partnered by Greville Starkey).

Another good horse to appear at Birmingham in 1964 was Sweet Moss, winner of that year's Dee Stakes, Dante Stakes and Gordon Stakes, who started the heavy odds-on favourite for the Midland Breeders' Stakes. It was also the richest ever running of the race, being worth £2,038 18s to the winner. Sweet Moss never gave his supporters an anxious moment, winning comfortably by two lengths in the hands of Willie Snaith.

Birmingham's first National Hunt evening meeting took place on Wednesday 13th May 1964. The winners included Joss Merlyn, ridden by Michael Scudamore, who beat Honey End by a length in the Harborne Handicap Chase. It also witnessed what must rank as the one of the heaviest lumps of overweight to be carried in post-war racing. Eleven-year-old Great Scot was the horse so lumbered. Allocated 10st 4lb in the Sheldon Handicap Hurdle, his owner-rider's 7lb claim should have reduced the weight to a mere 9st 11lb. However, Great Scot's podgy partner was far in excess of that and weighed out no less than 40lb overweight, meaning the poor horse had to lumber 12st 9lb round two miles and five furlongs of Bromford Bridge. Anchored by his heavyweight burden, Great Scot not surprisingly trailed in last of the twenty-one runners.

Two months later, Birmingham staged its first ever Saturday evening fixture, which brought doubles for both Lester Piggott and Greville Starkey. That night the Migil Five performed live on the mound in the centre of the course, giving a fine rendition of their chart hit 'Mockingbird Hill' to an appreciative audience.

The added entertainment provided by leading pop groups between races encouraged many teenagers to give racing a try. The Swinging Blue Jeans were among the other hit-makers to appear.

Willie Snaith, won on Sweet Moss.

To attract the families, ladies were given free admission to selected meetings and a play area was created in the course enclosure so that young children could be left in the care of attendants while mom and dad were off enjoying themselves.

So now Birmingham seemingly had it all. More prize money, big Bank Holiday crowds, lots of evening meetings, pop groups on the mound, top horses, leading jockeys. Everything was going great.

Or was it?

The beginning of the end

By this time the average attendance for a 'regular' Bromford Bridge fixture was down to around 5,000, leading Chairman Lord Willoughby de Broke to comment, "Over the years it has become obvious that people in the area are not interested in racing." In addition, the cost of staging a meeting had trebled since the war to some £3,000 per day, excluding prize money.

Meanwhile, Birmingham Corporation was keen to acquire the 180-acre site for housing development as part of its slum clearance programme. Due to a housing shortage, new properties were badly needed and the Corporation proposed building an estate of 1,900 homes on the racecourse land. The Birmingham Racecourse Company had earlier rejected an offer from a conglomerate of major oil companies who wanted to use the site as a terminal base, but they were more sympathetic to what the Corporation had to say.

In 1964 the Birmingham Racecourse Company recommended to its shareholders the sale of the racecourse to the Corporation for £1,250,000. In fact, the recommendation was more of a *fait accompli*. With a general election being imminent, the Racecourse Company was anxious that a change of government could scupper the deal, hence they hastily agreed it before fully consulting the shareholders. The pill was sweetened somewhat by a dividend in excess of £20 per share, an offer that most shareholders felt they couldn't refuse. It was agreed that Bromford Bridge racecourse would close the following June.

In some ways the news of its closure came at an opportune time. In April 1963 the Levy Board, which had taken over responsibility for a major part of racing's finances since the legalisation of betting shops two years earlier, had decreed that there were just too many racecourses. In a cost cutting exercise it earmarked a dozen for closure, stating that they would no longer receive any financial support after 1966. Several courses had accepted their fate and chosen not to fight, including Lewes, Lincoln, Bogside, Woore and Rothbury. Birmingham itself had not been one of the twelve selected courses, although two other major tracks, Hurst Park and Manchester, had already been sold for housing development.

Birmingham's shareholders planned to invest the proceeds of the sale in a new 'supercourse' combined with a sports centre, golf course, sailing club and athletics track to be built on land near Tamworth, which would eventually replace both Bromford Bridge and Wolverhampton's Dunstall Park. The chairman of the Levy Board appeared to be all for it and intimated that if the two courses were to be sold off and a new combined racecourse built in more congenial surroundings, the Levy Board would be prepared to offer financial assistance. It was estimated that to purchase the site and lay out a racecourse would cost in excess of £2 million, possibly a good deal more. There was much excitement as negotiations were instigated and plans were drawn up.

Unfortunately, the most the Levy Board was prepared to offer in terms of "financial assistance" was a mere drop in the ocean and, despite all the enthusiasm and

In the paddock at Bromford Bridge in 1964.

good intentions, the scheme never really got off the ground. By October 1964 it had fallen through completely.

The last few months

There were massive fields for the final autumn meeting, 133 runners in all, with four of the six races having fields of 24 or more. By contrast, the three chases on the first day of the November meeting attracted a total of just six runners, with the Coleshill Handicap Chase being declared void after none of the horses that had been entered was declared to run.

At the December meeting, Eric Cousins' Commander in Chief, winner of the 1963 Cambridgeshire and previously a winner on the Flat at Birmingham, captured division one of the Yuletide Novices' Hurdle in the hands of Terry Biddlecombe. George Owen's Peacetown, who had finished third in that year's Grand National, won the Ashby Handicap Chase, ridden by Roy Edwards.

Sadly, the 1965 January meeting was abandoned for the third consecutive year. February's survived and, in stark contrast to the November fixture, runners were plentiful, with the Graveley Maiden Hurdle having to be run in four divisions. Honey End won the final running of the Withington Handicap Chase, partnered by Michael Scudamore.

Birmingham's last Easter fixture brought success for Frankie Vaughan and Terry Downes. No, not the actual entertainer or boxing champion but horses named after them. Frankie Vaughan, with Jock Wilson up, won the two-year-old auction maiden plate, while Terry Downes, ridden by Irish champion jockey John Roe, won the Warwickshire Handicap. This was one of three winners for Roe over the two-day meeting. There was also an Easter Monday double for Wordsley-born apprentice Geoff Baxter, completed by Ledsam Lad, trained by Reg Hollinshead for the city's former Lord Mayor, Dr Louis Glass.

Birmingham's last National Hunt meeting took place on the evening of Friday 21st May 1965. Bishop Auckland trainer Arthur Stephenson and stable jockey Paddy Broderick combined to win the first two races. The last race was division two of the Farewell Novices' Hurdle, won by Penisola, owned and trained by Bryan Marshall at Lambourn and ridden by Johnny Haine.

On Monday 21st June 1965 Birmingham staged its final fixture, an evening meeting beginning at 7.00pm. Some 9,400 racegoers, almost twice the average number, were there to witness its demise. Surprisingly, the race card contained no farewell message from the directors. The only clue to the course's closure came in the naming of the last race, the Farewell Plate.

That day's *Sporting Chronicle* previewed the final meeting under the headline 'Farewell To Birmingham', commenting: "The history of racing at Birmingham, which has been one of stops and starts for more than 100 years, looks like coming to an end for once and for all.

"Modern economic conditions make it seem impossible that another course will be laid out within the confines of the city after Bromford Bridge has gone the way of Manchester, Hurst Park, Lewes and Lincoln, and another step is taken towards the centralisation of racing."

The article concluded: "While recognising the inevitability of answering the demands of the twentieth century, one cannot help regretting that no horses will ever more race in this spot of the Midlands after tonight."

Lester Piggott rode a double that night, including the five-furlong Bromford Handicap on the popular eight-year-old Selly Oak, scoring his fifth course victory. Penisola, winner of the last race over jumps at Birmingham, won the penultimate Flat race, the Henley-in-Arden Handicap, over one mile five furlongs, in the hands of Stan Clayton.

The very last race run at Birmingham was the Farewell Maiden Plate, for two-year-olds over five furlongs. It took place in pouring rain and was won by Sir Edwin McAlpine's Welshman, ridden by Greville Starkey, who had had his first ride in public at Birmingham back in October 1955. Welshman, an 11 to 2 chance, won by six lengths from the 6 to 4 favourite Philistine (Bobby Elliott), with Peintre Bleu (Colin Moss) a further four lengths away in third. Just for the record, the last horse past the post was called Plantation Inn.

It was a sad occasion not only for the racegoers but also for Francis Ford, who had carried out the role of clerk of the course since 1953. His grandfather John Ford and great-uncle Stanley Ford had opened the course in 1895 and had both served as clerk of the course, as had his father Stanley B. Ford. It was equally sad for Reg Stonebridge, who had been Bromford's groundsman for thirty-four years; and for Hal Walker, a bookmaker there since 1924.

Lord Willoughby de Broke ceremoniously handed over the winning post to Councillor Bond, chairman of the city housing committee. Former Lord Mayor of Birmingham and racehorse owner Dr Louis Glass – his two-year-old Forward ran in the Farewell Maiden Plate – said, "This is a very sad business, but housing is more important."

Lester Piggott, succinct as ever, observed: "No one likes to see a course closing, especially a jockey. Birmingham has been one of my good courses."

The racecourse's effects were sold off by public auction in September 1965. The catalogue comprised an Aladdin's Cave of treasures including turnstiles, weighing scales, water heaters, folding beds, mirrors, lampshades and iron gates, complete with safety locks. The largest item, the Bromford grandstand, went to Hednesford Raceway, a stock car racing circuit near Cannock. Erected in the home straight it was always known as 'The Bromford Stand' and was much loved by the stock car racing enthusiasts. It remained there for many years until being burned to the ground by vandals in 1990.

The following year work began on providing homes for 7,500 people and in due course the once broad, green acres of Birmingham Racecourse gave way to the Bromford housing estate.

The names of equine racing heroes were perpetuated by the likes of Reynoldstown Road, Tulyar Close and Arkle Croft, while other parts of the estate were named after racecourses, such as Doncaster Way, Sandown Road and Cheltenham Drive. Derby winners Papyrus, Trigo, Hyperion and Pinza joined Grand National heroes Sundew, Kilmore, Sprig and Ayala to serve as a permanent reminder that this had once been home to the Sport of Kings.

Auctioning off the racecourse's items.

Top: The start of the Meriden Fillies' Maiden Plate, 29th August 1961.
Middle: The Sollihull Handicap Hurdle, 15th January 1962. Left to right:
Fen Street (Derek Ancil up, the winner), Red Holly (John Kenneally),
Givus Light (Johnny Gilbert) and The Mexican (John Buckingham).
Bottom: The Rugby Amateur Riders' Stakes, 24th April 1961, Markless,
ridden by Simon Chamberlayne, beats My Own (Mr John Lawrence).

The Tile Hill Plate for two-year-olds, 24th April 1961. The favourite Del Silva (right), ridden by Russ Maddock, beats Scarlet Cloak (Doug Smith).

The Charlecote Novices' Chase, 12th November 1962. Son of Tam (David Nicholson) leads Red Ripple (Tim Ryan, far side) and Joss Merlyn (Tim Brookshaw) over the last fence. Joss Merlyn got up to win the race by half a length from Red Ripple with Son of Tam third.

The Sutton Handicap Hurdle, 14th November 1961. Jumping the second flight are the blinkered Royal Abundance (Brian Delaney) who finished fifth, and the winner, Autumn Flight (Ron Harrison).

In the winner's enclosure. Auctioning the winner of the selling race.

A packed betting ring at Bromford Bridge.

Tote punters place their bets.

KEEP FAITH IN CLAIR SOLEIL
Kingfish Should Run on for Bromford Victory

By MAJOR KETTLE

CLAIR SOLEIL is napped to take advantage of the 6lb. he's in receipt from Limeville and win the Packington Novices' Chase of £1,000 at Bromford Bridge's opening stage to-day. The ex-champion hurdler fell at the "water" at Newbury, where his jumping was below par. I expect a greatly-improved performance this time.

Pivot in Replay

e to solve Aston Villa's centre-)lay with Stoke City at Molineux

If from their 3-0 defeat at n Charlton.

e As centre-forward Johnny ll King, who has missed the last two games owing to a knee and t ankle injury, is still unfit no t changes are expected.

r Aston Villa: Sims; Lynn, Ash- r field; Birch, Saward, Crowe; j Smith, Sewell, Hitchens, Myers- cough, McParland.

c Stoke City: Hall; McCue, Allen; Cairns, Thomson, Sellars; Cole- man, Bowyer, Wilshaw, Kelly, Oscroft.

This valuable race should be among the most exciting on the card as Renaldo, Misty Vision and Flame Royal also take part in it, all these having done well since put to the major obstacles.

It was not before time that Renaldo won at Windsor, for he had run very promising races against Double Star at Sandown and earlier on when opposed to The Fosse here in November.

Limeville, second in the Imperial Cup last season, showed at Kempton Park on Boxing Day that he is going to challenge for top-honours as a two-mile chaser.

SLOW PACE

Due to the slow early pace at Kempton, Limeville jumped stickily but, once warmed up, buckled to with a will.

Misty Vision was an easy winner of a novice chase at Dunstall Park, but he's taking on better class to-day, while Flame Royal's second on that same course to The Bell, though a creditable effort, has not been enhanced by Saturday's failure of Oleins Way at Newbury.

I prefer to judge Clair Soleil on his third to Double Star and Brunel II at Newbury in November and expect him to exert his undoubted class over this line-up.

BLUNDERED

Turning my attention to the final race, the Knowle Maiden Hurdle (Div. II), I cannot help but feel that Kingfish will compensate owner-rider, Mr. Rodney Mansfield, for a most unlucky defeat by Reprieved at Leicester last week.

In that race Kingfish disputed the lead to the last flight but a blunder here lost him some ground. He ran on to such good purpose on the flat that

Turn to Back Page

It's Keame Dancer at Willenhall

GOOD sport is offered to race-goers at Willenhall tonight where the best wager on the card can be found in the top class event through Mrs. L. Booth's Keame Dancer, a speedy son of Imperial Dancer, who is noted for his early pace. He recently returned from resting and was installed an even money favourite on Monday, his first appearance on this track for several months. He trapped well but was baulked twice by Black Marsh and was beaten into fourth place. This time he is the only

WINNERS !

THE Sporting Buff's grey-hound service provided another profitable week-end. Five winners were named at Perry Barr and three each at King's Heath and Leicester. The Perry Barr successes were:—

Kilcaskin Kourier (5-2), Winnies Lassie (2-1), Noisy Sam (nap, 4-5), Flyaway Prince (4-5), and Careless Blue (4-5).

wide runner in the field and although he will be challenged by Leagh Swank and Balardo in the initial stages, he should never be headed.

Extract from the Sporting Buff on Tuesday 14th January 1958. That day's fixture had to be abandoned.

Clerk of the course Francis Ford (second left) and the stewards inspect the course as another fixture is lost.

*An overhead view of Bromford Bridge in 1966 during the
construction of the housing estate.
The paddock can be seen, just below centre.*

Part of the paddock as it looks today.

BROMFORD BRIDGE POST WAR BIG RACE WINNERS

City of Birmingham Cup (3yo Handicap) (1 mile 2 furlongs)

Year	Winner	Weight	Jockey	SP
1946	Arromanches	8-8	G Richards	7-4fav
1947	Early Harvest	9-1	K Gethin	5-1
1948	Star of Gujrath	9-1	C Smirke	5-4fav
1949	Ridge Wood	9-0	G Richards	100-30
1950	Sinless	9-2	P Maher	7-4fav
1951	Highcrest	8-4	G Richards	5-1
1952	Norooz	8-5	R Fawdon	11-2
1953	Pearl Stud	8-6	G Richards	11-4
1954	Tuppenny Fare *	7-11	B Swift	4-1
1955	Saykash	7-12	G Lewis	3-1jtfav
1956	Trent Bridge	7-10	E Smith	25-1
1957	Sovereign Flame	8-6	J Purtell	13-2
1958	Kabale	8-1	A C Rawlinson	10-1
1959	Decree	9-0	W Rickaby	15-2
1960	Silent Waters	7-10	Donald Morris	100-7
1961	Jacqueline Ann	7-11	J Wilson	8-1
1962	Authorise	7-11	P Tulk	20-1
1963	Saltarello	8-12	D Yates	4-6fav
1964	Forthright	8-3	R Hutchinson	5-1
1965	Dites	8-6	B Taylor	100-30

* In 1954, Boreas came in first but was disqualified.

Festival Stakes (6 furlongs) Festival Maiden Stakes (3yo) from 1961

1951	Bob Cherry	4-9-7	N Sellwood	5-2
1952	Grey Sovereign	4-9-7	E Fordyce	9-2
1953	Set Fair	4-9-7	E Smith	7-4fav
1954	King Bruce	3-8-7	F Durr	6-4fav
1955	Pappa Fourway	3-8-7	W H Carr	4-5fav
1956	Prairie Emblem	3-8-0	P Robinson	6-4fav
1957	Vigo	4-9-7	L Piggott	1-1fav
1958	Right Boy	4-9-7	F Durr	7-2
1959	Capuchon	3-7-10	P Tulk	11-2
1960	Red Gauntlet (w.o.)	3-7-7	R P Elliott	walk over
1961	Marsolve	9-0	W Rickaby	11-8fav
1962	Spring Wheat	9-4	E Smith	7-1
1963	Teetotal	8-6	W Elliott	100-8
1964	Sylvan Prince	7-12	K Temple-Nidd	10-1

Warwickshire Breeders' Foal Plate (2yo) (5 furlongs)
(Warwickshire Breeders' Stakes from 1959) (First run 1904)

1946	Marriage Day	8-11	G Richards	4-11fav
1947	Henley-in-Arden	8-4	D Smith	4-5fav
1948	Gay Street	8-4	T Lowrey	33-1
1949	Fair Coup	8-11	M Beary	6-1
1950	Idolatry	8-1	P Maher	4-1

1951	Mountain Ash	8-4	G Richards	2-1fav
1952	Trial by Jury	8-4	A P Taylor	8-1
1953	Crimson	8-1	R Parnell	3-1
1954	Constable	8-4	Sir G Richards	2-5fav
1955	Lady Midge	8-1	E Mercer	7-2jtfav
1956	Colosseum	8-4	W Rickaby	10-11fav
1957	Pebble Ridge	8-2	J Mercer	11-2
1958	Marsh Meadow	9-4	R Fawdon	11-2
1959	Bourbon	8-4	E Mercer	8-11fav
1960	Parmene	8-1	E Hide	5-2fav
1961	Zebra	8-4	W Rickaby	7-1
1962	Harbinger	8-6	J Mercer	6-4fav
1963	Fideve	8-9	L Piggott	6-5fav
1964	Silent Trust	8-9	L Piggott	4-6fav

Midland Breeders' Foal Plate (3yo) (1 mile 2 furlongs)
(Midland Breeders' Stakes from 1960) (First run 1909)

1946	Croupier	9-5	M Beary	2-1
1947	Merry Quip	9-5	T Weston	4-6fav
1948	Jacket	8-4	E Smith	7-1
1949	Forethought	8-4	E C Elliott	11-10fav
1950	Sultan Blanc	8-9	E Britt	11-8fav
1951	Chiaroscuro	8-4	L Piggott	12_-1
1952	Rawson	9-5	F Hunter	8-13fav
1953	Tudor Sovereign	8-4	A Breasley	20-1
1954	Coronation Scot	9-0	D Smith	11-4
1955	Tamerlane	9-9	A Breasley	8-11fav
1956	Rustam	9-7	D Smith	4-6fav
1957	London Cry	9-7	A Breasley	9-4jtfav
1958	Trimmer	8-9	S Clayton	9-2
1959	Dickens	9-7	S Clayton	2-9fav
1960	Saint Anne	8-8	L Piggott	1-25fav
1961	Just Great	9-7	A Breasley	4-11fav
1962	Valentine	9-7	D Smith	4-1
1963	Crevette	9-4	D Smith	15-8
1964	Sweet Moss	9-7	W Snaith	30-100fav

Guernsey Stud Produce Stakes (2yo) (5 furlongs) (First run 1911)

1946	Ranjit	9-9	E Britt	8-11fav
1947	Bodala	8-2	G Richards	9-4
1948	Companion-way	8-4	T Lowrey	6-4fav
1949	Rare Bird	8-1	E Smith	9-2
1950	Rambling Vista	8-4	A Ireson	20-1
1951	Zabara	8-1	D Smith	5-2
1952	Chartair	8-4	F Barlow	2-1fav
1953	Big Berry	8-1	P Newson	15-2
1954	Queen's Orders	8-1	J Mercer	2-1fav
1955	La Fresnes	8-11	D Smith	8-11fav
1956	Seven Up	8-6	D Smith	15-8
1957	Medina	9-4	A Breasley	1-3fav
1958	Donna	8-1	E Mercer	8-11fav
1959	Tudor Court	8-4	E Smith	5-6fav
1960	Ribelle	8-9	J Lindley	8-13fav
1961	Windmill	9-0	J Lindley	4-5fav

Shakespeare Stakes (1 mile 5 furlongs)

1949	Vic Day	4-9-5	E C Elliott	10-11fav
1950	Vic Day	5-9-7	E C Elliott	7-1
1951	(dead heat)			
	Strathspey	6-9-7	A Breasley	100-30
	Chinese Cracker	3-8-8	E C Elliott	7-4
1952	Philantrope	5-9-7	W Rickaby	15-8
1953	Westinform	4-9-7	T Gosling	9-2
1954	Philos	4-9-7	F Barlow	6-1
1955	Chatsworth	5-9-7	F Barlow	1-33fav
1956	Zarathrustra	6-9-7	W H Carr	2-9fav
1957	Brave Buck	3-8-5	S Clayton	100-30
1958	Midlander	3-7-8	D Smith	4-1
1959	Come to Daddy	4-8-4	A J Russell	15-8
1960	Induna	7-9-4	W Guest	1-8fav

Union Stakes (6 furlongs)
(Renamed as Stanley Ford Stakes in 1954)

1947	Vagabond II	7-9-0	W R Johnstone	10-11fav
1948	Delirium	3-8-10	C Smirke	9-4
1949	Luminary	3-8-12	E C Elliott	1-4
1950	Abadan	8-8-12	G Richards	5-4fav
1951	Lady Godiva	3-7-12	P Evans	100-6
1952	Grey Sovereign	4-9-7	E Fordyce	2-1
1953	Rose Coral	3-8-2	D Smith	2-1jtfav
1954	Dumbarnie	5-9-7	F Barlow	100-30fav
1955	Live Spirit	5-9-7	W H Carr	2-1
1956	Matador	3-8-12	E Smith	2-7fav
1957	Arcandy	4-9-6	T Gosling	13-8
1958	Right Boy	4-9-6	L Piggott	2-5fav
1959	Marsh Meadow	3-8-10	R Fawdon	4-1

Midland Cesarewitch Handicap (2 miles)

1946	Lady Crusader	4-7-9	E Smith	11-2
1947	Avon Prince	4-7-10	D Smith	5-1
1948	Garter Club	6-8-9	J Sirett	7-2
1949	Fidonia	5-8-7	W H Carr	3-1
1950	Father Thames	4-8-3	W Rickaby	11-2
1951	Sarda II	6-8-2	G Richards	100-30
1952	Misty Light	5-7-6	J Mercer	100-7
1953	Eynsford	4-7-6	J Wilson	6-1
1954	Windless	3-7-11	E Smith	13-2
1955	Shirley Pat	4-8-3	A Russell	12-1
1956	Closebeck	4-7-2	N Pearson	8-1
1957	Hollyhock	5-7-10	E Hide	100-9
1958	Seadon	3-7-4	M Hayes	7-1cofav
1959	Grecian Granite	4-7-1	R Singer	100-8
1960	Curry's Kin	3-7-0	D Cullen	33-1
1961	Mr Pharoah	4-6-10	A Gibbons	13-2
1962	Tropical Sky	3-7-11	R Hutchinson	10-1
1963	Roxburgh	8-7-6	D W Morris	100-7
1964	French Patrol	3-8-3	W Williamson	5-1

Midland Cambridgeshire Handicap (1 mile, straight)

1946	Eric's Folly	7-8-9	E C Elliott	10-1
1947	Solfax	3-7-11	D Smith	100-3-fav
1948	Wisley	3-7-10	E Smith	7-1
1949	Refund	3-8-3	G Richards	8-1
1950	Valdeso	3-8-2	K Gethin	100-30fav
1951	Dorogoi	8-7-10	J Sime	4-1
1952	Capsize	4-8-7	J Mercer	11-2
1953	Dumbarnie	4-8-12	Sir G Richards	5-2
1954	Whippy	4-7-3	A Shrive	12-1
1955	Opera Score	4-8-0	E Smith	20-1
1956	Variety King	4-8-9	A Breasley	3-1fav
1957	Nicholas Nickleby	6-8-5	A Breasley	15-2
1958	Small Slam	3-7-11	E Smith	20-1
1959	Gold Miner	3-7-13	D Smith	4-1fav
1960	Connaissance	4-9-7	W Rickaby	100-7
1961	Redoubt	4-8-12	J Mercer	10-1
1962	Mustavon	7-9-4	L Piggott	4-1fav
1963	Gelert	4-8-0	P Newson	10-1
1964	Ruby Wedding	3-7-4	P Cook	100-7

Champion Trial Hurdle (2 miles)

1948	D.U.K.W.	5-11-6	J Maguire	5-1
1949	Shining Gold	6-12-0	A P Thompson	2-1
1950	Desir	6-11-8	F T Winter	20-1
1951	Secret Service	8-12-5	B Marshall	10-1
1952	Sir Ken	5-11-9	T Molony	2-5
1953	Sir Ken	6-12-5	T Molony	1-4fav
1954	Sir Ken	7-12-5	T Molony	8-13fav
	1955-56 Abandoned			
1957	Wayward Bird	8-11-8	D Ancil	100-7
	1958 Abandoned			
1959	Tokoroa	8-11-12	T Brookshaw	11-10fav
1960	Saffron Tartan	9-11-12	T P Burns	10-11fav
1961	Costa Brava	7-11-8	H J East	100-6
	1962-64 Abandoned			
1965	Magic Court	7-12-5	J FitzGerald	4-11fav

Withington Handicap Chase (4 miles and a few yards)

1953	Glen Fire	10-11-8	M Scudamore	8-1
1954	Crudwell	8-12-0	R Francis	9-2fav
	1955-56 Abandoned			
1957	Rondino	8-10-1	G Mann	6-1
1958	Mr Gay	11-11-0	D Ancil	5-1
1959	Oscar Wilde	9-11-9	R E Jenkins	4-1
1960	Clover Bud	10-10-3	T Taaffe	9-4fav
1961	Jimuru	10-11-1	Mr J Leigh	20-1
	1962-63 Abandoned			
1964	Popham Down	7-10-3	G W Robinson	11-2
1965	Honey End	8-10-8	M Scudamore	9-1

A GROUNDSMAN'S MEMORIES

When Glyn Betteridge set out to write his book, he invited people to contact him with their memories of Bromford Bridge. Among the replies he received was this one from **Bob Healey**....

"I have many happy memories of my time at Bromford Bridge after my demob from the Royal Navy in 1949. After a life in submarines the outdoors appealed to myself and a couple of friends also. We went along for an interview and the three of us were taken on as ground staff. The rest of the men employed at the course were a mixture of the likes even the Navy could not produce, all from Summer Lane area, as rough as they come but everyone a super character.

"We had Old Jack, a jockey from days past, who could make a stable look like the Ritz with his knowledge of bedding a horse down in the straw. He used to collect a fair living in tips from the trainers. Then there was Little Tich, a 4ft nothing little fellow whose claim to fame was dodging work but being able to produce all types of mushrooms from the two spinneys growing along the straight mile.

"The head groundsman was Reg Stonehouse, an ex pioneer man from the army. Reg had to be a tough boss with the Summer Lane boys and this led to more than one middleweight contest at the six furlong gate, but everything taken into consideration, the life at Bromford was a happy one, despite the poor wages. Our wages used to be subsidised on race days. The punters could lose more money on the floor than they could to the bookies, and cleaning up after racing used to be worth good money, especially if you worked in Tatts or the Silver Ring.

"We used to have days away from the course gathering gorse bushes from the hedgerows by Elmdon Airport. This was used to make the hurdles, a full time occupation for an old chap from Coleshill who worked there. Between race days I used sometimes to build fences, go out mowing, help in the stables, paint, and dozens of other duties, but on race days my job was on the starting gates. The day before the meeting we used to go out and put up and test the gates.

"On race days we always had some incident or other. At the six-furlong gate one afternoon, Charlie Smirke's horse went into the gate, turned round, knocking the jockey off, and managed to get his teeth trapped in the gate. If the gate had gone up the horse's neck would have been broken. I took the horse by his bridle and slowly turned him out of the gate, gave Charlie a leg up and off they went. The next race, Charlie came over to me and gave me paper money from his riding boot and told me he was trying in the last. I had a bet, he tried and won, and we became good friends."

THE RACECOURSE TIPSTERS

You hardly see any racecourse tipsters today. They've nearly all been replaced by premium rate telephone lines and even the few that do exist are but pale imitations of the characters of yesteryear. Without them, the racecourse seems a more sterile place, devoid of that special atmosphere that the tipsters created.

Newmarket and Epsom may have had Prince Monolulu – the man who'd always "gotta horse" - but Birmingham had its fair share of tipsters too. Two of the most memorable were the "Shilling Shocker" and Michael Lynch. We are indebted to author David Ashworth for sharing his memories of the latter, on which the following is based.

Your Old Pal **Michael Lynch** was a small, wrinkled man who wore a surgical boot due to a badly bent leg. He also wore a trademark brown trilby. By his side stood a board on which the words "Michael Lynch, Jockey" were written. To back up this claim, he would open his bag and produce three or four faded mounted photographs, each showing a jockey of indeterminate features sat astride a horse and being led into the winner's enclosure.

Even though his gammy leg was reputedly the legacy of a car accident, no matter which racecourse he happened to be at, "Your Old Pal Michael" would insist that this was the very place where he broke it, thus ending his career in the saddle.

Once a crowd had gathered round he'd begin his banter. "You see these photos? That's me there," he'd proclaim, pointing to the victorious rider. "I was a jockey for twenty-three years. I rode for nobility – Lord Derby, the Aga Khan, Captain Boyd-Rochfort."

Then he'd take out what appeared to be a thick roll of five-pound notes, but which, in all probability, were no more than half a dozen fivers stuck on top of sheets of paper. "I'm not going to win this much today," he'd say, waving it around, "nor this much," as a wad of tenners was produced. The crowd grew more animated.

"I know what you're asking yourselves," he'd continue in a serious, lets-drop-the-showmanship voice. "Where did old Michael get a pile of money like that from?" Then he'd pause, as if defying anyone to contradict.

"I'm right aren't I? That's it, have a good look. I won't be here much longer. I'm a busy man. You think this is a lot of money? Pah!" He'd wave the money dismissively and make a spitting gesture.

Old Michael would adjust his hat, turn sideways to the onlookers, and contemplate the tarmac. "Ladies and gentlemen," he'd resume earnestly, "I've come here today to give you *one horse*." He'd pause again.

"I know that surprises you. Some of you want miracles. You want old Michael to tell you all six winners on the card. Well if that's what you want you'd better turn to your Newsboy or your Robin Goodfellow because I can't do it. Ladies and gentlemen, they don't run their horses for the likes of you and me. I cannot give you all six winners. But I've got one horse today and when it wins – and make no mistake, it *will* win – and I ought to know because I came up here with the trainer this morning – when it wins I'm not going to win this much," he gestured to the rolls of fivers and tenners.

"Ladies and gentlemen, I'm going double nap and when this horse wins," and at this juncture he'd produce a sheaf of twenty-pound notes as thick as a house brick and fan through it with his thumb, "*this* is what I expect to be taking home."

"I know what some of you are saying," he'd sigh, like a preacher despairing of the ignorance of his flock. "How do we know old Michael won't lead us up the garden path? Ha! Those of you who were here with me last time know. Those of you who saw me at Newmarket in July when I gave three winners know.

"What's that? You want to see my credentials?" He'd jab a forefinger impatiently at the photographs. "These are my credentials. You just go and see Lord Derby, the Aga Khan, or Captain Boyd-Rochfort and ask them if old Michael Lynch ever let them down.

"Put your money on with confidence with your old pal Michael. Now who'll give me half a crown for my card? Come on, I've only got a few left."

The crowd began to disperse, some laughing uncertainly, while others pressed forward almost against their will to buy the card. Another man muttered that he'd seen old Michael travelling up on the train alone, yet he still shuffled forward to part with his half-crown.

****

Nobody who was on the racecourse during the fifties and sixties would have heard of Leonard Cave. But they'd all remember his alias – the **Shilling Shocker**.

In stark contrast to Prince Monolulu's lavish feathers and finery, the Shocker rarely dressed as though he was caning the bookmakers. Whereas other racecourse tipsters worked in half-crowns, Shocker would happily pass on his 'good thing' for the price of a shilling.

There are many tales of the Shocker's exploits. Legend has it that he once got up on stage at Bromford Bridge and sang with the Swinging Blue Jeans, during their concert on the mound in the centre of the course.

Racegoer Ken Myatt recalls: "I remember seeing him one day at Worcester, wearing a striped jacket and cream trousers, looking as though he'd come straight from Henley Regatta. The only thing that let him down was the big holes in his socks!

"Phipps and Larden used to have a fish stall in the Bull Ring. The Shilling Shocker used to drop by from time to time. Arthur Phipps, being a generous sort, always used to give him two bob for a tip – even though he never backed it. One day the Shocker said to him: 'Arthur, I can't get a cup of tea with two bob.' 'No,' replies Arthur, 'and I can't get a winner with your tips!'

"I don't think he ever had a proper job from the time he came out of the army. He used to earn his money playing the piano in local pubs."

Most of those who remember the Shilling Shocker are convinced he's been dead for years, but Leonard Cave, now aged 82, is still going strong.

Born in London's Old Kent Road, he came to Birmingham just after the Second World War. He chose Birmingham, he insists, because of its location. There were plenty of racecourses in the Midlands.

"Before the war I did anything to get a few shillings, but I've been a tipster all my life. When I was down in London, that's when I learned to play the old Joanna. I played everywhere. Somebody always used to take a collection for the pianist.

"I called myself the Shilling Shocker. I did all the Midlands tracks and up as far as Haydock. I used to like Ascot and Goodwood because, being a Londoner, everyone knew me. And I always used to do well at Cheltenham.

"Even dealing in shillings I could take twenty or thirty quid in a day. You had your ups and downs but if I tipped a winner, they'd give you a bung. I've had some good days and some bad days in this game."

Now, though, those days are over. It's been a good few years since the Shilling Shocker was last seen on a racecourse. Today he lives modestly in senior citizens' accommodation in Birmingham and no longer follows racing.

"I've been away from it such a long time, I wouldn't know anyone," he says. "I don't even watch it on the telly now. When I had a pitch I used to love to get out and have a go, but that's all gone. Things of the past."

So, what inside sources did the Shilling Shocker have? Who were his contacts with all the hottest news and latest information? In which stables did he have his 'moles'? Where did he get his tips from? He laughs, then admits: "Out of the paper, the same as everyone else!"

Just as reports of the death of Mark Twain were greatly exaggerated, so Leonard Cave is keen to stress that he remains a going concern. "I'm supposed to have passed on but I'm still about, don't worry. We're still getting by."

THOSE NEARBY

This book covers horse racing in Birmingham and its immediate environs. One of the main problems was defining what constituted 'immediate'.

We wanted to mention some of the local places that staged horse racing at one time or another. However, we were keen to avoid encroaching on other books which we knew to be either nearing completion or in their embryonic stages. For example, John Griffiths is well advanced with his history of racing in and around Walsall.

Flat Racing enjoyed long histories in some towns. Bewdley first raced in 1815 and from 1857 to 1869, while Lichfield ran from 1774 to 1894.

As steeplechasing gained popularity during the mid-nineteenth century, many 'one-off' fixtures cropped up throughout the country, never to be heard of again. Others lasted longer, with local venues including Alcester (1837-46), Kenilworth's at the Bowling Green Inn (1843-50), Nuneaton (1856-58), and Upton-on-Severn's at Fish Meadow (1862-70). Kidderminster's began at Hoo Brook in 1844, then moved to Stone Village, where they continued until 1884.

After some consideration we decided to provide brief histories of five West Midlands venues that staged racing during the nineteenth century.

BRIERLEY HILL

An advertisement appeared on the front page of *Aris's Birmingham Gazette* for a meeting to be held over a new racecourse at Brierley Hill on Monday 25th and Tuesday 26th September 1820. The races comprised, on the first day, a Plate not exceeding £50 for ponies and, on day two, a similar Plate for Galloways. Entries, which cost 10s 6d, were to be made to the Clerk of the Course, Mr. John Light, of Level Iron Works. In addition, an "Ordinary" would be provided each day at the Three Furnaces and Old Bush Inns, at 5s each.

From thereon, Brierley Hill's annual race meetings always took place on a Monday and Tuesday in late September, being part of the entertainment of the local wake. In 1849 it was held on 24th and 25th September, adjacent to Round Oak Station, nearly opposite the Round Oak Inn. Each day started with a race for a new saddle and bridle. The *Worcestershire Chronicle* reported that that year's meeting "afforded some excellent sport to a numerous assemblage of persons; the weather being favourable on the whole and particularly on the latter day, there was a more than usual attendance of pleasure seekers."

Brierley Hill races continued during the 1850s. An advertisement for the 1856 meeting, scheduled for 22nd and 23rd September, states that it was to be held "over the Old course."

Race meetings took place at the back of the Three Furnaces Inn, Level Street, the last being on Monday 24th and Tuesday 25th September 1860. The Three Furnaces Inn was run by John Oakes, who also acted as a steward at the meeting, the starter being Henry Keeten of the Forge Tavern in Birmingham.

PENN COMMON

Until the coming of the golf club, a two-day race meeting was held at Penn Common, on the southern outskirts of Wolverhampton. Most races were run in heats over distances of about two miles.

The races were invariably plates or matches between two horses, a "plate" being for a guaranteed cash prize. The entrance fee for the races was usually half a guinea, payable at the Fox and Goose public house two or three days before the meeting.

In the post-Napoleonic period there was also a race for horses belonging to the Himley and Enville troop of Yeomanry Cavalry, a locally raised defence force. The horses had to have attended at least three field days and could be entered by officers, N.C.O.s or privates. The race was won in 1822 by Mr Aston's unnamed bay mare, with Mr Brewster's horse coming in second.

There were booths selling liquor (licence fee 10s 6d, payable to the clerk of the course) and the amusements of the local fair. A good time was had by all – including the pickpockets.

The races continued until the late nineteenth century, catering mainly for ponies and Galloways. James Lakin, a local entrepreneur who later purchased the Penn Brewery building, was among those who regularly took part.

The outline of the racecourse can still be seen from the air in dry summers. Though no longer staging races, it has at least survived as an area of public open space.

Penn Racecourse

REDDITCH

Racing at Redditch dates back to 1839 when a two-day meeting was held on 16th and 17th September. The races included the Cavalry Cup, the Hewell Stakes and the Hack Stakes. A Tradesmen's Plate was introduced to the programme in 1844 and the annual September meeting trundled on in this fashion until 1848.

After a six-year break, the Redditch meetings resumed at Ipsley in 1854 with a two-day fixture on 5th and 6th June. The programme included two hurdle races, one of which was won by Ducrow, the mount of Bob Sly, Jun. Two years later, Sly came close to winning the Grand National, being beaten just half a length on Minerva. George Stevens, who beat Sly in that 1856 Grand National on Freetrader, was himself among the winning jockeys at Redditch's 1858 meeting, taking the Sweepstakes on Swiftmoor.

Redditch continued to hold Flat racing at Ipsley until 1869, the final meeting taking place on 17th May. There were four races that day, including the Licensed Victuallers' Plate for hunters, over a mile and a half, which attracted a field of thirteen runners, victory going to an unnamed three-year-old filly by The Lawyer.

National Hunt racing at Ipsley, which had commenced in 1868, continued until the last meeting was held on 26th October 1886. A "Worcestershire Hunt" fixture took place at Ipsley on 4th April 1887 but that appears to have been the end of Redditch's racing history.

STOURBRIDGE

The earliest race meetings took place on Stourbridge Common. An article by Thomas Millward of Wollescote Hall in 1711 refers to the instigation of a horse race for the "encouragement of ye breeding of good horses." A group of twenty gentlemen contributed one guinea apiece "for buying a plate of 20 guineas value to be run for three years successively from ye date hereof on Stourbridge Heath."

The race took place on the last Tuesday in May and was run in three heats. Half an hour was allowed in between heats "for rubbing and refreshment of ye coursers." Among the more unusual conditions was: "ye winner of ye said plate in each year shall pay to ye steward 5 shillings for weighing and 5 shillings for drum, horn or trumpet and 10 shillings more for ye use of ye poor of ye town."

On 28th and 29th October 1822, after several failed attempts in the preceding years, racing was established at Pedmore Common, the village of Pedmore lying a mile and a half south east of Stourbridge.

The *Worcestershire Chronicle* reported of the 1850 meeting, held on two days in late August: "These annual sports commenced on Monday, and drew together an immense assemblage of the industrial classes from the neighbourhoods of Kidderminster, Bromsgrove, Dudley, Brierley Hill, Birmingham, and other locations in this densely populated district.

"The day was exceedingly fine, and the atmosphere clear, rendering the view of the surrounding country from the course altogether magnificent. In fact, the sight of the congregated thousands on Pedmore Heath this day, combined with the delightful weather, was highly exhilarating to the warm-hearted residents who thus annually provide for so seasonable a holiday.

"The meeting was graced by the presence of many elegantly dressed ladies, both on the Stand and the course, and there was also a tolerable sprinkling of the aristocracy, and several handsome equipages. Booths, shows, and stands formed a long and continuous line on the upper ground of the course, while of travelling wonders Batty's menagerie towered high above the rest. The promenade of a moderate-sized elephant from the latter establishment among the company, who helter-skeltered in all directions on its approach, was amongst the novelties of the occasion."

Although the weather on the second day was not as good, there was a larger attendance. The Gold Cup Stakes, a two-mile handicap, was won by Lord Stamford's Cingari, ridden by sixteen-year-old John "Tiny" Wells from Sutton Coldfield, who was still eight years away from riding the first of his three Epsom Derby winners. Wells also rode the winner of the last race, the Himley Stakes, on Mr John Fowler's Cosachia, causing the *Chronicle's* reporter to enthuse: "Wells displayed for a mere child some extraordinary jockeyship and, as also in the Cup race, was greeted with much cheering."

The last recorded meeting on Pedmore Heath took place on 12th and 13th July 1858 when there were four races each day. Jockey David Plumb dominated the meeting by riding five of the eight winners, but it was left to reigning champion George Fordham to round off proceedings by winning the Pedmore Stakes on Rio.

Although the meetings were popular, the increasing requirement for housing eventually saw their demise. By then, however, National Hunt racing had grown in prominence, with a meeting having taken place at nearby Enville on 22nd January 1849. The first actual Stourbridge Hunt steeplechase meeting had been held at Pedmore the same year, on 2nd April 1849, on a course

PEDMORE RACECOURSE

To Norton

N

Pedmore Common
(Now Stourbridge Golf Course)

Winning Post

Grand Stand

Racecourse Farm

Racecourse Lane

that had been extended from the Flat racecourse.

The final Stourbridge Hunt meeting was held at Wassel Grove Farm on 13th April 1874 and consisted of eight races. Captain Bulkeley rode two winners, the Red Coat Steeplechase on Vivandiere and the Enville Steeplechase on Baronet. The only professional jockey to win a race that day was William Daniels, who landed the three-mile Pedmore Steeplechase on Star Thistle. Alas, the winner of the final race run at Stourbridge remains a mystery. The Tally-ho Steeplechase was worth less than £20 to winner and consequently the result was not recorded in the *Racing Calendar*.

TAMWORTH

The first Tamworth Steeplechase meeting comprised just one race. *The Observer* reported in March 1836: "This race came off on Wednesday week, and the novelty of the affair, and the number of horses entered, attracted at least a thousand persons, comprising many ladies in their carriages, and sportsmen belonging to the Atherstone and Meynell Hunts."

There were six runners and the starting point was near to Stalfold, by No Man's Heath. The course was "over a light country of about three miles, with some moderate fences, and a brook at the finish, which was close by Wiggington." The race was won by Mr Choice's black mare The Infant, with Hannah second and Pompey third.

The next racing at Tamworth took place in April 1843, April 1844, and on 24th March 1845, when Neptune Stagg won both heats of the Hack Stakes on Go-a-head.

After a lapse of several years, racing returned to Tamworth on 29th March 1864, though the exact venue is not recorded. A woman, Mrs Mary Bartrave, of Hopwas, was killed when the stands collapsed on Easter Monday 1866. Racing finished there the following year, on Monday 12th April, when Mr George Darby won the Members' Plate on Catspaw.

A new course was then opened at Lady Meadow, just off Lady Bridge, Bitterscote, in an attractive setting with the River Tame bordering one side. Racing commenced there on 13th April 1868 and continued, holding mixed meetings (Flat racing and jumping), until the final two-day affair on 14th and 15th April 1879. Both days of that last meeting comprised two Flat races, each over two miles, and a pair of two-mile hurdle races.

Pony racing went on at Fazeley throughout the 1860s, and also in 1894 and 1895, which may well have been the final horse racing of any kind at Tamworth.

*K.O. from K.B.O. Len Stephens and his mount K.B.O. go their separate
ways in the Moseley Handicap Hurdle at Bromford Bridge on
18th January 1949.*

GLOSSARY OF RACING TERMS

RACING terminology is often a very confusing and daunting language. The following glossary should help to clarify various terms that may not be fully understood or adequately explained in the book.

ADDED: Money forming part of the prize money and made up of owners' entry and forfeit money which is over and above the stake money.

BAY: Colour of horse. Brown, with black mane, tail and legs.

CLASSICS: Comprises the Two Thousand Guineas, the One Thousand Guineas, the Derby, the Oaks and the St. Leger.

CLERK OF THE COURSE: The official responsible for the general arrangements.

COLOURS: Worn by jockeys. These were first recorded in 1762 and were made of silk material. This has now been generally replaced by satin nylon.

COLT: Male ungelded horse up to four years old. After the age of four he is known simply as a horse or as an 'entire'.

CONDITIONS RACE: Governed by a set of conditions, e.g. for horses that have not won a race of more than a certain value.

DAM: The mother of a horse.

DEAD HEAT: Applies where two or more horses cannot be separated at the finish.

DISTANCE: This has more than one meaning. Firstly, the length of a race. Secondly, the distance measured between horses during and at the end of a race. (Formerly, when there was more than 30 lengths between two finishers in a race, it was officially designated 'a distance'.) Thirdly, "at the distance" is a term meaning that the horses are 240 yards from the winning post. Thus, a race that is described as being "twice round and a distance" means that the runners would start 240 yards before the winning post and then complete two laps of the course to finish.

ENCLOSURE: The typical British racecourse is modelled on the old class system, arranged in such a way that patrons of the most expensive enclosures, generally Members or "Club", can move through Tattersalls and the Silver Ring, whereas patrons of the cheaper enclosures cannot move upwards.

FIELD: The number of horses in a race, e.g. in a field of nine.

FILLY: Female horse up to four years old. After the age of four she is known as a mare.

FURLONG: A furlong measures 220 yards. There are eight furlongs in a mile.

GALLOWAY: A breed of tough fast ponies that originated in Scotland.

GELDING: A castrated horse.

HAND: The height of horse is measured from the point of its withers (shoulder) in 'hands'. A hand measures four inches.

HANDICAP: Horses are given different weights so that, in theory, they will all finish level at the end. The better the horse, the more weight it is allocated.

JOCKEY CLUB: Until the formation of the British Horseracing Board (BHB) in the 1990s, the Jockey Club was the governing body of racing.

JUVENILE: A two-year-old horse.

MAIDEN: A horse of either sex that has never won a race.

MR: When a jockey has the prefix 'Mr' in front of his name, it denotes an amateur rider.

NURSERY: A handicap race confined to two-year-olds.

ORDINARY: A public meal provided at a fixed time and price in a tavern, etc.

PADDOCK: The area around which horses are paraded and mounted by their jockeys prior to a race.

PLATE: A race in which the prize or prizes of definite value are guaranteed by the Race-fund. The entrance fee, forfeit, subscription or other owners' contribution goes to the Race-fund. It originally applied to races where a piece of plate, usually a cup, was the prize. A plate is also the name given to a shoe worn by a horse for racing.

POINT-TO-POINT: Steeplechases, usually organised by a Hunt, confined to amateur riders and horses that have been "regularly and fairly" hunted.

RACING CALENDAR: Founded by John Cheney in 1727, this was essentially a list of all matches and other horse races run and was intended as a reliable reference for all races throughout the country. Weatherbys took over the control of the Racing Calendar in 1773.

SCURRY: Normally refers to a race over two miles, rather than three or four miles, which were the traditional steeplechase distances during much of the nineteenth century.

SELLING RACE: The winner is normally auctioned off immediately after the race. Sellers are a valuable source of income to the racecourse as it receives a proportion of the selling price.

SILVER RING: The cheapest enclosure at a racecourse. The name is derived from the cost of admission, which in earlier times were usually florins (10p) and half-crowns (12.5p), rather than paper money.

SIRE: The father of a horse.

SOVEREIGNS or 'SOVS': Refers to £s, as in the amount of prize money.

STALLION: An entire horse (i.e. not gelded) used for breeding.

SWEEPSTAKE: A race in which the entrance fee, forfeit, subscription, or other contribution of three or more owners go to the winner or placed horses. Any such race is still a sweep-stakes even when money or other prize is added.

TATTERSALLS: The public enclosure where the betting ring is located. It is named after Richard Tattersall (1724-1795) and abbreviated to "Tatts".

TOTE or TOTALISATOR: A pool betting system that operates in competition to the book-makers.

TRIPLE CROWN: Comprises the Two Thousand Guineas, the Derby and the St. Leger.

WAKE: An annual festival held in a town or village, lasting anything from a single day to a whole week.

WALKOVER: A 'race' where only one horse is declared to run.

WARNED OFF: Banned from attending any race meeting under the Rules of Racing, from training or holding a licence for any post connected with racing

YEARLING: A horse of either sex between the first New Year's Day after foaling and the following 31st December.

BIBLIOGRAPHY

MUCH of the research for this book was compiled from reference material at Birmingham's Central Library, such as the Birmingham Journal, Birmingham Gazette, the Observer, the Sporting Buff, back copies of the Birmingham Post, Birmingham Evening Mail, Baily's Magazine, plus various periodicals.

Other references have been obtained from:

BAYLES, F. H.: *The Racecourses of Great Britain and Ireland* (c1906)
BLACKER, Brigadier C. H. 'Monkey': *The Story of Workboy* (1960)
DARLING, Sam: *Sam Darling's Reminiscences* (1914)
GREEN, Reg: *A Race Apart. The History of the Grand National* (1988)
HAMMOND, Chas: *Jump Jockeys 1830-1950* (2003)
HAMPSON, Martin: *Harborne. The Second Selection* (2002)
HERBERT, Ivor: *The Queen Mother's Horses* (1967)
HIDE, Edward with Mike CATTERMOLE: *Nothing to Hide* (1989)
HOLLAND, Anne: Steeplechasing. *A Celebration of 250 Years* (2001)
JONES, Douglas V.: *Sutton Park. Its History and Wildlife* (1982).
JONES, John Morris: *From Hall Green and Hereabout*
MARSH, Richard: *A Trainer to Two Kings* (1925)
MORTIMER, Roger: *The History of the Derby Stakes* (1973)
MORTIMER, Roger, Richard ONSLOW & Peter WILLETT:
    Biographical Encyclopaedia of British Flat Racing (1978)
MUNROE, David Hoadley: *The Grand National 1839-1930* (1931)
PITT, Chris: *A Long Time Gone* (1996)
RICHARDSON, Charles: *The English Turf* (1901)
RICHARDSON, John Maunsell & Finch MASON:
    Gentlemen Riders Past and Present (1909)
RICKMAN, Eric: *Come Racing With Me* (1951)
RICKMAN, John: *Homes of Sport: Horse Racing* (1952)
SMYLY, Patricia: *Encyclopaedia of Steeplechasing* (1979)
TANNER, Michael: *The Champion Hurdle* (1989)
WELCOME, John: *The Cheltenham Gold Cup* (1973)
WELCOME, John: *Fred Archer. His Life and Times* (1987)

INDEX

Abadan 167
Abdale, George 76
Acrobat 87
Adamas 72-3, 90
Adams James 'Jimmy' 71, 85, 92, 94, 97
Ancil, Derek 171
Anthony, Jack 158
Anzio 172
Apostacy 159
Arcandy 177
Archer, Fred 37, 86-7, 90, 97, 99-101
Archer, William 25, 31, 33-4, 36-8
Authorise 165
Avenger 159
Aylesford, Lord 71, 111, 113, 131, 150
Baird, George Alexander
         'Mr Abington' 98-100
Bandalore 171-2
Barker, Arthur 99
Barlow, Frank 176
Barnabo 85
Barratt, Lowther 188
Barrett, George 102-3
Barsac 155
Baxter, Geoff 195
Beardsworth, John 12
Beary, Michael 161, 165
Beasley, H R (Bobby) 171-2, 186
Beasley, Pat 'Rufus' 162
Beaver II 187
Becher, Capt Martin 19
Beechey, E 85
Bicester, Lord 169
Biddlecombe, Anthony 185
Biddlecombe, Terry 185, 195
Birmingham (horse) 12
Black Diamond 188-9
Blacker, Brig C H 'Monkey' 174
Blagrave, Herbert 166-7
Bletsoe, Morgan 124
Bletsoe, H Bryan 126
Blue Prince 159
Bob Cherry 176

Bold Biri 188
Bolton, Henry 45-7
Boothman, Peter 179
Bovril III 158
Bowen, George 164
Boyce, Charles 26
Boyd-Rochfort, Cecil 166, 181-2
Brantingham 137
Breasley, Arthur 'Scobie' 166-7, 178, 180-1,
183, 188
Bricett 168-9
Bridgwater, Ken 39
Broadwas 159
Brockton, William Rippon 94
Broderick, Paddy 195
Brooke, Geoffrey 180, 186
Brookes, Fred 159
Brookshaw, Tim 171, 179, 188
Brown, Eric 159
Brown, Harry Atherton 124, 137
Brown, Jesse 132
Bugle March 88, 94
Bullock, Johnny 174
Burns, Bob 44, 89-90
Burns, T P (Tommy) 171, 185
Butchers, Don 159
Butters, Frank 163
Cannon, Joe 39, 71, 111
Carfax 138
Carr, W H (Harry) 166, 177, 181
Casamba 184
Case, Thomas 107-8
Cave, Leonard 210-1
Cazalet, Peter 186, 188
Chamade 69
Chandley, Seth 153
Chatsworth 181
Cherry Ripe 129
Childs, John 94
Chinese Cracker 167
Churchill, Sir Winston 188
Clanricarde, Marquis of 104
Clay, T 46

Clayton, Stan 196
Coloured School Boy 167
Come to Daddy 182
Commander in Chief 186, 195
Common 129
Congress 112
Conjuror II 158
Connolly, Mick 185
Constable 178
Cook, Paul 167, 189
Cordrey, Chris 180
Corfu 71, 92
Costa Brava 172
Coulthwaite, Tom 158
Counsellor 75
Cousins, Eric 195
Coventry, Arthur 93, 97, 112
Crickmere, John 16
Crudwell 170, 175
Crump, Neville 174
Cundell, Frank 178, 189
Dabbs, Arthur 39
Dainty 111
Dandolo 137
Daniels, William 91, 111, 123, 216
Darby, George 92, 216
Darling, Sam (1796-1881) 15, 30
Darling, Sam (1826-1860) 36
Darling, Sam (1852-1921) 87
Davis, Henry 94
Day, Reg 165
Deceitful 56, 60
Deceiver 30
Decree 165
Denman, Robert 76
Dewhurst, Cecil 158
Dick, Dave 186
Dickens 182
Didoric 159
Disturbance 86
Dites 166
Dodona 71
Dodgson, John 77
Donoghue, Steve 127, 156-8, 161-2, 173
Doubtful 68
Dowdeswell, Jack 141
Drifter 137
Drum Beat 177
Durr, Frank 176-7
D.U.K.W. 169

Dumbarnie 176-7
Easterby, Peter 167
East Lancashire 85
Eborneezer 172
Ede, George 'Mr Edwards' 41-2, 70
Edmunds, Jim 49, 148
Edwards, Roy 195
Elliott, Charlie 161, 167
Elliott, R P (Bobby) 185, 192, 196
Elsey, Captain Charles 162
Emblem 34, 69, 71
Emin 155
Ennis 177
E.S.B. 174-6
Escott, John 72-3, 90
Farrell, Paddy 184
Farrney Fox 185
Father O'Flynn 103, 113, 124
Fawcus, Jack 159, 172
Fawdon, Richard 'Snowy' 165
Featherstone, George 145-7
Fidonia 166
Fighting Charlie 192
Filmer-Sankey, Billy 158
Finlay, Fred 153
Finnure 169
FitzGerald, Jimmy 172
Flatman, Elnathan 'Nat' 76
Flattery 103
Ford, Francis B 196
Ford, John 151, 196
Ford, Stanley 151, 196
Ford, Stanley B 172, 196
Fordham, George 215
Ford of Fyne 155
Forewarned 158
Four Ten 176
Foster, Eric 138
Fox, Freddy 157, 161
Francis, Dick 175
Franc Picard 38, 68
Frankie Vaughan 195
Freebooter 168
Freeman, Arthur 186
French Patrol 167
Gallery 168-9
Galloway Braes 175
Gamecock 102
Gazey, George 125
General Saxham 158

Gethin, Ken 165-6, 173-4
Gifford, Josh 179, 187
Gilbert, Geoff 177
Glass, Dr Louis 195, 197
Glen Fire 175
Golden Miller 161
Golden Ray 156
Goldsmith 41-2, 68
Goodwill, Arthur 'Fiddler' 189
Goodwin, John 70, 91
Gosling, Tommy 177
Gowing, Frederick 137
Graham, George 128-131
Graham, Isabella 128-130
Graham, Young Robertson 128-130
Grakle 159
Great Scot 192
Great Span 159
Grecian Granite 166
Green, Chris 37-8
Green, George 126
Gregalach 159
Gretton, Frederick 128-9
Greville-Nugent, Sir Reginald
    'Mr St James' 93
Grey Sovereign 176
Grudon 124, 155
Haine, Johnny 195
Halford, Mr C 39
Hall, Charlie 184
Hall, Sam 167
Hanlon, John 34
Happy Home 168-9
Hardy 130, 136
Harrington, Lord 98
Harrison, Maurice 143
Hassall, Fred 123-4
Hastings-Bass, Peter 176
Hathaway, Joseph 111
Hide, Edward 178
Highland Mary 99
Hippolyte 70
Hobson, Fred 70
Hollinshead, Reg 195
Holman, George 68-9
Hornbeam 180-1
Honey End 187, 195
Horton, John 136
Humble Bee 111
Hunt, Captain George Warwick 68

Hutchinson, Ron 176
Iles, Harry 136
Ilex 103
Induna 185
Isaac 15, 30
Isinglass 129
Isonomy 129-30
Jack Horner 158
Jaipur 186
Jenkins, R E 'Taffy' 176
Joel, Jim 186
Johnny Longtail 112, 123
Johnstone, Rae 167
Jones, Arthur 171
Jones, Herbert 91, 156
Jones, John G 91
Jones, Robert (Bobby) 162
Joss Merlyn 179, 192
Juggler 93
Keeten, Henry (Harry) 52, 54, 56
Kellsboro Jack 159
Keogh, Murtagh 160-1
Kerstin 176
Kilpatrick, Alec 174
King Bruce 176, 181
Kingsley, Maurice 170
Knock Hard 170
Koko 138, 161
Kowloon 130, 136
Lady Diane 157
Lady Gundrede 123-5, 155
Lady Wildair 76
Lakin, James 213
Lambton, Hon. George 100
Lamplugh, Harry 38, 49, 68
Last 137
Lazy Boots 159
Lea, Jack 49, 148
Leader, Ted 159
Limber Hill 175
Little, Captain Josey 26-7
Little Dwarf 56, 60
Little Yeoman 41
Livesey, John 31
Live Spirit 181
Loates, Charles 100, 155
Loates, Samuel 156
Lord, Mr E H 124, 155
Lowe, Mr Gus 97
Lowrey, Tommy 165

Luminary 167
Lynch, Michael 209-10
Lynham, Fred 71, 111
Lynn's Own 187
Madden, Otto 155, 56
Magic Court 172
Magnetic Fin 168-9
Maidment, Charles 104
March Past 176
Marks, Doug 180
Marplot 100
Marsh, Richard (Dick) 110-1
Marshall, Bryan 169, 195
Marsh Meadow 182
Mason, Francis 'Tich' 137, 139, 157
Masters, Tommy 185
Matador 177
Mawson, George 104, 155
Mayou, Samuel 21, 24-5
May Wood 143
McCall, George 156
McComb, Sammy 148
McMorrow, Leo 168-9
Meanwood 70
Melleray's Belle 138
Melsom, Samuel 53
Mercer, Joe 166, 181
Mercer, Syd 39, 175, 179, 182
Merry Deal 171
Migil Five 193
Milburn, George 176
Millbanks, Sammy 189
Miller, Wally 147
Molony, Martin 169
Molony, Tim 169-70, 174
Moore, Garrett 93
Moose 49, 70
Morning Star 71, 111
Morrow, Bert 174-5
Mould, David 188
Mount Eagle 14, 19
Mr Gay 176
Mrs Starr 91-2
Mullane, Jimmy 188
Mustavon 167
Needwood 37
Newey, Alf 126
Nicholson, Herbert 'Frenchie' 161
Nicolas Nickleby 166
Nightingall, Arthur 103

Noholme 170
Norooz 165
Norris, Graham 160
Nucleus 180
O'Brien, Vincent 170
Olliver, Tom 20-1, 27
Opera Score 166
Oscar Wilde 176
Our Jim 52-3
Owen, George 159
Owen, Captain Roddy 113
Oxford 128
Oxley, John 166
Page, John 44, 49-50, 69-70, 123
Page, Joseph 44, 49, 121-3
Paget, Dorothy 161, 169, 178
Pappa Fourway 177
Paradox 129
Parker, John 25, 32
Patron Saint 159
Payne, Bill 156-8
Payne, Fred 148
Peacetown 195
Pearce, William 126
Peel, Captain William 25-7
Penarth 68
Penisola 195
Pennington, G W 'Bobby' 158
Perryman, Richard 'Dick' 161-2, 165
Persse, Atty 173
Philip, Roy 138
Philology 153
Pickernell, Thomas 'Mr Thomas' 70, 87, 112
Piggott, Keith 138
Piggott, Lester 162, 173, 177-8, 185, 188-9, 192-3, 196-7
Piggott, Victor 138
Pillory 102
Plumb, David 215
Pointsman 175, 183
Popham Down 192
Porter, John 100, 128-9
Prendergast, Paddy 180
Pretty Boy 49
Pretty Doe 24
Price, Ryan 179, 187
Privy Councillor 185
Pucka Belle 159
Queen, HM The 166
Queen Mother, HM The 186

Quelle Chance 172
Quibble 94, 97
Ranunculus 158
Rawlinson, Anthony 165
Raymond, Bruce 180
Really True 159
Red Gauntlet 185
Red Knob 42, 122
Red Splash 161
Rees, Bill 186
Reiff, John 156
Reugny 71, 86
Reynoldstown 159
Richards, Charles 24, 28
Richards, Cliff 162
Richards, Gordon 158, 161-7, 173, 178, 185
Richardson, John Maunsell 27, 71
Rickaby, Bill 165-6, 181, 185
Ridge Wood 165
Right Boy 177
Rimell, Fred 141, 159, 167, 171
Riste, Jonathan 103
Robinson, Peter 178
Robinson, G W (Willie) 172, 192
Rockquilla 159
Roe, John 195
Roimond 168-9
Roman Hackle 161
Rondetto 187
Rory O'Moore 17
Rosebery, Lord 134, 162
Rowland Roy 169
Royal Mail 159
Royal Toy 138-40
Ruby Wedding 167
Ruddyglow 158
Rupununi 172
Russell, Alec 182
Russian Hero 168-9
Rustam 180
Ryan, Denis 186
Saffron Tartan 171
Sail, Jack 142-3
Salterello 166
Sankey, Mr J 32, 122
Sardis 153
Saunders, William 15, 25
Scott, Sir Edward 18, 20, 26
Scudamore, Michael 175, 192, 195
Sellwood, Neville 176

Selly Oak 188-9, 196
Sensier, Billy 98, 112-3
Sergeant Buzfuzz 137
Set Fair 176
Sharpe, William 77
Snaith, Willie 181, 192
Sneyd, Major Fred 166
Sparkling Flame 171
Spartan General 189
Stagg, Neptune 26, 31, 75, 216
Starkey, Greville 187, 192-3, 196
Star of England 33-4
Stephens, William 103, 112
Stephenson, Arthur 195
Stephenson, Willie 170, 180
Sterling 128-30
Stevens, George 33-4, 68-9, 214
Sting 67
Stonehouse, Reg 197, 208
Stott, Billy 139
Strathspey 167
Sturrock, Terry 108
Summer Lightning 155
Sum Total 130, 136
Sun Hat 188
Sweet Moss 192
Swinging Blue Jeans 193
Tamerlane 180
Tasker, John 34
Taxidermist 183
Taylor, Brian 116, 188
Taylor, Henry (Harry) 86
Taylor, Lynn 187
Taylor, William 24, 26-7
Teal 174-5
Teme Willow 159
Terry Downes 195
The Chandler 26
The Colonel 34, 70-1, 102
The Comet 34, 68
The Fosse 183
The Nun 69, 110
Thomas, Arthur 172
Thompson, Arthur 174
Thrale, Peter 173
Thrown In 161
Tibere 160
Tiger 69
Timber 179
Tipperary Boy 36-7

Title Deed 182
Tokoroa 171
Topthorn 21, 24
Trelawny 183
Trent Bridge 165
Trigg, Charles 156
Tulk, Paul 165
Tulyar 174
Turkey Buzzard 157
Turnell, Bob 187
Underwood, Grenville 171
Vagabond II 167
Valdeso 166
Valentine 186
Variety King 166
Varmint 28
Vic Day 167
Vigo 177
Vilmoray 176
Wales, David 189
Wales, Walter 189
Walker, Charles 34
Walker, Hal 197
Walker, John Shaw 20, 24, 26
Wallis, Mr F 19
Walwyn, Fulke 159, 161, 172, 183
Watts, Jack 97, 99
Waugh, Tom 185
Wayward Bird 171
Weever, Edwin 67
Weld, Charlie 185
Wells, Bernard 148
Wells, John "Tiny" 73, 215
Welsh Abbot 177
Welshman 196

Weston, Tommy 161
Whalley, Albert "Snowy" 157
What a Myth 188
Wheeler, John 69-70
White, Walter 34, 38, 85-6
Whitehouse, George 14-5, 17, 77
Wiggan, John 74, 87
Wightman, Bill 176
Wilkinson, Benjamin "Jumbo" 172
Wilkinson, Clive 90
Williams, Evan 159
Williams, Ian 50
Williamson, Bill 167
Willoughby de Broke, Lord 164, 172, 183, 193, 197
Wilson, E P "Ted" 69-70, 97, 112
Wilson, Jock 195
Winter, Fred 172, 183, 188
Withington, Fred 172
Wood, Arthur "Stosher" 130, 136
Wood, Charles 100
Woolf, Jack 186
Woolley, Bob 187
Wootton, Frank 156
Wootton, Stanley 173
Worcran 186
Workboy 174
Wragg, Harry 161-2, 173, 178-9
Wragg, Sam 162
Wright, Stanley 171
Xanthus 69
Yates, Arthur 27, 94, 113
Yates, David "Flapper" 166
Zarathrustra 181
Zabara 173-4